HOLY WARS

HOLY WARS

The Rise of Islamic Fundamentalism

by Dilip Hiro

ROUTLEDGE

New York

Published in 1989 by

Routledge
An imprint of Routledge, Chapman and Hall, Inc.
29 West 35th Street
New York, NY 10001

Library of Congress Cataloging-in-Publication Data

Hiro, Dilip.
    Holy wars : the rise of Islamic fundamentalism / Dilip Hiro.
        p.   cm.
    Bibliography: p.
    Includes index.
    ISBN 0-415-90207-X. — ISBN 0-415-90208-8 (pbk.)
    1. Islamic fundamentalism—Middle East—History—20th century.
2. Islam and politics—Middle East—History—20th century.
3. Middle East—Politics and government.   I. Title.
BP63.A4M534 1989
297'.09—dc20   89-10190
                                                                              CIP

To
Carol B.

CONTENTS

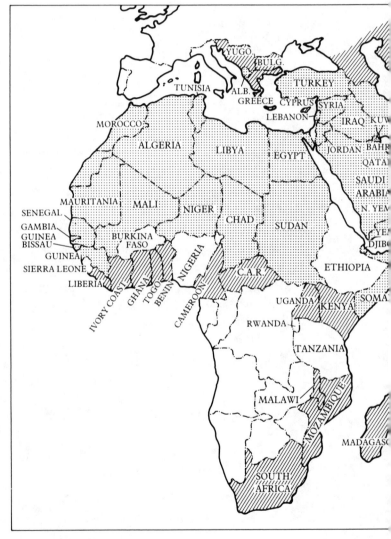

The Muslim World

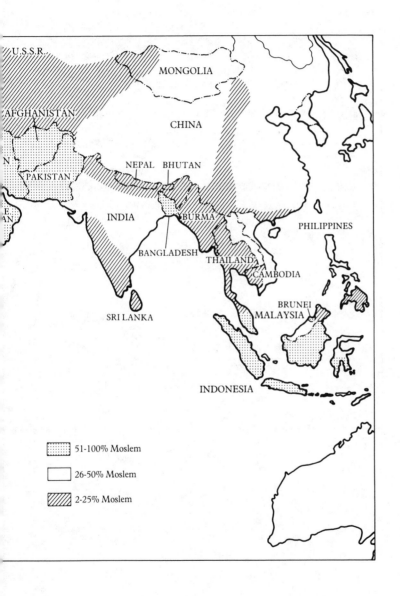

U.S.R.

MONGOLIA

AFGHANISTAN

CHINA

N

PAKISTAN

NEPAL   BHUTAN

E
AN

INDIA   BURMA

PHILIPPINES

BANGLADESH

THAILAND

CAMBODIA

SRI LANKA

BRUNEI
MALAYSIA

INDONESIA

51-100% Moslem

26-50% Moslem

2-25% Moslem

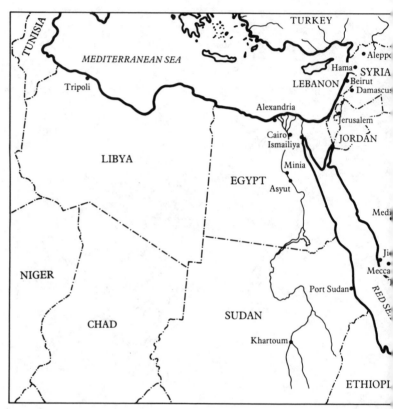

Heartland of Islam

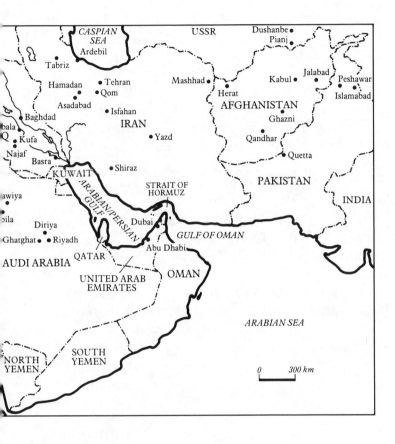

CASPIAN
SEA
USSR
Dushanbe •
Pianj

Ardebil
Tabriz •
Hamadan • • Tehran
• Qom
Mashhad •
Herat
Kabul • Jalabad
Islamabad •
Peshawar

Asadabad
• Isfahan
AFGHANISTAN
Ghazni

Baghdad •
bala
Q
• Kufa
Najaf
IRAN
• Yazd
Qandhar •
Quetta •

Basra
KUWAIT
• Shiraz
Diriya
Ghatghat • • Riyadh
ARABIAN/PERSIAN GULF
STRAIT OF
HORMUZ
Dubai •
Abu Dhabi •
GULF OF OMAN
PAKISTAN
INDIA

awiya
bila

AUDI ARABIA
QATAR
UNITED ARAB
EMIRATES
OMAN

NORTH
YEMEN
SOUTH
YEMEN
ARABIAN SEA

0   300 km

A NOTE ON THE
ISLAMIC CALENDAR

The Islamic calendar is lunar. It dates from 15 July A.D. 622, the day of the hijra (migration) of Prophet Muhammad from Mecca to Medina, and is denoted by A.H.: After Hijra.

On average a lunar year contains 354 days. The Islamic lunar months, with their duration, are: Muharram (30 days), Safar (29), Rabia Awal (30), Rabia Thani (29), Jumada Awal (30), Jumada Thani (29), Rajab (30), Shaaban (29), Ramadan (29), Shawal (30), Dhu al Qaada (29) and Dhu al Hijja (30).

Since a lunar year is shorter than a solar year by eleven days, it takes thirty-four years to equal roughly thirty-three solar years. That is, there is an approximate difference of three years between a lunar century and a solar one.

To convert an Islamic lunar year date to a Christian solar date, divide it first by 1.031, and then add 621 or 622.

GLOSSARY OF ARABIC
AND PERSIAN WORDS

aal: of a family or tribe
abi/abu: father
adha: sacrifice
ahl: people
akbar: great
akhbar: report
al/el/ol/ul: the
Alawi: follower or descendant of
 Imam Ali
alim (pl. ulama): religious–legal
 scholar
amal: hope
amr: command
ansar: helper (of Prophet
 Muhammad)
ashura: (lit.) tenth; (fig.) tenth of
 Muharram
asr: period or age
Ayatollah: sign or token of Allah
azhar: resplendent

baath: renaissance
bacha: son
bait: place or house
balaghe: eloquence
basij: mobilization
bast: sanctuary
beduin (sing. bedu): nomads
bida: innovation
bin: son
bint: daughter
bismillah: in the name of Allah

chador: (lit.) sheet; (fig.) veil

daawa: call (of Islam)
dar: house or realm

dervish: mendicant
din: faith

-e: of
eid: festival
Eid al Adha: the Festival of
 Sacrifice
Eid al Fitr: the Festival of
 'Breaking the Fast'
emir/amir: one who gives amr
 (command); commander

faqih: religious jurist
fatwa: religious ruling
fedayin (sing. fedai): self-sacrificers
fitna: sedition or civil strife
fitr: breaking the fast

hadd: (lit.) boundary; (fig.)
 punishments contained in the
 Sharia
hadith: action or speech of Prophet
 Muhammad or an Imam
hajj: pilgrimage (to Mecca)
haram: religiously forbidden
harb: war
hazrat: title for a prophet or imam
hijab: screen or veil
hijra: migration or flight
hizb: party
Hizbollah: Party of Allah
hojatalislam: proof of Islam
hukumat: government

ibn: son
ihtisab: observance of religious
 morality

ihya: revival
ijma: consensus
ijtihad: interpretative reasoning
ikhwan: brotherhood or brethren
illahi: divine
imam: (lit.) one who leads prayers
   in a mosque; (fig.) religious
   leader
inqilab: revolution
islam: state or act of submission
   (to the will of Allah)
isma: impeccability (of Shia imam)
ittilaat: information

jahiliya: (lit.) period of ignorance;
   (fig.) pre-Islamic era
jamaat: society
jamiyya: society
jihad: (lit.) struggle in the name of
   Allah; (fig.) holy crusade or war
jumhouri: republic

kayhan: world
khalifa: caliph or deputy
khalq: people
kharaji: outsider or seceder
khums: one-fifth (of gains)

madhhab: (lit.) adopted policy;
   (fig.) a school of jurisprudence
madrasa: religious school
mahdi: one who is guided by Allah
majallat: review
majlis: assembly
maqam: ritual place
marja: source
maslah: beneficial
mawali (sing. mawla): clients or
   associates
medina: city
mubarak: blessed
mufti: one who delivers fatwas,
   religious rulings
muhajirin (sing. muhajir):
   migrants
muhammad: praiseworthy or
   blessed

muhtasib: one who supervises
   religious–moral behaviour
mujahed (pl. mujahedin): (lit.) one
   who volunteers for jihad; (fig.)
   holy warrior or crusader
mujtahid: one who practises
   ijtihad
mullah: cleric or preacher
muminin: believers
muntazar: awaited or expected
muqaddas: holy
murid: disciple or follower
murshid: master or guide
Muslim (pl. Muslimin): one who
   accepts Islam
mustazafin (sing. mustazaf): the
   needy or the oppressed
mutlaq: absolute
muttawin (sing. muttawi): (lit.)
   one who enforces compliance;
   (fig.) religious police
muwahhidin (sing. muwahhid):
   unitarians

nabi: prophet
nahaj: path
nasr: victory
nizam: order

parcham: flag
pasdar (pl. pasdaran): guard

qanun: positive law (subordinate
   to the Sharia)
qisas: retribution
qiyas: analogy
quds: holy
quran/koran: recitation or
   discourse

rahbar: leader
rasul: messenger
riba: usury

salaf: (lit.) roots; (fig.) ancestor
salafiya: ideology of following the

precedents of the first generation of Muslims

salat: prayers

salih: pious

sawm: fasting during Ramadan

sayyid: (lit.) lord or prince; (fig.) title applied to a male descendant of Imam Hussein

sazman: organization

sejah: army

shah: king

shahada: (lit.) act of witness; (fig.) central precept (of Islam)

shaikh: (lit.) old man; (fig.) a title of respect accorded to a wise man

Sharia: sacred law of Islam

sharif: noble

shia: partisan or follower

shirk: idolatry

shura: consultation

suf: wool

sufi: follower of sufism, the Islamic mystic path

sultan: ruler

sunna: tradition or beaten path

sunni: one who follows sunna

talfiq: synthesis of rulings of different schools of law

tanzimat: reorganization

taqlid: imitation or emulation

tariq/tariqa: road

tudeh: masses

ulama (sing. alim): body of religious–legal scholars

umma: community

usul: root

vahid: unit

vali: lord

vilayat: rule

wa: and

waqf: religious endowment

watan: homeland or nation

-ye: of

zakat: alms or charity

zaman: present time

INTRODUCTION

In recent times Islamic Fundamentalism has had a bigger impact on the West than any other Third World movement. This is partly because many of the countries experiencing it are situated in the strategically important Middle East and partly because several of these states are rich in oil, a commodity upon which western economies are heavily dependent.

Popular belief in the West tends to associate Islamic Fundamentalism with the Iranian revolution of 1979, and sees it as a movement of fanatics bent on harming western interests. Yet the oldest Islamic fundamentalist state of present times, Saudi Arabia, is firmly allied with the West. In Afghanistan, western arms and funds have played a crucial role in bolstering the Afghan fundamentalist camp in its war against the Marxist regime in Kabul.

One of the salient features of Islamic history is that it offers many examples of revivalist movements. It is in the nature of any major religion to revitalize itself periodically. But Islam is special. For it is more than a religion. It constitutes a complete social system that embraces all Muslims, all those who have accepted Islam. It is indeed a civilization that applies to all times and places.

Such a comprehensive system sets standards and norms for its followers in every aspect of life. Being human, they fail to live up to these stringent, all-pervasive standards. And every so often an extraordinarily pious leader rises and calls for an end to back-sliding.

Fundamentalism is the term used for the effort to define the fundamentals of a religious system and adhere to them. One of the cardinal tenets of Islamic Fundamentalism is to protect the purity of Islamic precepts from the adulteration of speculative exercises. Related to fundamentalism is Islamic revival or resurgence, a renewed interest in Islam. Behind all this is a drive to purify Islam in order to release all its vital force.

In medieval times this drive for purification meant ridding Islam of superstition and/or scholastic legalism. That is, the fundamentalist response was purely internal. Today the response is both internal and external: to release Islam from its scholastic cobwebs as well as to rid it of ideas imbibed from the West.

There is no distinction between religion and politics in Islam. Besides being a messenger of God's word, Prophet Muhammad was an administrator, judge and military commander. Islamic law consists of the Quran and the Hadiths (the Sayings and Doings of Prophet Muhammad). It is therefore essential to offer an outline of Muhammad's life; and that is what I do in Chapter 1 of this book.

After Prophet Muhammad's death in 632, Islam expanded widely and rapidly, to the east and west of the Arabian Peninsula, and was adopted by peoples who had their own long-established traditions and religions. It was through the rise of Sufism that Islam was often able to absorb the pre-Islamic beliefs and practices of the new converts. Thus Islam adapted itself to widely differing cultures and, after the first generation of Arab military conquerors, Sufi leaders frequently became its most effective missionaries. In the process, however, Islam became diluted. This in turn led to the emergence of revivalist movements, concentrating on either injecting orthodoxy into Sufism or purifying Muslim practices. This forms the gist of Chapter 2.

The next chapter deals with Islam in modern times when the Muslim world found itself on the defensive wherever it came into contact with Christian power, political or commercial. This was as true of the Ottoman Turkish empire in Istanbul vis-à-vis European powers as it was of the Mogul empire in Delhi in its dealings with the British East India Company. A multifarious response to the rising dominance of western powers in the Islamic world was articulated by the pan-Islamist Jamal al-Din Afghani (1838–97): a defensive call to arms, a concerted attempt to learn the secrets of western strength, and adoption of western modes of thought within Islam. Muhammad Abdu (1849–1905), Afghani's most renowned disciple, became an eminent Islamic reformer of Egypt, and was followed by his brilliant acolyte, Muhammad Rashid Rida (1865–1935).

It is against this background that case studies of Egypt, Syria, Libya, Saudi Arabia, Iran and Afghanistan are presented. Each of these is different. In Egypt, the birthplace of the Muslim Brotherhood, Islamic Fundamentalism has been a feature of the political landscape since the 1930s. At different times it has been wooed, co-opted or suppressed by the regime. With the advent of Muhammad Anwar Sadat as President in 1970, the moderate segments of the fundamentalist movement were co-opted into the political–religious establishment while its radical offshoots resorted to armed resistance and assassinations, including that of Sadat himself. This mixed picture is at variance with the movement's fortunes in Syria: there it has been murderously hostile to the Arab Baath Socialist Party regime of President Hafiz Assad and his predecessors. In Syria, therefore, Islamic Fundamentalism has developed purely as a movement of resistance. (It is debatable whether Islamic Fundamentalism is in power in Libya. Colonel Muammar el Qadhafi's interpretation of the Islamic law, Sharia, is so unconventionally liberal that most fundamentalist thinkers have come to regard him as an embarrassing aberration.)

A similar contrast comes to the fore when one examines the fundamentalist regimes of Saudi Arabia and Iran. Saudi Arabia is a monarchical autocracy without constitution or parliament. Iran is a republic with a constitution and a vigorous parliament elected by universal suffrage. The histories of the two countries, too, are wide apart. In a modern re-enactment of the events of Arabia in the days of Prophet Muhammad in the 620s, Abdul Aziz ibn Saud, acting as a fervent Islamist, subdued and unified the feuding Arabian tribes, nomadic and sedentary, to forge the state of Saudi Arabia in 1932. Iran, on the other hand, had been the centre of the Safavid empire since the early sixteenth century. It underwent many decades of secularization under the Pahlavi dynasty (1926–79) before a revolutionary movement ushered in an Islamic regime under Ayatollah Ruhollah Khomeini. In that sense the Iranian example parallels that of most of the Islamic Conference Organization's forty-five members. The latter countries, too, experienced modernization and secularization, albeit as the colonies of European nations.

Afghanistan is a case unto itself. An independent country, which escaped European domination, political or economic, its religious establishment played a major role in the overthrow of King Amanullah in 1929 when he tried to accelerate the tardy processes of modernization and secularization. In today's Afghanistan, ruled by a Marxist regime, Islam has emerged as an ideology of armed resistance. But the leftist government has shied away from total confrontation with orthodox clerics or Sufi leaders. Having taken spectacularly secular steps in the immediate aftermath of the Saur Revolution of April 1978, the authorities have been retracing their path, wooing clerics, building new mosques, and decrying the insurgents as unIslamic.

In short, while there is a general agreement on the basic principles of fundamentalism, the manner in which the movement is conducted varies widely from country to country. The mere fact that Islamic Fundamentalism is the creed of the Saudi and Iranian regimes does not imply that they act in unison abroad or follow identical policies at home.

It is along these lines that I offer an exposition of Islamic Fundamentalism as an idea and a movement.

1
THE RISE OF ISLAM: SUNNISM AND SHIAISM

Islam emerged out of a rudimentary beduin society in Arabia in the first quarter of the seventh century, and created from scratch an entire social order. How this came about, and how Islam developed after the death of its founder, Prophet Muhammad, form an important body of learning for the believers. The events of early Islam offered precedents upon which subsequent Muslim societies strove to organize themselves. It is to this seminal period of Islam that contemporary Muslims return for answers to such basic questions pertaining to a political–administrative entity as power, legitimacy, relations between the ruler and ruled, law and order, and social harmony.

Islam, in Arabic, means state of submission; and a Muslim is one who has submitted – to Allah, the one and only God. By putting all believers on an equal footing – submission to Allah – Islam created a confraternity above the traditional bonds of clan and tribe. The faithful were united in their belief in Allah and his precepts, as conveyed through Muhammad (literally, praiseworthy), his messenger.

Muhammad was born on 22 April A.D. 570 (or A.D. 571) to Amina bint Wahb and her husband Abdullah of the Hashim clan of the merchant tribe of Quraish in Mecca, a trading post in western Arabia of some 5,000 people, which was also a place of pilgrimage for the worshippers of idols at the sanctuary of Kaaba, a small square temple containing the sacred Black Stone, which was probably a fallen meteorite. Over many centuries the animistic beliefs of Arabia's nomadic tribes had developed into the worship of idols often placed around a rock or tree regarded as sacred,

the Black Stone at Kaaba being a prominent example of
this. Muhammad grew up to be a sturdy man of average
height with a curved nose, large eyes, sensuous mouth and
thick, slightly curly hair. He was a quiet man, serious,
reflective, given to speaking briefly and pointedly. When he
was about forty his introverted, religious nature drove him
to periodic retreats to a cave in the hills near Mecca to
engage in solitary contemplation. During one such period
of prayer and meditation he became aware of a 'Presence'
telling him, 'Muhammad, thou art the Messenger of Allah.'
In the course of a subsequent retreat, according to Muslim
tradition, the first divine revelation 'came down' to
Muhammad on the night of 26–27 Ramadan, the ninth
month of the Islamic calendar.[1] Over the next twenty years
or so, these revelations, delivered in rhythmic prose, continued. These were taken down by his followers on palm
leaves, camel bones or patches of leather, and compiled
into 114 suras (chapters) of varying lengths to form a book
of some 6,616 verses, called the Quran (literally, recitation
or discourse), which took a definitive form a few years after
Muhammad's death.

In 613 Muhammad ibn Abdullah began to preach the
divine revelations to a small body of relatives and friends.
His message to his followers was: abandon all forms of
idolatrous worship and surrender yourself completely to the
omniscient and omnipotent, yet compassionate, Allah. He
warned the wealthy that considering the accumulation of
riches as an end in itself and being niggardly would lead
them to catastrophe. Since Muhammad's monotheistic
teachings were antithetical to the polytheistic idol worship
practised at Kaaba, he angered the Meccan merchants who
profited by the arrival of the pilgrims. Also, by demanding
unequivocal acceptance of one God, Muhammad created a
loyalty which went beyond traditional allegiance to the
clan, and this upset powerful clan leaders who also resented
Muhammad's strictures against their unshared riches.

By 619 hostility towards Muhammad and his small band
of followers – forty men and twenty women – had reached
a point where they were often harassed and attacked. In

620 during their visit to Kaaba some members of the Khazraj tribal federation from the oasis of Yathrib, known in Aramaic as Medinta, or City (later to be called Medinat al Nabi, City of the Prophet, or simply, Medina), about two hundred miles north-east of Mecca, embraced Islam. On their return to Medina they won more converts, and the following year they brought to Mecca some of the new converts, including two members of the Aus tribal federation, which had maintained a long feud with the Khazraj. In June 622 a secret meeting of seventy-five Medinese Muslims promised to protect the Muslims of Mecca if the latter decided to migrate to Medina. During the next several weeks the Muslims of Mecca quietly slipped out of the town and headed for Medina, with Muhammad and his companion Abu Bakr being the last to leave.

In Medina the feuding Aus and Khazraj tribal federations welcomed Muhammad as an arbiter. Their subsequent acceptance of Islam brought an end to their conflict: they were now all believers, Muslims. Gradually Muhammad assumed the authority of a civil and military governor of Medina.

Divine revelations continued to 'come down' to Muhammad, but they were now full of legal and moral guidelines. These were well suited to the need of the time for a framework for an orderly and pious existence within society. Thus the Medinese section of the Quran is concerned with commenting on current affairs and providing a corpus of law. Firstly, it deals with the external and internal security of the Islamic umma, community. The task of protecting the umma from external threats lies with the whole community. The best way to assure the security of the person and property of individuals at home is seen to lie with the old tribal custom of retribution, set down in the Quranic verse: 'A life for a life, an eye for an eye; a nose for a nose, an ear for an ear; a tooth for a tooth, and for wounds retaliation.'[2] The only modification is that in case of an unintended murder the aggrieved party must accept the blood price. Secondly, family life is regulated. Women are given the right to own and inherit property, an improvement on the situation then prevailing in Arabia. They are also awarded the same rights in marriage and divorce as men. The obligations of the husband are defined; and a man is allowed a maximum of four wives with the proviso that 'if you fear you will not be equitable [to them], then only one [wife]'.[3] Thirdly, the Quran lays down ethical and legal injunctions. It forbids intoxicants, flesh of swine, games of chance and hoarding. It condemns fraud, slander, perjury, hypocrisy, corruption, extravagance and arrogance. It prescribes punishments, among others, for stealing, murder and adultery. Cutting off of hands is the penalty for thieving. If adultery is proved for married women through the testimony of four witnesses, then 'detain them in their houses until death takes them or God appoints for them a way'. Furthermore, 'And when two of them commit indecency, punish them both.'[4]

In Medina Muhammad laid the foundations of the Islamic umma and Dar al Islam, Realm of Islam. A written document issued by him, most probably in 627 and later called The Constitution of Medina, is enlightening. It can be summarized as follows. First, the believers and their dependents form a single community, umma. Secondly, each clan or subdivision of the umma is responsible for blood money and ransoms on behalf of its members. Thirdly, the members of the umma must show solidarity against crime, and must not support a criminal even when he is a near kinsman where the crime is against another member of the community. Fourthly, they must maintain solidarity against unbelievers in war and peace. Finally, in case of a dispute arising between members of the community, it should be referred to 'God and to Muhammad for a decision'.[5]

Following a series of victories on the battlefield, Muhammad expanded his domain, and defeated the Quraish in Mecca. In January 630, at the head of an army 10,000 strong, he entered Mecca. He had the 360 stone idols at the Kaaba overturned from their pedestals, and the pagan Quraish were forced to march past him in homage. He touched the Black Stone with his stick and shouted, 'Allahu Akbar!' (God is Great!), the battle-cry of Islam.

The ranks of Muhammad's followers swelled, with the polytheist nomads converting to Islam in droves. Delegation after delegation from various parts of the Arabian Peninsula, the land of Arabs, arrived in Medina imploring the Prophet to include them in the Islamic umma. Muhammad welcomed them, aware that the nascent state of Medina needed all the protection he could muster in order to survive his death.

Islam thus evolved differently from Judaism and Christianity, the other monotheistic faiths which existed in Arabia and the surrounding lands and which were mentioned many times in the divine revelations to Prophet Muhammad. According to Bernard Lewis, a historian, in the case of Islam, religion was the state – with its Prophet acting as the military commander, making war and peace, collecting taxes, laying down the law and dispensing justice. In contrast, Christ made a distinction between what belonged to God and what belonged to Caesar at the very outset. Since then Christianity has recognized two separate authorities – Church and State – existing sometimes in harmony and sometimes in conflict. As for Judaism, the situation is unclear: classical, rabbinical Judaism emerged only after the Hebrew state had ceased to exist. Judaism, therefore, falls uneasily between Islam and Christianity as far as relations between the state and religion are concerned.[6]

Muhammad realized that the best way to ensure the survival of the Islamic umma was by inculcating the new converts with a sense of solidarity which transcended traditional loyalties, and which was so ritualized that it impinged on everyday life. Out of this emerged the five pillars of Islam, a compendium of individual and social obligations, prescribed by Prophet Muhammad in a hadith (saying): shahada (literally, act of religious witness; figuratively, central precept); salat (prayer); zakat (literally, purification; figuratively, obligatory charity); sawm (annual fast of Ramadan); and the hajj (pilgrimage to Mecca).[7]

A Muslim is enjoined to recite the shahada, the central precept of Islam: '*la ilaha illallah, muhammadur rasulullah*' ('There is no god but Allah, Muhammad is the messenger of Allah'). To embrace Islam it is enough to say the shahada before witnesses. After the public ritual it is left to the individual to decide the frequency with which he wishes to practise it in private.

The prayer is performed both individually and collectively. Its public performance on Fridays and religious days strengthens group solidarity. The specific bodily movements – standing, bowing, kneeling, prostrating – that the faithful undergo in the course of the prayer in the congregation engender discipline in the same way as a troop drill. By specifying that the believer must cease all other activity and turn to prayers at least three times daily, Muhammad wanted to remind his followers that Allah's claims were uppermost. The practice of all Muslims standing together at the same level in a mosque or on a prayer ground, irrespective of their social status, underlined the equality of all before Allah. Mosques are remarkable for their simplicity and provision of a single-level floor for prayers. The sermon that follows the Friday prayer has an important social and religious purpose. For it deals not only with some religious aspects of the faith but also the current socio-political situation. Today in the Islamic Republic of Iran, for instance, the Friday sermon is the prime vehicle for the leaders to educate and inform the populace on current affairs, internal and external.

The requirement on zakat, charity, mentioned in the Quran as 'the freewill offerings' for 'the poor and needy . . . the ransoming of slaves, debtors, in God's way, and the traveller', was refined later as obligatory charity amounting annually to 2.5 per cent of the believer's wealth.[8] The underlying principle is that a Muslim should purify his wealth by paying his dues to the umma, which spends the resources on aiding the indigent.

Fasting during Ramadan, the ninth month of the Islamic

(lunar) calendar, requires that the believer must abstain from food, drink and sex between sunrise and sunset. By so doing a Muslim learns to exercise control over his physical requirements. This ascetic practice by individual Muslims helps transform the Islamic umma into a self-disciplined community.

The hajj is enjoined upon those who can afford it. The pilgrimage is undertaken in Dhu al Hijja, the final month of the Islamic calendar. It begins with circumambulating the Kaaba in Mecca and ends with sacrificing an animal in Mina, ten miles away, with prayers offered at Arafat and Muzdilfa in between. The hajj rituals, which can be completed in five days, are derived from the practices already common among the inhabitants of Arabia before Prophet Muhammad's days. By incorporating pagan traditions the hajj helped to solidify the newly emergent Muslim community; and by undertaking the hajj the umma became conscious of its own existence as a powerful social force. In modern times the gathering of over two million Muslims from all over the world sharpens the sense of Islam's universality.

Prophet Muhammad himself prescribed the hajj rituals after his last pilgrimage to Mecca in early 632. He was then at the zenith of his power, the most powerful man in Arabia, and a highly respected religious figure at home and abroad. The numerous Arabian tribes, which had hitherto spent much of their energy in bloody feuding, were now united under his leadership. But Muhammad knew that this unity was tenuous, and that the only means by which he could ensure the survival of the Medinese nucleus of the Dar al Islam after his death was by keeping up an expansionary drive – a strategy which also appealed to his beduin followers eager to appropriate the (legitimate) booty from successful campaigns.

After his return to Medina from the hajj Muhammad prepared to attack Syria. But, following a sudden and severe illness, he died on 8 June 632, leaving behind no male child. Had Muhammad left a worthy son behind, it is likely that the umma would have chosen him the successor, thus setting a precedent, and sparing subsequent Muslim generations the internecine conflicts which centred round succession, the single most contentious issue in Islamic history.

The custom in Arabia was that when a tribal chief died he was succeeded by the best-qualified person in the leading family or the tribe, and the decision was taken by a meeting of all adult males of the family or tribe. There are several versions of events during Muhammad's illness and after his death, culled from written and oral historical records. The description offered here is what passes for the 'standard account' of the accession of the next three successors to Prophet Muhammad.

During Muhammad's fortnight-long illness intense rivalry broke out between his close aides. The main contenders for the succession were Abu Bakr, father of Aisha, the Prophet's youngest (and favourite) wife; and Ali ibn Abi Talib, the Prophet's cousin married to his daughter Fatima. Whereas Abu Bakr led the public prayers during Muhammad's illness, the Prophet chose Ali, then aged thirty-three, to wash his body, a singular honour.

While Ali and other Muslims were busy mourning the Prophet's death and burying him, the Medinese followers of the Prophet, known as ansars (literally, helpers), held a meeting at Saada banu Saqifa. Hearing this, Abu Bakr and Umar ibn Khattab – father of Hafsa, the Prophet's other wife – rushed to the Saqifa assembly. They forestalled a move by the assembly to have a Medinese Muslim, an ansar, succeed the Prophet. They argued that only someone who was a Meccan from the Quraish tribe, to which Prophet Muhammad belonged, would be acceptable as the leader to the nomadic tribes. They won the argument. The assembly chose Abu Bakr as the leader, and conferred on him the title Khalifa (Caliph, or successor) of the Messenger of Allah. The oldest among the contenders for the caliphate, Abu Bakr, a merchant, was one of the early converts to Islam, the companion of the Prophet during the latter's migration from Mecca to Medina, and the leader of the hajj of 631.

Abu Bakr died two years later in 634. But before his death he nominated Umar ibn Khattab as his successor. Still, before assuming the high office, Umar sought and secured the community leaders' approval. This disappointed Ali, who largely withdrew from public life, devoting himself to teaching, and compiling an authoritative version of the Quran.

In 636 Umar's troops defeated the Byzantine forces in Syria, and the following year they inflicted defeat on the Sassanids at Qadisiya on the banks of the Euphrates, seizing (present-day) Iraq and part of Iran. Four years later Umar's forces conquered Egypt. The sustained expansion of the Dar al Islam through the waging of jihad, holy war, helped Umar to hold together the coalition of Arabian tribes under his leadership. He combined the expansionist drive with a well-designed plan to maintain a large standing army and inculcate it with Islamic teachings and practices. He forbade the conquering soldiers from colonizing the captured territories. He levied land tax on the landowners in the seized territories as well as a poll tax on the inhabitants. He compiled a register of the men in the armies, all of them belonging to the tribes of Arabia, and paid them fixed stipends derived from the taxes on the conquered peoples. He maintained the troops in garrison towns which he furnished with mosques and reciters of the Quran in order to indoctrinate the soldiery. In other words, he intensified the holy struggle while strengthening the ideological basis of Islam.

Umar was equally relentless at home; and his harshness aroused more fear than affection. Following the practice of Prophet Muhammad and Abu Bakr, he acted as the chief judge. He was conscientious, yet not all his judgments were flawless. Every so often Ali would point out the drawbacks in his verdicts. One such judgment so infuriated the plaintiff, named Firuz, an Iranian slave of an Arab resident of Medina, that he murdered Umar in November 644.

On his death-bed Umar nominated an electoral college of six to choose the successor, the college including Ali ibn Abi Talib and Uthman ibn Affan, a member of the

Ummayad clan (of the Quraish tribe), who was married to Ruqaiya and Umm Kulthum, daughters of Prophet Muhammad. Thus Umar was less arbitrary than Abu Bakr. The caliphate was offered to Ali but on two conditions: he was required to rule according to the Quran and the Prophet's Practice, Sunna, and accept the (recorded) precedents set by the previous caliphs. Ali rejected the second condition. He had in the past publicly criticized some of the actions of Abu Bakr and Umar; and being a man of integrity, he refused to compromise his principled stance by concurring with all their decisions. The caliphate was then offered to Uthman on the same conditions. He accepted without hesitation.

This choice sowed the seeds of dissension in the Dar al Islam. Ali became the focus of opposition which grew as Uthman began favouring fellow Ummayads brazenly. Ali's Islamic credentials were unmatched. He had adopted Islam when he was a boy; he was steeped in the Quran. An extremely pious man who never failed to observe Islamic rituals and practices, he had emerged as an uncompromising idealist, the conscience of Islam, a believer who had let the opportunity to become the caliph pass because of one unacceptable condition. Along with his piety and idealism went striking looks: a stocky, broad-shouldered man, he wore a long beard.

Uthman relaxed his predecessor's policy of banning the Arabians from colonizing the conquered territories, particularly in the fertile region of Mesopotamia, present-day Iraq. The subsequent rise of an affluent, absentee landlord class in Mecca, Medina and Taif caused much resentment. Many Quranic reciters objected strongly to the growing Ummayad monopoly of top administrative posts. The soldiers complained bitterly against paltry stipends and demanded a return to the customary booty of successful campaigns. The simmering discontent boiled over in open conflict between the Muslims of Arabia, civilian and military, and the local inhabitants in the Iraqi garrison towns of Kufa and Basra.

Matters came to a head in mid-656 when rebel troops

from Egypt combined with dissidents from Basra and Kufa and surrounded Uthman's house in Medina, demanding his abdication. Ali interceded on the mutineers' behalf, but failed to resolve the crisis. In June a group of rebel soldiers attacked Uthman's house and killed him. Ali condemned the assassination, but made no effort to apprehend the murderers.

Calling Ali the 'First among the Muslims', the rebels and most of the adult male Medinese elected him the caliph, thus recovering for the community at large the right to choose the caliph – a right which had been usurped earlier both by a living caliph (Abu Bakr) and a college appointed by the living caliph (Umar). So, after a lapse of twenty-four years, the highest office in Islam was offered, unconditionally, to Ali. He accepted it. But by now the conflict within the Dar al Islam had proliferated to such an extent that he was compelled to channel most of his time and energy into subduing the opposition.

Muwaiya ibn Abi Sufian, the Ummayad governor of Syria and a brother-in-law of Prophet Muhammad, and Aisha, the surviving wife of the Prophet, refused to acknowledge Ali as the caliph, and demanded that Uthman's murder be avenged. The assassins sought refuge in the argument that since Uthman had not ruled according to the edicts of the Quran, and had therefore ceased to be a member of the Islamic umma, murdering him was a legitimate act. Throughout the centuries assassins and armed insurgents in Muslim societies have offered this rationale for their actions: the ruler, having disobeyed the Word of God, the Quran, has ceased to be Islamic. A recent example was the assassination in 1981 of President Sadat of Egypt by fundamentalist soldiers.

When Ali refused to concede the demand of Aisha to punish Uthman's assassins, she rushed to Basra to raise a force against the new caliph. Ali withdrew to Kufa, a stronghold of his supporters. In the ensuing battle near Basra in December 656 Ali vanquished Aisha's partisans, but was courteous to the Prophet's widow. Most military governors now swore allegiance to Ali.

In 658 the armies of Ali and Muwaiya clashed at Siffin on the banks of the Euphrates, a battle in which Ali's forces soon established their superiority. Then Muwaiya's men induced intervention by the Quran – literally – by sticking pages of the holy book on their lances. This led to a ceasefire.

After several months of negotiations Ali and Muwaiya agreed to refer their dispute and the issue of the caliphate to two arbiters, one appointed by each side. The arbitration that ensued has become the most tangled tale in Islamic history due to the partisan descriptions offered by various interested parties of the course of events and the motivation of the participants.

To start with, several hundred of Ali's militant followers, arguing that there was no provision for arbitration in the Quran, abandoned Ali and set up a camp near Baghdad. They came to be called Kharajis, Outsiders or Seceders. Ali defeated them in July 658. Yet enough survived to continue the Kharaji movement, which believed among other things that any pious Muslim was worthy of becoming caliph. (In this they differed from Shiat Ali – Partisans of Ali – who insisted on the sanctity of the lineage of Prophet Muhammad through his daughter Fatima and her husband Ali as a prerequisite for the caliphate.)

One version of the arbitration has it that the arbiters agreed that both the contenders be deposed and that a new caliph be elected by an assembly of notables. Ali's representative, being senior in age, was the first to speak before such a gathering. He declared the deposition of both rivals. Then Muwaiya's representative rose but, instead of inviting nominations for the caliphate, announced that Muwaiya was the rightful caliph. The meeting broke up in pandemonium. Ali stuck firmly to his office. The treachery of Muwaiya's representative has been much condemned by Shiat Ali – or simply Shias – and left a deep mark on them. This continues. The consistent refusal of Ayatollah Khomeini, a Shia, to accept mediation in the Iran–Iraq War stems from a deep mistrust of mediators rooted in Ali's experience after the Battle of Siffin.

The surviving Kharajis were out to avenge the deaths of their comrades by Ali's forces. Ali was therefore high on their hit list. One of them, named Ibn Mujlam, fatally stabbed Ali on 19 Ramadan 40 A.H./March 661 as he was praying in his mosque in Kufa. Ali's assassination was a great blow to those who had supported him all along in his claims to the caliphate. In another context his departure marked the end of the thirty-year-long rule by four 'Rightly Guided' caliphs based in Medina.

Muwaiya was proclaimed caliph in Jerusalem; and Hassan, the oldest son of Ali, in Kufa. But this duality did not last long. Muwaiya, a scion of the Ummayad clan, part of the long-established upper class of Arabian society, enjoyed greater prestige and military power than Hassan. His emissaries persuaded Hassan to retire to Medina on a comfortable pension with the promise that after Muwaiya's death the caliphate would return to the Hashimi clan, whose stature had risen sharply due to the popular acceptance of one of its sons, Muhammad, as the Messenger of Allah, and the involvement of the clan members in promoting the new, vigorous religion of Islam. Hassan died of poisoning in 669. Muwaiya reneged on his promise, and nominated his son, Yazid, as caliph during his lifetime. He thus set up a dynasty, something that had not happened so far in the Dar al Islam. This practice undercut the tradition of choosing the most able and pious Muslim from among the Hashimi or Ummayad clan as the leader of the Islamic umma. Dynastic rule continues to be opposed by many present-day Islamic thinkers on ideological grounds.

By the time Muwaiya died in 680 the Ummayads had consolidated their power. Yet Shias were still adamant in their argument that because Ali had been the divinely appointed successor to Prophet Muhammad, and because Allah's message had been clearly received by Ali and his family, only the descendants of the first truly Muslim family were fit to rule the Dar al Islam.

From this arose the concept of Imamat. That is, only those who were in the lineage of Prophet Muhammad – and thus of Fatima and Ali – can govern Muslims on behalf of Allah, and that the imams, religious leaders, being divinely inspired, are infallible. This view was not shared by Sunnis – or more specifically Ahl al Sunna, People of the Sunna, the Beaten Path or Tradition – who regard caliphs as fallible interpreters of the Quran, the Word of Allah. Unsurprisingly, Sunnis revere the Prophet and the four 'Rightly Guided' caliphs, whereas Shias venerate only the Prophet and Imam Ali, and Ali's descendants. Sunnis believe in three basic concepts: monotheism, that is, there is only one God; prophethood, which is a means of communication between God and humankind; and resurrection, that is, souls of dead human beings would be raised by God on the Day of Judgement and their deeds on earth judged.[9] Shias believe in these as well as in Imamat and social justice. However, in the late seventh century, Shiaism was more a school of thought than a well-defined sect.

Following Muwaiya's death Yazid became the caliph. Hussein, the oldest surviving son of Ali, then living in Medina, staked his claim to the caliphate on the grounds that it belonged to the House of the Prophet, of which he was the most senior male member, and that Yazid was a usurper. His stance won him swift and fervent messages of support from Kufa, a stronghold of Ali's supporters, coupled with exhortations to claim the caliphate, and rekindle the glory that had visited the Dar al Islam during Imam Ali's reign. The news of this reached Yazid. He rushed a trusted aide, Ubaidullah ibn Ziyad, to Kufa. Ibn Ziyad employed the age-old tactics of co-option and repression, and neutralized the anti-Yazid forces. By then the unsuspecting Hussein, acompanied only by his family and seventy-two retainers – forty horsemen and thirty-two footmen – was well advanced in his march to southern Iraq.

On 1 Muharram 61 A.H./8 May 681, Hussein's entourage was intercepted near Karbala, some thirty miles from Kufa, by Yazid's soldiers. For the next eight days their commander tried to obtain Hussein's unconditional surrender through negotiations. He got nowhere. Hussein's belief in his right to the caliphate was total. He refused to budge even when he knew that his forces were no match for

Yazid's, and that defeat and death were inevitable. This disregard for pragmatism, which demands the sacrifice of exalted principles on the altar of realism, was a manifestation of the idealism that fired Hussein, and made him the most revered martyr in Islam, particularly among Shias. He resolved to battle and perish, rather than surrender or retreat, in the cause of justice, which he felt had been denied to him, as well as in the belief that his martyrdom would revitalize the claim of the House of the Prophet to the caliphate. On the morning of 10 Muharram, Friday, Hussein led his small band of warriors to confront Yazid's 4,000 heavily armed troops, mounted and infantry. To match the occasion he donned the sacred mantle of his grandfather, Prophet Muhammad. Hopelessly outnumbered, Hussein's partisans fell one by one. The last was Hussein. He was decapitated, and his severed head was presented to Yazid.

A narrative of the dramatic events of these ten days of Muharram is recited annually, wherever Shias live, by professional readers in mosques and meeting halls, and mounted as the second act of the most celebrated passion play of Islam, accompanied by frenzied grief and tears, wailing and self-flagellation: an annual ritual which sets Shias firmly apart from Sunnis. This popular ritual revives the memory of Imam Hussein and brings to life the early history of Islam, offering current Shia leaders the opportunity to draw lessons from the heroic tragedy of a man of charisma and extraordinary piety – the chief one being that the true believer should not shy away from challenging the established order, with arms if necessary, if it has become unjust and oppressive even if the chances of overthrowing it are slender. No wonder, then, that those rulers who wish to lead their citizens away from the Islamic path attempt to suppress the ritual. In 1939 the Iranian Shah, Reza Pahlavi, banned self-flagellation in public on 10 Muharram, and tried to stop the public performance of Shia passion plays preceding the mourning.

At Yazid's court in 681 the fact that Imam Hussein was a direct descendant of Prophet Muhammad weighed heavily on the ruler. Yazid allowed a safe passage to Medina to all the surviving women of the Hussein family as well as to Ali Zain al Abidin, Hussein's seriously wounded son, considered dead by Yazid's troops, and an infant grandson, Muhammad al Baqir. Zainab, Imam Hussein's sister, upheld the Shia cause until Zain al Abidin had fully recovered. From then on Shias attracted dissident and revolutionary elements in the Dar al Islam.

Imam Hussein's martyrdom was an important milestone in Islamic history and not merely in terms of the final defeat of the Hashimi clan by the Ummayads. The clash between the corrupt, cynical Yazid and the self-righteous, pious Hussein was part of the same dialectic which had earlier pitted the pragmatist Uthman against the idealist Ali: the dialectic of an ideology which had succeeded. The basic question, in the words of Malise Ruthven, a historian of Islam, was: 'Could the new solidarity of the umma, based on the common observance of the Quran and the Prophet's Sunna, be the ideological base for a new Islamic order, or would the order first have to establish itself on the basis of Quraishi – and specifically Ummayad – power?'[10] The real life answer was, as is often the case, a compromise between the two polarities. But the dialectic continued, and remains unresolved. 'The problem of finding a balance between the ideal and the real, the perfection of Islam and the human and material facts of life, became the stuff of Islamic history from the Prophet's time down to the present.'[11]

Within the opposition Shia camp itself a conflict developed. While Zain al Abidin accepted the Ummayad rule, Muhammad ibn al Hanafiya, a son of Ali by a Hanafi woman, revolted against the Ummayads in 687. The revolt failed, but social conditions for dissidence remained fertile. Under the Ummayads society had become stratified: Ummayad aristocrats at the top, and the conquered non-Arab peoples, called mawalis (clients) at the bottom – with Arab ansars (helpers) and nomadic tribes in between. The discrimination practised against non-Arab Muslims by the Ummayads ran counter to the teachings of the Quran, and was a source of much disaffection among the mawalis, who were attracted to the Shia camp.

In line with the Shia tradition, Ali Zain al Abidin named his son Muhammad al Baqir as his spiritual heir before his death in 712. Since Baqir continued the quietist stance of his father, activist Shias lent their support to his younger half-brother Zaid ibn Ali. Zaid raised a banner of revolt in 740, but was struck down. Later, in 743, his son, Yahya ibn Zaid, revolted in Khurasan, the easternmost province of the Dar al Islam which now included all of Iran, but was defeated.

These failures did not arrest the sharpening of the contradictions within the system. The pious were scandalized by the corruption and luxury of the Ummayads, whose empire now spanned Spain in the west and Sind in the east. In Damascus, the capital, much of the administration was in the hands of the Christian clerical families who had run the country under the Byzantine emperors, a situation which the Islamic scholars found intolerable. The Damascus of the 730s was a far cry from the simple egalitarianism of Medina a century before. Little wonder that the garrison towns in Iraq and Khurasan seethed with discontent. Increasingly in the 730s and 740s intellectual energy was channelled into the subject of the right to rebel against an unjust ruler.

It was against this backcloth that in the late 740s a second series of revolts was launched under the leadership of Abu Muslim who, interestingly enough, was a former slave of Ibrahim, the Imam of Hashimis and a descendant of Abbas, uncle of Prophet Muhammad. These revolts were joined by the garrison tribes of Khurasan and backed by urban Islamic intellectuals who were bitterly critical of the Ummayads' worldly ways. Abu Muslim won the support of Shias by declaring that the Ummayad caliph would be replaced by a member of the House of the Prophet. Thus the Hashimi rivalry with the Ummayads, the ideological revulsion against the corrupt rulers who had deviated from Islam, and the Shia yearning for the return of the caliphate to the House of the Prophet coalesced to produce a formidable force. The insurgency gathered momentum and succeeded in overthrowing the Ummayads in 750.

What followed the Ummayads was called the Abbasid caliphate, named after Abbas, the Prophet's uncle. The Abbasid revolution was hailed by both religious intellectuals and non-Arab Muslim masses. It was the first victory of fundamentalism in Islamic history. The Ummayads had deviated from the true ways of the Quran and Sunna, and were overthrown. Those who replaced them, the Abbasids, pledged to stick strictly to the Quran and Sunna. They also promised to treat mawalis, non-Arab Muslims, on a par with Arabs, and choose judges from among those who had studied the Quran and the Prophet's practices.

Since Abbas al Hashimi was one generation older than Prophet Muhammad, the Abbasid claim of belonging to the House of the Prophet was invalid. Still Jaafar al Sadiq, the Sixth Shia Imam, acquiesced in Abbasid power. In return the Abbasid caliph honoured Sadiq while keeping him under discreet surveillance. This was the beginning of an uneasy co-operation between the Shia Imam's followers and the Sunni state.

But not all Shias followed Jaafar al Sadiq. Within a few decades of seizing power the Abbasids imitated the dictatorial style of the Sassanids whom they had overthrown, and let the administration fall into the hands of the bureaucrats who had served the Sassanid emperors. The Islamic militants, who had been fervent supporters of the Abbasids, felt betrayed. In 786 Shias revolted in Hijaz, the region which includes Mecca and Medina. They were suppressed by the Abbasid caliph.

Over the next several generations three branches of Shiaism crystallized: Zaidis or Fivers, Ismailis or Seveners, and Imamis or Twelvers. Zaidis share the first four Imams with Twelvers[12] and follow a different line beginning with Zaid, son of Zain al Abidin. Ismailis share the first six Imams with Twelvers[13] and then follow a different line beginning with Ismail, the older, militant son of Jaafar al Sadiq, who pre-deceased his father. Those who followed Musa al Kazim, the younger, moderate son of Jaafar al Sadiq, came to be known as Jaafaris – and later as Twelvers.[14] They believe that Muhammad al Muntazar (literally, The Awaited Muhammad), the infant son of the Eleventh Imam, went into occultation in 873, thus acquiring the title of Hidden Imam, leaving behind four special assistants.

By then the effective power of the Abbasid caliph had declined, with the Dar al Islam's eastern region being increasingly usurped by semi-independent Iranian dynasties. Indeed, in 932 Baghdad fell into the hands of Ahmed Muizz al Dawla, a Buyid king, who was a Twelver Shia. But neither he nor his descendants attempted to institute Shiaism at the caliph's court or abolish the Abbasid caliphate. Thus a division of power came about – the Buyid king exercising political authority, and the Abbasid caliph spiritual.

Such an arrangement was contrary to true Islam and was disapproved of by the Ismailis, the most militant of the Shias. They too challenged the Abbasids but with a view to overthrowing them. They succeeded in Tunisia. There, led by Ubaidullah al Mahdi and aided by Berbers, they seized power in 909, and established themselves as the Fatimid (derivative of Fatima, wife of Ali) caliphate. This signified a successful Shia fundamentalist challenge to Sunni Abbasid rule which was considered by the Fatimids as unjust. Its importance rose when in 969 the Fatimids captured Egypt and became rivals to the Abbasids. In the new palace city of Al Qahira (Cairo) they founded the mosque and theological college of Al Azhar which became the leading centre of Shia learning.

During the Buyid hegemony in Baghdad (932–1055) four collections of Shia hadiths – Sayings and Doings of Shia Imams – were codified. In legal terms this put Shias on a par with the already existing four Sunni codes of the Sharia, canon law: Hanafi, Maliki, Shafii and Hanbali. The Buyids were overthrown by the Seljuks from central Asia, who were Sunni.

The loss of Jerusalem, the third holiest city of Islam, to Christians in the First Crusade (1095–9) created a crisis in the Islamic world. To the extent that it gave impetus to revivalist impulses among Muslims it initially aided the

Fatimids and their vision of Islam more than the others. The Fatimids were bent on bringing all Muslim lands under the sway of their Imams. They made much headway. At its peak the Fatimid domain extended from Tunisia to Sind including Egypt, Syria, Hijaz, Yemen and Oman – leaving only Iraq and Iran under Abbasid control.

It was from this base that Salah al Din Ayubi (also known as Saladin), a Kurdish general who had risen from the ranks of the Seljuk army, mounted his attack on the Fatimids in 1171, and ended their Shia rule. With this Sunnism once again became the dominant force in Islam. Today Shias are no more than twelve to fifteen per cent of the global Muslim population of some 950 million.

Summary

Muhammad was born in a feuding, polytheistic tribal society. In order to forge a unified monotheistic community under his leadership he prescribed a comprehensive set of rituals and practices, a meticulous code of moral–ethical behaviour and strict ground-rules for the running of a political state. His revelations of the Word of God, the Quran, and his personal practices, Sunna, became the foundations for the ordering of the Islamic umma.

By advocating strict adherence to the Quran and Sunna, Ali came to represent the idealist polarity in Islam. The pragmatist polarity was represented by those who succeeded Prophet Muhammad as caliphs. Indeed the third caliph, Uthman, stretched pragmatism so far as to trigger off a determined campaign by groups of militant soldiers against him, ending in his assassination. With this, Shiat Ali, Partisans of Ali, became the first fundamentalists in Islamic history. Ali's son Hussein took up arms against Yazid, an unjust ruler, even though the odds against him were desperately high. He thus turned the concept of martyrdom into a tactic to achieve an ideal Islamic order.

Shias, the early fundamentalists, drew the bulk of their support from pious Muslims and non-Arab Muslim clients, who felt discriminated against by Arab Muslims. Though the times have changed, the fundamentalists' constituencies have not. Today the alienated class of recent migrants to cities from villages provides the popular backing for the fundamentalist movement which is led mainly by low- and medium-ranking clerics and pious professionals and traders.

Shias were an important part of the coalition which engineered the Abbasid revolution against the Ummayad caliphs who had deviated widely from the true Islamic path, thus scoring the first fundamentalist triumph in Islam. But it was not long before the Sunni Abbasid caliphs too began slipping away from the Quran and Sunna, thus allowing Shias to become the sole repositories of the vision of ideal Islam. This role, coupled with the martyr complex inspired by Imam Hussein, turned Shias into valiant soldiers. The consequences were the subjugation of the Sunni caliph in Baghdad by a Twelver Shia king in 932, and the emergence of an Ismaili Shia caliphate, the Fatimids, in Cairo in 969. Shia domination lasted many generations, losing its grip first in Baghdad in 1055, and then in Cairo in 1171. But, oddly enough, Salah al Din Ayubi, the Sunni general who defeated the Shia caliphate in Cairo, was riding the wave of Islamic revivalism which swept the Muslim lands in the wake of the loss of Jerusalem to Christians in 1099.

2
ORTHODOX ISLAM AND SUFISM

In a general sense, while the Ummayad era (661–750) was a period of expansion for Islam, the Abbasid age was a period of consolidation. The early Ummayads were committed to keeping the Arab conquerors separate from the conquered people. They confined their soldiers to garrison towns and forbade sexual liaisons between them and non-Arab women. They provided protection to the non-Muslim population on payment of a poll tax, a practice initiated by Prophet Muhammad after his victory at Khaibar, an oasis populated largely by Jewish tribes. They were lukewarm to the idea of converting native populations to Islam.

In time, however, lured by the advantages, financial and otherwise, which stemmed from embracing Islam, the conquered peoples opted for Islam in large numbers, and came to be known as mawalis, clients. With this, social distinctions between Arab Muslims and non-Arab Muslims diminished. The tribal habits and simple rules of the Arabs intermingled with the more complex rules and regulations of the agrarian societies of Mesopotamia and Iran. The Ummayad caliphs took the easy way out by adopting the legal and administrative practices of the Byzantine and Sassanian emperors they had overthrown. This went down badly with pious Muslims. They wanted specifically Islamic solutions to the problems thrown up by the conquest of vast non-Arab lands and peoples. With the later Ummayads encouraging mass conversions in the conquered territories, Islam spread to villages among non-Arab peasants; and this made the need for an Islamic legal and administrative system more urgent. The Ummayads failed to meet this need. So the religious intellectuals sided with the Abbasid revolutionary forces as they rebelled against the Ummayads.

The early Abbasids concentrated on developing Islam as a social system and thus consolidating the empire. It was a complex and demanding task which took nearly two centuries to accomplish. It was performed by Islamic intellectuals. They found that of the 6,616 verses in the Quran only eighty concerned legal issues, and these were mainly about women, marriage, family and inheritance. But since Prophet Muhammad had ruled a political entity there was an oral record of what he had said and done as judge and administrator. After his death elaborate means had been employed to collect his sayings and doings, called the Prophet's Practice, or Sunna. (Later, in the mid-ninth century, some 2,700 sayings and doings of the Prophet were to be codified, and published in six canonical collections, called Hadiths, Reports, the most famous collections being by Muhammad al Bukhari (810–870). In short, the Quran is the Word of Allah, and the Hadiths explain the Quran.

Among the first to codify the Quran and Sunna was Abu Hanifa al Numan (699–767), an Iranian merchant resident in Kufa. His madhhab (legal school) was adopted by the Abbasids. Later another canonical school was pioneered by Malik ibn Anas (714–96), a lawyer in Medina. The environment in which these scholars worked is reflected in the character of the documents they produced. The Hanafi code is liberal and oriented towards urban society whereas the Maliki is conservative and suitable for pastoral communities.

But the alim, the religious–legal scholar, who was to make the greatest impression on the legal–administrative apparatus of the Abbasid empire was Muhammad ibn Idris al Shafii (767–820), a student of Malik ibn Anas in Medina who later settled in Cairo. He founded the science of religious jurisprudence, fiqh, on four pillars: the Quran, the Prophet's Sunna as recorded in the Hadiths, the consensus (ijma) of the community, and analogical reasoning (qiyas). So far, ijma had been construed as consensus of *ahl al hall wal aqd*, those who loose and bind, a term which embraces various types of representatives of the community, including religious intellectuals, but Shafii enlarged it to include the whole community. Analogical reasoning allowed the community to incorporate new situations into the system of the Sharia, Divine Law, without disturbing the primacy of the Quran and Sunna. It also permitted individual opinions and differences, something sanctioned by the hadith: 'The differences of opinion among the learned within my community are [a sign of] God's grace.'[1] By pursuing this method the ulama could merge Prophet Muhammad's teachings, Arab traditions and non-Arab traditions into a single canonical system applicable to the life of all Muslims, Arab and non-Arab. Thus Shafii's systematization of the Sharia provided the foundation upon which a common identity of Muslims scattered around the world could be built.

The other school which has survived is that of Ahmad ibn Hanbal (780–855). He was against a legal superstructure built upon the Quran and Sunna, and argued that a legal decision must be reached by referring directly to the Quran and Sunna instead of a body of religious jurisprudence derived from them. According to him, the Quran and Sunna were the law itself, not merely the source of it. His fundamentalist approach proved unpopular in the sophisticated societies of the Fertile Crescent – comprising present-day Iraq, Syria, Jordan, Lebanon and Egypt – but found its followers among the nomadic tribes of the Najd region of Arabia.

Over the next several generations most of the Sunni ulama in the Dar al Islam settled for one of these four schools which set the boundaries of the Sharia, from the fundamentalist Hanbali code to the liberal Hanafi. In order not to upset the consensus thus arrived at with some new radical innovations, the ulama from the tenth century onwards declared that the doors of ijtihad, creative interpretation, in Islam had been shut. The cumulative effect of this stance was to prove detrimental to Islam. It became rigid and reflected the status quo, and declined perceptibly in the latter centuries of the second (Christian) millennium as the pace of technological development in the West quickened and rivalry between the Ottoman caliphate and European powers sharpened.

Hanafi's school, adopted by the Abbasids, became established in West Asia. The Maliki school, native to Medina, spread to north and central Africa. The Shafii school, originating in Egypt, reached southern Arabia, and from there spread along the monsoon route to East Africa and South-East Asia. The Hanbali school, on the other hand, remained confined to the Najd.

The Sharia, Divine Law, governs the life of a Muslim completely. Religious jurisprudents, called faqihs, studied all human actions and categorized them as: obligatory, recommended, allowed, unspecified, undesirable and prohibited. From this they graduated to prescribing exactly how the obligatory, recommended and allowed acts were to be performed. They began to ascribe profound meanings to certain obligatory acts. The simple edict by Prophet Muhammad that a believer must undertake ritual ablution with water (or sand) before prayers became enmeshed into a profound debate on the purity and pollution of the human body. Religious jurisprudents conducted minute examinations of all bodily functions – eating, drinking, breathing, washing, urinating, defecating, farting, copulating, vomiting, bleeding, shaving – and prescribed how these were to be performed, the main stress being on keeping the body 'pure'. Along with this went a code of social behaviour which too was all-encompassing. The twin codes were so demanding that, even with the best will in the world, a believer could not abide by them all the time. On the other hand it was the introduction of these codes into the lives of those who had embraced Islam that led to common behavioural patterns among Muslims whether they lived in the Mauritanian desert or the Indonesian archipelago.

The speed with which this process took root varied from region to region. In general, the farther away a territory was from the Islamic heartland in West Asia the longer was the period before Islamization took firm root. It also depended on how Islam was brought to a region: whether by armed conquest or economic contacts with Arab traders arriving either overland or by sea.

For instance, in sub-Saharan Africa Islam spread through the trade routes serviced by the Arabs from the north. Here, often an African tribal chieftain would embrace Islam to raise his social and political status by joining a superior, larger civilization with a written scripture. He would start by accepting an amulet or costume, graduate to offering prayers, and then replace the local taboos with Islamic ones in his personal life. His example would be emulated by his followers. Only after Islamic culture had thus become established in the tribe would the religious jurisprudence, fiqh, be applied.

The same process was at work in the major Indonesian islands of Java and Sumatra. These were under Hindu or Buddhist influence when Arab traders arrived in the thirteenth century. Islam percolated from the coast into the interior through the trade network. The Islamization process, which began seriously in the fourteenth century, has yet to be completed. In Java and other major islands the hill people in the hinterland are either animist or Christian or 'nominal Muslims' called *abangan* (whereas orthodox Muslims on the coast are known as *santri*). In the interior Islamic practices and worship exist alongside those rooted in animism, Hinduism or Buddhism.

The fiqh is less a system of law, with a developed apparatus of procedure and enforcement, than a process of socialization and acculturation which progressively transforms human societies in a more or less autonomous manner [notes Malise Ruthven]. In time the process of Islamization takes root, imposing a degree of cultural homogeneity. Observance of the Divine Law becomes a social factor functioning more or less independently of the state.[2]

Islam spread among those societies where existing religious faith involved either idol-worship or a personality cult. This was as true of the Arabia of the seventh century as of the Java of the thirteenth. As a result, those who adopted Islam, for whatever reasons, missed the psychic satisfaction they had derived from worshipping idols, or objects of nature, or even some superior human being; practices strictly forbidden by the Quran. Furthermore, the Allah portrayed in the Quran was a severe entity who aroused awe and reverence among the believers rather than love or affection. To the bulk of new converts Islam came across as a creed concerned primarily with precise and overt observance of the Quranic edicts, and pursuing of political power. Strict obedience to Allah's commandments and meticulous observance of religious rituals left many believers spiritually and psychologically unfulfilled. The debates about the finer points of the Quran and Sunna, which deeply engaged the ulama, left the largely illiterate body of the faithful cold and bewildered. At the very least the Muslim masses needed a humane, charismatic Islamic leader whose words and actions would infuse their new faith with warmth. In the early days of Islam the tragic figure of the idealist, uncompromising Ali became the personality from whom many of the fresh converts drew living inspiration. Later Imam Hussein and his martyrdom provided the spiritual sustenance to this body of believers. After Hussein's death in 681 no equivalent figure emerged to satisfy the spiritual needs of such Muslims.

Some Muslims sought solace in undertaking ascetic exercises and arduous spiritual practices, believing that such means would bring them closer to the Deity. They were inspired by the example of Prophet Muhammad who used to withdraw into a cave and undertake nightly vigils, and by the practices of Christian hermits. Like the adherents of the Eastern Orthodox Church they came to believe that Allah, or the Ultimate Reality, could be apprehended only by direct personal experience. They therefore stressed meditation and contemplation of the Deity, and regarded direct involvement in worldly affairs, or pursuit of political power, as distractions from the path of seeking Allah within. Through their practices they injected warmth, piety and altruistic love into Islam. They came to be known as sufis – from the term *suf*, wool, linked to the woollen garments the pioneers among them wore as a sign of asceticism. Hassan al Basri (d. 728), who adopted the path of simple asceticism, was the first known sufi personality.

In time two kinds of sufis emerged: ecstatic and sober. The ecstatic Al Hussein ibn Mansur al Hallaj (857–922) declared 'I am the Truth', and was executed as a heretic. Among sober sufis Abu Hamid Muhammad al Ghazali (1058–1111) was the most prominent. His personal experience led him to conclude that mysticism was a meaningful way of perceiving the Ultimate Reality, even though it did not enable the believer to learn anything about Allah, or the Ultimate Reality, over and above what was already in the Quran. He thus tried to fit the mystical experience within the limits of the Sharia. His greatest contribution to Islam was to write *Ihya Ulum al Din* (Revival of the Religious Sciences), a manual for everyday existence which blended institutional religion with individual virtue.

While Shafii had built a legal superstructure on the foundation of the Quran and Sunna, Ghazali tried to integrate the whole legal system with a spiritual infrastructure originating in Prophet Muhammad's mystic consciousness. In *Ihya Ulum al Din* Ghazali urged the faithful to be aware of God's presence while undertaking not only prayers and fasting but also such mundane actions as eating, washing and sleeping. His work became the living document for the sufi orders which sprang up soon after his death.

The first sufi brotherhood was Qadiriya, founded by Abdul Qadir al Gailani (1077–1166), who was based in Baghdad. It was later to spread as far as West Africa and South-East Asia. It is a more orthodox order than the subsequent ones and stresses piety and humanitarianism.

In the absence of any social organization outside the folds of the extended family, sufi orders provided the only platform for social solidarity. A brotherhood consisted of aspirants (murids) or mendicants (dervishes) who took an oath of allegiance to the guide, known as shaikh, pir or murshid. (Women were admitted as associate aspirants.) The shaikh headed a hierarchy within the order which was linked by a chain of inherited sanctity (baraka) or kinship to the founding saint. This chain went back to the early sufi founders, such as Hassan al Basri, and through them to the House of the Prophet or Prophet Muhammad himself. It was a common practice for a sufi brotherhood to establish its own convents.

As long as the Shia Buyid monarchy flourished in Baghdad and the Fatimid caliphate in Cairo, a great deal of the ideological–spiritual energy of the Islamic world was channelled into the Sunni–Shia feud. But once the Buyids had been replaced by the Sunni Seljuks in 1055, and the Fatimids by Salah al Din Ayubi in 1171, and the supremacy of Sunnism had been re-established, sectarian disputes virtually ended. Since sufi orders were generally free of sectarian influences they became the recipients of the intellectual energy which had been previously expended in Sunni–Shia disputation. This gave a fillip to sufism.

The overthrow of the Sunni Abbasids in 1258 by the invading Mongols led by Hulagu Khan created an ideological and intellectual vacuum in which sufism thrived; and so did Shiaism. During this period of rapid expansion sufi orders took on board both orthodox and dissident ideologies.

An example of a dissident order was Bektashi in Turkey. Its excessive respect for the House of Ali bordered on Shiaism, and not surprisingly many of its followers belonged to the Alevi (a variation of Shia) sect. An example of a mainstream brotherhood was Naqshbandi, established by Yusuf al Hamadani (d. 1140) but named after Baha al Din Naqshband (1318–89), a mystic born in Tajikstan and buried near Bukhara. Naqshbandis believed that there was no tariqa (road) outside the Sharia, and followed the maxim, 'The exterior is for the world, the interior for Allah.' Believing that piety was best expressed through social activity, they opposed withdrawal from the world. That the Naqshbandi order was free of the Sunni–Shia divide was obvious from its genealogy: Abu Bakr, Ali, Salman al Farsi (a companion of the Prophet), Jaafar al Sadiq and Abu Yazid al Bistani. Naqshbandis are noted for their silent remembrance (dhikr) in mosques undertaken to induce a state of collective ecstasy.

From about the mid-twelfth century onwards sufism became so prevalent as to be indistinguishable from main-stream Islam. Sufis ceased to be apolitical, and became involved in political–military campaigns. For instance, in 1453 sufi dervishes participated in the successful seizure of Constantinople by the Ottoman Turks. In 1501 the sufi order of Safavi, based in Ardebil, captured Tabriz and laid the foundation of the Safavid dynasty in Iran.

There was all along a certain tension between the ulama – steeped in scriptures and conscious of their role as the only qualified spiritual guides – and sufi shaikhs, who invariably invoked a call by Allah or the Prophet in a dream or vision to take up the mantle of spiritual leadership (without the rigorous book learning of the conventional ulama). Sufi shaikhs were frequently credited with miracu-lous powers; and it was widely believed that their inherited sanctity, which survived their death, stayed on around their tombs. This turned their tombs into shrines where saint-worship was practised, much to the chagrin of the ulama. While saint-worship was heretical in Islam it appealed to most of the new converts from the societies which were steeped in this tradition. Thus sufism became a bridge between pre-Islamic creeds and Islam, helping to win converts to Islam and retain them.

Also, while the conventional ulama, in their capacity as religious jurisprudents or judges, could not provide a model for social behaviour to the faithful or encourage more devotional forms of worship, the sufi shaikhs were not so inhibited. They bent rules to suit local customs.

Whereas Islamic rituals were by and large austere, sufi orders provided a framework within which rich and colour-ful liturgical practices were spawned in the form of the devotional rituals of novices. The ecstatic sufi orders were particularly suitable for this purpose. The Rifaiiya broth-erhood, originating in Iraq, was a case in point. Its followers went into frenzies during which they would ride dangerous animals, walk into fires, ravage venomous rep-tiles, or mutilate themselves by placing iron rings in their ears, necks or hands – to demonstrate the supremacy of mind over matter. Given the frequent appearance of devils and angels in the Quran it required no major dispensation to let African pagan cults co-exist with Islamic rituals. Sufi silent prayers were conducted with the dual purpose of remembering Allah and propitiating savage pagan gods and goddesses.

Sufism grew rapidly between 1250 and 1500 when the caliphate was based in Cairo under Mamluk sultans, and when Islam penetrated central and western Africa, and southern India and South-East Asia, along the land and sea routes used by Arab traders. Islam came into contact not only with paganism in Africa but also the advanced religions and civilizations of Hinduism and Buddhism in Asia.

In fact the first encounter between Islam and Hinduism had occurred in 711 when Islamic forces from Arabia had arrived in Sind by sea. Their rule lasted until 828. A later Islamic incursion occurred through the Khyber pass along the Afghanistan–Indian border when the invader Mahmud of Ghazni (an Afghan city) incorporated Punjab into his realm. But it was only in 1206 that Qutb al Din Aibak, a Turko-Afghan, established a Turko-Afghan sultanate in northern India.

Islam's egalitarianism proved particularly attractive to lower caste Hindus and outcastes. But a bridge between polytheistic Hinduism and monotheistic Islam was needed to win converts to the new faith. It was provided by such sufi orders as Qadiriya, Chisti and Naqshbandi. The Qadiriya brotherhood, having originated in Baghdad, had spread to India and from there to eastern Afghanistan. The Naqshbandi order, having grown up in Tajikistan, had found its way through proselytized Tartars into Turkey (where Ottoman sultans were to base the caliphate from 1517 onwards), and also into India through its Turko-Afghan and Mogul invaders. Theologically, these brother-hoods subscribed to the 'unity of being' thesis articulated by Muhyi al Din al Arabi (1165–1240). According to Arabi, there was no duality between Allah and his universe. Instead, Allah and his creation were part of a continuum, or 'unity of being', composed of different grades of reality. Man was the microcosmic being through whom Allah contemplated himself. Thus divinity and humanity were two distinctive aspects which found expression at every level of creation – divinity corresponding to the covert side of reality and humanity to the overt.

Sufi shaikhs in India extended Arabi's thesis by arguing that since Allah was the only reality, all physical objects were mere 'appearances' (an idea remarkably similar to the Hindu concept of the world being an illusion, *maya*), which could be revered as manifestations of the divine will. From this the acceptance of Hindu pantheism was only one short step. It was thus that sufi shaikhs built a theological bridge which enabled disaffected Hindus to cross over to Islam and synthesize some of the pre-Islamic practices with the Islamic ones.

The process of synthesis between Islam and Hinduism found its apogee during the reign of Jalal al Din Muhammad Akbar (1556–1605), a grandson of Zahir al Din Muhammad Babar, who founded the Mogul dynasty in India in 1526. Akbar cultivated sufi shaikhs, and was close to the Chisti brotherhood which was renowned for its universalist outlook. He tried to overcome the differences between Hinduism and Islam by treating his Hindu and Muslim subjects as equals, something which was not sanctified by the Sharia, and which had not been attempted by any of the previous Muslim rulers. Akbar got around the problem by declaring himself to be the chief and absolute mujtahid, practitioner of ijtihad, thus inadvertently ending the virtual ban on ijtihad that the ulama had maintained since the tenth century. He then changed those parts of the Sharia which discriminated against his non-Muslim subjects. He abolished the poll tax, and declared that Hindu women did not have to embrace Islam when marrying Muslims. His actions amounted to a gross deviation from Islam, and caused consternation among orthodox ulama.

In 1581 he went so far as to launch his own faith, Din Illahi (Divine Faith), by synthesizing Islam with other religions. It was founded on the twin pillars of reason and asceticism. It praised the sufi attributes of devotion, piety, kindness and yearning for Allah, and condemned imitation and blind application of Islamic jurisprudence, which were the hallmarks of the Islamic establishment in India and elsewhere. Din Illahi had the full backing of the crown. Yet it failed to catch the popular imagination. It was adopted mainly by courtiers who treated the Emperor Akbar as their religious guide.

Orthodox Islamic circles considered Din Illahi heretical. For it implicitly challenged the claim of Islam to be the final and most authentic faith bestowed upon humanity by Allah. A fundamentalist reaction was bound to follow; and it did. But, interestingly enough, it was led by a Naqsh-bandi shaikh, Khwaja Abu al Muayyid Radi al Din Baqi-billah (1563–1603). He won recruits to his order from among Akbar's courtiers. However, an open attack on the dilution of Islam and the ingression of esoteric practices into sufi orders had to wait until after Akbar's rule had given way to Nur al Din Selim Jahangir's (1605–27). It was mounted by Shaikh Ahmad Sirhindi, a disciple of Baqibillah. He blamed Arabi's 'unity of being' doctrine for opening the floodgates of Hinduism into Islam and dissolving the monotheistic faith of Prophet Muhammad into the polymorphous structure of Hindu society. He reiterated the Naqshbandi position: the only way to perceive the Deity was through the Sharia, and (as elaborated earlier by Abu Hamid al Ghazali) the believer's mystical experiences had to be adapted to the Sharia and its external forms so as to avoid a relapse into heterodoxy or getting lost in individualistic eccentricities. He countered Arabi's 'unity of being' doctrine with his 'unity of witness' thesis. It differentiated absolutely between Allah and his creation, and rejected the concept of continuum. While Arabi had argued that reality was the mirror through which Allah contemplated himself, Sirhindi reasoned that reality was a reflection of Allah but was at the same time quite apart from him. In short, in Sirhindi's view, the Sharia was supreme both in the believer's inner mystical experiences and his outward practices. Such an uncompromising stance precluded any chance of reconciliation between Islam and Hinduism. He was called the Mujaddid Alf-e Thani, Reformer of the Second (Islamic) Millennium.

By arresting the synthetic tendencies in the Indian Muslim community, Sirhindi placed a stamp of rigid orthodoxy on Islam in India, and sowed the seeds of Muslim communalism which resulted three and a half centuries later in the creation of Pakistan, a homeland for the Muslims of the Indian subcontinent.

The heyday of Sirhindi and the Naqshbandi order came during the rule of Muhyi al Din Aurangzeb (1658–1707), a grandson of Jahangir. Inspired by Sirhindi's ideology, Aurangzeb set out to purify the Muslim community by strictly implementing the Sharia. He actively pursued the Quranic edict of suppressing evil and enjoining virtue. He appointed censors to check alcoholism and sexual vices. He banned prostitution and hashish cultivation, and actively discouraged music. He strictly prohibited the construction of roofs over saints' graves and the use of such tombs as places of pilgrimage, a fairly common practice among Indian Muslims. He provided free kitchens, inns and subsistence allowances to indigent Muslims and withdrew taxes not sanctioned by the Sharia. He reintroduced the poll tax on Hindus, thus ending the equal treatment accorded to them since the days of Akbar. He replaced the Hindu solar calendar with the Muslim lunar calendar.

Aurangzeb's policies helped to rid Indian Islam of the heterodoxy and superstition that had crept into it since the early thirteenth century. They also enabled the Islamic state to reassert its authority over its non-Muslim citizens. In the process, however, the state lost much of the good-will that Akbar's policies had engendered among the Hindus – who constituted three-quarters of the total population. The result was a series of revolts by Hindus and Sikhs (followers of a monotheistic faith which originated as a Hindu reform movement in the late fifteenth century), which debilitated the Mogul empire and, after Aurangzeb's death in 1707, showed to the Muslims that they were a vulnerable minority.

Faced with the prospect of a declining Mogul empire, Shah Waliullah of Delhi (1703–64), an eminent Naqshbandi shaikh educated in Mecca and Medina, argued that what Aurangzeb had achieved was insufficient, and that since Islam had been weakened by the infusion of Hindu customs and beliefs the only solution lay in further intensifying Islamic reform. He believed that the essence of Islam was eternal, but not its detailed practices. Hence there was a need for perpetual ijtihad, creative reasoning, a stance totally at variance with the religious establishment. He proposed that the conclusions of the four (Sunni) legal schools be sifted with the texts of the Quran and Hadiths – a fundamentalist position. To help this process, and bring ordinary educated Muslims (totally dependent on their local mullahs for guidance) into direct contact with the Quran, he translated the Holy Book into Persian, the language of the literate Muslims, an unprecedented step. More importantly, he argued that with the Islamic umma enlarging and progressing there was constant need for ijtihad to cope with the new problems arising. He was probably the first Islamic thinker to articulate that religious thought had to interact with changing social conditions.

But the disintegration of the Mogul empire continued. It was under attack by Hindu and Sikh kings as well as by British East India Company forces. With this the reformism preached by Waliullah turned into militancy under the leadership of Ahmad Barelvi (d. 1831), a disciple of Waliullah's son Abdul Aziz. He broadened the base of the reformist movement by attracting supporters from the three leading sufi orders – Naqshbandi, Qadiriya and Chisti – and harnessing them within the framework of renewed Sharia orthodoxy. Thus was born the Tariq-e Muhammadiya, Way of Muhammad, an order which coupled sufi discipline with Sharia orthodoxy. Since the Sikh rulers had taken to persecuting Muslims, Barelvi declared a jihad against them in 1826. Later he led his followers to the Indo-Afghan border region with a view to founding an Islamic state on a 'liberated territory', thus emulating the example of the hijra (migration) of Prophet Muhammad from Mecca to Medina.

His venture met with initial success. But when he attempted to impose Sharia taxes on the resident Pathan tribesmen of the region, they abandoned his camp. The Sikh army battled with Barelvi's forces and defeated them in 1831. Barelvi was executed. But Tariq-e Muhammadiya survived as a militant movement and played a substantial role in the major Indian rebellion of 1857 against the British. This was an instance where a reformist movement in Islam proved to be double-edged: against adulteration of Islamic practices among Muslims as well as against Western Christian forces.

It was not only the periphery of the Dar al Islam which experienced moral and scriptural back-sliding, but also the Islamic heartland. Those who attacked this tendency vociferously were often the followers of Ahmad ibn Hanbal, the founder of the Hanbali legal school. In so far as the Hanbalis referred directly to the Quran and Sunna to reach legal decisions they stood apart from the other three schools which had codified the Sharia into a comprehensive jurisprudential system. In the late fourteenth century Taqi al Din ibn Taimiya emerged as an eminent Hanbali reformer. Though he started as a member of the Qadiriya sufi brotherhood he later severely condemned the practices of saint-worship and tomb cult. He opposed the contemporary ulama's assertion that the doors of ijtihad had been closed. In jurisprudence he placed the Quran and Sunna far above ijma, the community's consensus, and stressed loyalty to salaf (ancestors) rather than to any specific legal school. The salafi concept was later to become the foundation of the fundamentalist movement among Sunnis. His views found a positive response among the Mamluk sultans in Cairo, the base of the caliphate from 1250 to 1517.

The situation changed when the Ottoman Turks became the leading power in the Dar al Islam: they were the followers of the Hanafi school. The Ottoman empire was founded by Osman I (1259–1326), a leader of Osmanli

Turks. When Muhammad II seized Constantinople/Istanbul in 1453 he became heir to the Byzantine empire. Under Selim I (1512–20) the Ottoman empire acquired Islamic primacy by usurping the caliphate from the Mamluks. The expansion continued under his successor Suleiman the Magnificent (1520–66), when the empire included Algeria, Libya, Egypt, most of Greece and Hungary, much of Persia and Arabia, and Syria. Transylvania, Wallachia and Moldavia were its tributary principalities. The growth and consolidation lasted until 1683 when the Ottomans reached, but failed to conquer, Vienna. By now the Ottoman empire spanned Africa, Europe and Asia, and had Muslim, Christian and Jewish subjects. The emperor was the protector of the Muslim holy cities of Mecca and Medina, which were also thriving centres of Islamic learning.

It was in Mecca and Medina, for instance, that Shah Waliullah had acquired his knowledge of Islam. Among his contemporaries was Muhammad ibn Abdul Wahhab (1703–87), a native of Najd, a Hanbali stronghold. Born into a religious family in Uyaina, Abdul Wahhab was inspired as much by Hanbal as by Taimiya. After his education in Mecca and Medina he returned to his home town. He was appalled by the prevalence of superstition, adultery and tribalism in his community, which had grown lax in its observance of Islamic rites and practices. He called for the discarding of all the medieval superstitions which had collected around the pristine teachings of Islam, and for the exercise of ijtihad. He opposed the codification of the Sharia into a comprehensive system of jurisprudence. He and his followers resorted to destroying the sacred trees and tombs of the saints. This upset the local community so much that its members drove out Abdul Wahhab and his supporters in 1744, an action reminiscent of the Meccans in the early days of Islam. They took refuge in the principality of Diriya where Abdul Wahhab made an alliance with the ruler, Muhammad ibn Saud. The followers of Abdul Wahhab, called Wahhabis, armed themselves and mounted a campaign against idolatry, the association of others with Allah, injustice, corruption and adultery. Regarding themselves to be the true believers, the Wahhabis launched a jihad against all others whom they described as apostates – a practice which had many precedents in Islamic history. But what was unprecedented was the degree of puritanism they wanted to impose on the community. Claiming authority from the Hadiths, they banned music, dancing and even poetry which had always been an integral part of Arab life. They prohibited the use of silk, gold, ornaments and jewellery. Parallels with early Islam were unmistakable. Yet there were important differences too. While Prophet Muhammad had wielded the sword himself, Abdul Wahhab let his principal ally, Muhammad ibn Saud, wage battles and govern the community of muwahhidin, unitarians, believers in the unity of Allah. Muhammad ibn Saud called himself Imam and each Imam chose his own successor, with the descendants of Abdul Wahhab, known as Aal Shaikh, providing the leading ulama to the government. As in the seventh century, so now: the zealot members of rejuvenated Islam expanded their domain rapidly.

But here too there were essential differences. For instance, when in 1802 Saud ibn Abdul Aziz, grandson of the founder of the Saudi dynasty, invaded Karbala and destroyed the shrine of Imam Hussein, robbing it of all finery, he ordered the killing of all the Karbala residents since, according to him, they were apostates.

The following year the Wahhabis seized Mecca and demolished all the domes over the graves of the leading figures of early Islam. In 1805, finding themselves besieged by the Wahhabis, the local Medinese destroyed the domes over all the tombs. These events signalled the victory of fundamentalist forces, and the emergence of a unified Arabia, including Mecca and Medina, ruled by its own Imam.

However, unlike the unified community under Prophet Muhammad, Muslims in the early nineteenth century were divided among various sects. The hegemony of Wahhabis, an extremist sect, over Mecca and Medina created unease among the pilgrims whose loyalties were spread over a whole range of orthodox sects and sufi orders. What was more, the Ottomans' loss of Mecca and Medina threatened the security and well-being of Damascus and Baghdad, which were intimately tied up with the pilgrimage trade. So the Ottoman sultan could not let Wahhabi actions go unchallenged. In 1812 Sultan Mahmud II (1808–39) despatched Muhammad Ali Pasha, governor of Egypt, to defeat the Wahhabis. He succeeded. By 1819 he had crushed the Wahhabis, destroyed Diriya, and taken the ruler Abdullah ibn Saud to Istanbul where he was executed. Thus ended a vigorous fundamentalist movement.

The logic of their convictions and geographical location had left the Wahhabis no choice but to march on Mecca and Medina and impose their vision of Islam, hoping thus to win converts to their camp. But since these settlements were part of the Ottoman empire a clash between Wahhabis and the Ottoman empire became inevitable; and so did the defeat of the Wahhabis. It is likely that had the Wahhabis by their example induced a similar movement in a key part of the Ottoman empire such as Egypt, Syria or Iraq, they would have set in motion forces that the Ottomans would have found difficult, if not impossible, to overcome. But they did not.

To be sure, Sultan Mahmud II was beset with intractable problems, unable to modernize the administration and military as he wished, and caught up in the shifting balance of forces within the ruling élite – not to mention the challenge of administering a large non-Muslim population in the empire. The issues were complex and overwhelming, and defied the simplistic solutions offered by Wahhabi fundamentalism.

Increasingly, as the Islamic heartland fell under western influence, the nature of the threats and dangers that Islam faced changed. Dilution and corruption of Islam began to occur not so much because of the ingression of the pre-Islamic practices of native populations as because of the infiltration of western secular ideas and practices, and political models, into the body politic of Islam. The Ottoman empire straddling Europe, Asia and Africa lay at the hub of this process.

3

ISLAM IN MODERN TIMES

Islam entered the modern age under the leadership of Ottoman Turks, with Istanbul as the capital of the caliphate. It is therefore crucial to study major developments within the Islamic empire as well as its relations with European powers.

Once the Ottomans failed to annex Vienna in 1683 they found themselves on the defensive *vis-à-vis* the empires of the Hapsburgs and Tsars. The Treaty of Kuchuk Kainarji of 1774 allowed the Russian Tsar to aid the Muslim Tartars, who were scattered from the Polish border to the Caspian Sea, including Crimea, to establish a semi-independent state under his tutelage. A decade later the Tsar annexed this state. In 1791 the Hapsburgs formalized their annexation of Belgrade. Clearly the Ottoman military was proving unequal to the task of fending off its European rivals.

Selim III (1789–1807) realized the need to modernize the army. He established a new militia and military schools with French instructors and training manuals. This upset the 50,000 professional soldiers and officers, called Janissaries, who had been the traditional armed force of the caliphate since 1259. The Janissaries allied with the ulama in arousing popular passions against military modernization, and deposed Selim III. The bureaucratic élite, the third centre of power which had been growing steadily, was not strong enough to alter the course of events. Selim III's successor, Mahmud II (1808–39), ended military reform.

What had struck a severe blow to Selim III's prestige was the occupation in 1798 of Egypt, a Muslim territory of his empire, by Napoleon Bonaparte. Then in 1830 France occupied another Muslim territory of the Ottoman empire: Algeria. It was apparent that Christian Europe, helped by striking advances in technology and administration, was forging ahead at the expense of the Ottomans. That Europe's rising supremacy stemmed from the rapid growth of capitalism, largely due to the discovery and development of the Americas, did not detract from the fact that the Ottoman power was on the decline.

There was a growing awareness in intellectual circles in the Ottoman empire of political and social malaise. The degree of stagnation of official Islam can be judged by the fatwa (verdict) issued by the Mufti (religious–legal jurist) of Cairo's Al Azhar early in the nineteenth century. 'The four orthodox schools are the best results, the finest extraction of all schools, because they count among their partisans many men dedicated to the search for truth and blessed with vast knowledge,' stated the Mufti. 'Deviation from these four schools shows the desire to live in error.' It was therefore obligatory to follow one of the four orthodox schools. He unequivocally rejected the claim to ijtihad, independent reasoning, in interpreting the sacred texts. 'No one denies the fact that the dignity of ijtihad has long disappeared and that at the present time no man has attained this degree of learning. He who believes himself to be mujtahid would be under the influence of his hallucinations and of the devil.'[1]

The reason for the suppression of independent thinking lay in the way that exercise of power had evolved in the Islamic world. The successors to the four Rightly Guided caliphs came to rely increasingly on sheer force to secure power and retain it. Yet they felt a periodic need for doctrinal legitimation. The only way to ensure this was by undermining independent thought on the doctrine. Time and again independent-minded thinkers were forced to retreat in the face of rigid official dogma sanctified by venal ulama whose sole argument was that opposition to the ruler would lead to chaos, which had to be avoided at all costs.

In the early nineteenth century, faced with unmistakable decline, the Ottoman intellectuals pondered the reasons for the growing strength of Christian European powers. Either Europeans had devised a system better than Islam or the Muslim community had failed to follow true Islam. Since none of them was prepared to concede the inferiority of Islam to any other social system the inevitable conclusion was that Muslims had deviated from the true path. So the stage was set for Islamic reform. Yet this time around the reform had less to do with theological or spiritual arguments and more with political power and policies. The numerous solutions offered boiled down to exhortations to Muslims all over the world to unite against European encroachment and/or to devise a strategy to study the sources of European power with a view to tapping them.

In the specific field of shoring up Ottoman military power, Mahmud II aligned more with the bureaucratic élite, committed to modernization, than with the coalition of the Janissaries and the ulama. The Janissaries suffered a severe setback in 1821 when they failed to curb a rebellion by the Greek subjects of the empire. It was a painful reminder to the sultan that the Islamic empire could no longer maintain its hold over its non-Muslim subjects. The standing of the Janissaries sank so low that when Mahmud II disbanded them in June 1826 the ulama uttered not a word of protest. This signalled victory for the state bureaucrats and their strategy of learning from the Europeans abroad, and making administrative and military reforms at home. Thus began the process of Tanzimat (literally, reorganization). Feudal tenure was abrogated and religious trusts reformed in 1827. Schools were opened in 1838 to train civil servants, doctors and military officers. Mahmud II prescribed the wearing of the fez instead of the assorted headgear used by various sections of Ottoman society. This signified symbolic equality for all Ottoman citizens, Muslim or non-Muslim, a concept which went down badly with Muslims at large. But these measures failed to appease the European powers. After annexing Bessarabia in 1812, Russia took over the Ottoman possessions in the Caucasus region in 1829.

Tanzimat gathered momentum under Abdul Majid

(1839–61). He laid down the doctrine of equality for all Ottoman citizens, irrespective of their religion, and the provision of security of life and property for all the inhabitants of the empire. In 1847 he founded military schools. Commercial and criminal codes, based on the Code Napoléon, were drafted in 1859. This meant limiting the Sharia to personal affairs. Control of education by the ulama was reduced when a ministry of education, formed in 1857, promulgated regulations for public instruction three years later. With the growing popularity of western dress in urban areas the ulama became differentiated from bureaucrats and military officers with whom hitherto they had been associated. Gradually the ulama came to be seen as diehard conservatives opposed to all innovations. Among the inventions they had (unsuccessfully) opposed was the printing press. Also the ulama came to be viewed as being concerned only with family matters and not with the believer's entire life.

European powers favoured Tanzimat; but that did not deter them from attacking the Ottoman empire. Tsarist Russia was the most aggressive, determined to act as the militant protector of 12 million Eastern Orthodox Christians under the Ottomans. It was at the same time consolidating and expanding its territories in central Asia inhabited by Muslims.

Taking their cue from Russian aspirations towards the Christians of the Ottoman empire, the leaders of the central Asian Muslims appealed to Sultan Abdul Aziz (1861–76) to establish himself as the guardian of the Muslims in Tsarist Russia. Abdul Aziz also became the recipient of appeals from the Muslims of India. There, after the failure of the 1857 uprising against the British – in which Muslim princes and kings played a leading role – depression had spread among Muslims as they pondered their fate as British subjects after having been the ruling caste for nearly seven centuries. To both the Indian and central Asian Muslims the Ottoman empire – containing the holy cities of Mecca, Medina and Jerusalem as well as the leading Islamic cultural centres of Cairo, Damascus and Baghdad –

was the prime embodiment of Islamic civilization and power.

But Abdul Aziz could do little. He was an extravagant ruler, heavily indebted to the European powers, and had no leverage over them. His impotence became embarrassingly obvious when in the last years of his reign, at Russia's behest, Bulgaria, Bosnia, Serbia and Montenegro rebelled against Istanbul. This caused such a tidal wave of disaffection that, following a fatwa against Abdul Aziz by the Shaikh al Islam, Wise Man of Islam, the supreme legal authority, Abdul Aziz was overthrown by Midhat Pasha, the leader of the Young Ottomans, a powerful group formed in 1859 with the main objective of securing an elected assembly for the umma of believers as a true application of the Sharia.

Midhat Pasha produced a constitution, an unprecedented development in Islam. Among other things it formalized the religious status of the Ottoman sultan. 'His Majesty the Sultan is, in his capacity as the Supreme Caliph, the protector of the Muslim religion,' it stated. The constitution, which included a Bill of Rights and stipulated an elected chamber, was promulgated by Abdul Hamid II (1876–1909) in December 1876.

In April 1877 the Russian army crossed the Ottoman borders with the objective of winning freedom for Slavs, and reached Istanbul. The sultan had to sign the humiliating Treaty of San Stefano in March 1878, which was revised in July by the Treaty of Berlin. According to it Cyprus went to Britain, and Tunisia to France. Furthermore, the sultan was obliged to engage financial and military advisers from Germany to implement reform, and allow judicial inspectors from European nations to travel through the empire to redress grievances.

The continued loss of territory coupled with growing intrusion into the internal affairs of the Ottoman empire by Europeans convinced Abdul Hamid II that the fifty-year-old Tanzimat programme had failed to reassure either the European powers or his Christian subjects. It was therefore time to change direction.

In February 1878 he suspended the constitution and dissolved parliament. He arrested Midhat Pasha and banished the Young Ottomans to different parts of the empire. He repudiated Islamic modernism and turned to traditional Islamic values and thought. But, interestingly enough, he continued to import western technology and methods. As it was, the ulama had no objection to the import of sewing-machines or railroads. At the same time they insisted that Islam had nothing spiritual to learn from the West – a position they still maintain.

Abdul Hamid II adopted the argument and policies first advocated by Ahmad Cevdet Pasha, who condemned Tanzimat leaders for destroying the cohesion of Ottoman society by implementing secular reform of the judicial system, and proposed that while the technological apparatus should be modernized, Islam in its traditional form should be maintained as the central system of Ottoman society. Indeed, Abdul Hamid II went one step further. He tried to regenerate cohesion in Ottoman society by activating the popular masses on a religious platform round the Islamic banner and harnessing their energies. In order to succeed in the venture he activated sufi brotherhoods and used them as channels of communication to reach the masses. His strategy worked since there had all along been a widespread current of Islamic feeling among the humbler subjects of the Ottoman empire.

He also tried to engender a pan-Islamic movement. In this he had the active backing of, among others, Jamal al-Din Afghani, a religious personality of varied talents: a scholar, philosopher, teacher, journalist and politician. He was born of Shia parents in Asadabad near Hamadan in western Iran, but claimed that his birthplace was Asadabad near Konar in eastern Afghanistan, and that his parents were Sunni.[2] By claiming Sunni background he could reach a wide audience. However, he did spend his childhood and adolescence in Kabul where he studied Islam and philosophy. At eighteen he left Kabul for pilgrimage to Mecca as well as Karbala and Najaf. Then he spent a year in India at a time when, following the failure of the 1857 Indian uprising against the British, there was strong anti-British feeling among Muslims. This left a deep mark on him.

On his return to Afghanistan in 1861 he became entangled in local politics. When his patron, Muhammad Azam, was ousted in 1869 by his half-brother, Sher Ali, Afghani was expelled from the country. He arrived in Istanbul, then in the throes of Tanzimat, and was well received by Sultan Abdul Aziz. Afghani, who favoured educational reform and scientific thought, was appointed to the Council of Education. In one of his lectures he referred to the esoteric meaning of the Quran, a concept regarded as heretical by Sunnis. This offended the ulama headed by the Shaikh al Islam, Hassan Fahmi, who was jealous of Afghani's scholarship and popularity. Afghani considered it prudent to leave Istanbul.

Soon after his arrival in Cairo in 1871 he was given a generous allowance by the ruler, Khedive Ismail. Among his students were Muhammad Abdu and Said Zaghlul Pasha: the former was to become the Grand Mufti of Egypt, and the latter a founder of the nationalist Wafd Party. Afghani encouraged patriotic resistance to growing British and French interference in Egypt's affairs, attacked Khedive Ismail for his extravagance, and proposed a parliamentary system of government which he saw as being in line with Islamic precepts. He thus proved to be an innovator in offering Islamic responses and solutions to contemporary problems.

When Tawfik succeeded his father, Khedive Ismail, in early 1879, the British advised him to expel Afghani. In September Afghani was deported to Hyderabad, India, and then to Calcutta, and kept under British surveillance. Here he attacked the Islamic modernist Sayyid Ahmad Khan for being servile towards the British and adopting a western lifestyle. He also condemned Ahmad Khan for persuading Indian Muslims to acquire British education and trying to offer a rationalist interpretation of the Quran. He advocated Hindu–Muslim unity in order to resist British rule. In Egypt, where Afghani had backed the nationalist movement led by Ahmad Urabi Pasha, anti-British feelings spilled over in an armed uprising in 1881–2 which was crushed. This marked the beginning of the British occupation of Egypt which continued until 1954.

Afghani turned up in Paris in January 1883. Four months later he published an article in the *Journal des Débats* in which he repudiated Joseph-Ernest Renan's arguments, delivered in an earlier lecture, that Islam and science were incompatible. While agreeing that, like other religions, Islam had been a barrier to scientific progress, he repudiated Renan's thesis that Islam was in this respect worse than other religions. Elsewhere he insisted that it was wrong to describe scientific study as antithetical to Islam, that it was indeed an integral part of Islamic civilization and that its loss was chiefly responsible for the decay that had set in in the Islamic umma.

He and Muhammad Abdu published a journal in Arabic, *Al Urwat al Wuthqa* (*The Indissoluble Link*). In it they supported Sultan Abdul Hamid II's pan-Islamist proclivities and elaborated their reformist ideas.

Following an invitation in 1886 by Iran's Nasir al Din Shah, Afghani went to live in Tehran. But his popularity there disconcerted the Shah. The next year Afghani left for the Uzbekistan region of the Tsarist empire. There he engaged in propaganda against the British in India, and this pleased the Tsar. Later, in Petersburg (now Leningrad), he persuaded Tsar Alexander II to allow the publication of the Quran and other Islamic literature for the first time in Tsarist history.

In 1889, on his way to the Paris World Exhibition, he met Nasir al Din Shah in Munich. Accepting the Shah's invitation, he returned to Tehran. However, his plan to reform the judiciary aroused the Shah's suspicion; and Afghani retired to a religious sanctuary near the capital. In early 1891, following his arrest, he was expelled to Turkey.

Afghani made his way to Basra. From there he attacked the Shah for giving the tobacco concession to a British company. His disciple, Mirza Hassan Shirazi, decreed that the faithful should stop smoking until the Shah had withdrawn his tobacco concession. This was the first time in

modern history that a religious leader had openly challenged the ruler in Iran. The popular response to Shirazi's
call was so overwhelming that the Shah cancelled the
tobacco concession in early 1892. Again this was the first
instance of public opinion in a Muslim country impinging
directly on royal decision-making.

From Basra, Afghani went to London where he carried
out a sustained campaign against the dictatorial rule of the
Shah, chiefly through *Diyal al Khafikyan* (Radiance of the
Two Hemispheres), a monthly journal published in Persian
and English. He thus helped to build a political reformist
movement in Iran under the leadership of the ulama which
was dedicated to the Shah's overthrow – a precursor of the
events of the late 1970s.

When Sultan Abdul Hamid II invited Afghani to Istanbul, he went. The sultan was liberal in his allowances to
Afghani, and tried to persuade him to cease his anti-Shah
propaganda. Afghani refused and sought, in vain, to leave.
In March 1896 the Shah of Iran was murdered by a
merchant who had once been a student of Afghani. About
a year later Afghani died of cancer.

Afghani was outstanding in more ways than one. He was
the first – and the last – Islamic figure who played an active
part in the religious–political life of the people in all the
important Islamic regions: Ottoman Turkey, Egypt, Iran,
India and central Asia. This gave him a truly pan-Islamic
perspective, and made him realize that all of the Islamic
umma was threatened by European powers. Not surprisingly, as Wilfred Cantwell Smith, an expert on Islam,
points out, Afghani was the first to use 'the concepts
"Islam" and "the West" as connoting correlative – and of
course antagonistic – historical phenomena'.[3]

Afghani was perceptive enough to realize that, of Britain
and Russia, Britain was the bigger threat to the Islamic
world. The British economic system was more advanced
along capitalist lines than the Russian, and it was Britain
which ruled both India and Egypt.

He was both a militant reformist of Islam and a vehement anti-imperialist. He wanted to goad the Muslim

masses and rulers into active resistance against European imperialism. While he used traditional Islamic language and constantly called on the dynamism and militancy of salaf al salih (the pious ancestors) to unite and resist the growing domination of the Islamic world by unbelievers, he also called on Muslims to revive scientific thought and reform their educational system – that is, to learn from the West.

Arguing for ijtihad, Afghani stated that each believer had the right and responsibility to interpret the Quran and Sunna for himself. He wanted the people to help themselves, and often quoted the Quranic verse: 'Verily, Allah does not change the state of a people until they change themselves inwardly.'

Afghani's influence was seminal in the creation of pan-Islamic nationalism and the reformist salafiya movement. In the dialect of Islam versus the West his position combined (in the words of Edward Mortimer) 'three types of Muslim responses to the West: the defensive call to arms, the eager attempt to learn the secret of Western strength, and the internalization of Western secular modes of thought'.[4]

Afghani was a genuine Islamic thinker. While he took an interest in certain western concepts, he never allowed western ideology to be the font of his inspiration. He remained rooted firmly in his Islamic heritage even though he spent some years in France, Britain and Russia.

In retrospect Afghani emerges as the modern progenitor of Islamic reform. His disciple, Muhammad Abdu, applied his general principles and guidelines to the specific task of law-making; and Muhammad Rashid Rida, one of Abdu's disciples, went on to offer a blueprint of an Islamic state suitable for the present day and age.

Muhammad Abdu, born into an Egyptian peasant family, came under Afghani's influence in the 1870s. When Egypt was occupied by the British in 1882, Abdu left for Paris where he assisted Afghani in publishing an Islamic journal. He parted with Afghani on the question of resisting the West. The militant Afghani believed in arousing

Muslim rulers and their subjects to fight the European forces whereas Abdu argued that Muslims must initially concentrate on educational and religious reform, and inculcate those aspects of western civilization which were in line with Islam.

Arguing that Islam was not incompatible with the basics of western thought, Abdu interpreted the Islamic concept of shura (consultation) as parliamentary democracy, ijma (consensus) as public opinion, and maslah (choosing that ruling or interpretation of the Sharia from which greatest good will ensue) as utilitarianism.

He returned to Egypt in 1888, and concentrated on educational and legal reform. After he had become the Grand Mufti he extended the concept of maslah to drafting laws based on the general principle of public morality. He even went so far as to state that if a particular Islamic ruling had become a source of harm – which it had not caused before – then it must be changed to suit contemporary conditions. He extended the concept of talfiq (choosing an interpretation from a legal school other than one's own) to produce a synthesis of different rulings and go beyond these to the original sources of the Sharia: the Quran, the Hadith and salaf al salih (pious ancestors) principles. While Afghani stressed the general militancy of the salaf of early Islam, Abdu focused on their impact on the shaping of the Sharia and their rationalism. Later, Abdu's approach to lawmaking was to be adopted by many Muslim states in the drafting of personal law.

Muhammad Rashid Rida, the best known of Abdu's disciples, carried the salafi principles further by researching what Prophet Muhammad and the salaf had done and said in order to apply it to contemporary conditions. In legal matters he preferred to follow the ideas of the salaf rather than formal legal schools. Like Ahmad ibn Hanbal he believed that the Quran and the Hadith were paramount because God could only be described by what he had done in the Quran, and Prophet Muhammad by what he had done in the Sunna. Also, when specific injunctions were found to be in contradiction, the best way that the believer

could solve the problem was by turning to the first principles as outlined in the Quran and the Hadith. He was thus
a supporter of the practice of ijtihad which he defined as
'independent reasoning from first principles'.

He outlined this and many other ideas in *Al Manar* (*The
Lighthouse*), the journal he published in Cairo after his
arrival there in 1897 from his native Tripoli, north Lebanon, where he had first met Abdu three years earlier.

While Egypt was occupied by Britain it was nominally
part of the Ottoman empire. By the early twentieth century
Abdul Hamid II's populist approach to Islam at home and
espousing of pan-Islamism abroad had proved inadequate
to revitalize the disintegrating empire. In 1908 the army
officers of the empire's European territories compelled
Abdul Hamid II to reinstate the 1876 constitution. The
next year they deposed him, hoping that this would
improve the health of the empire. It did not. The basic
problem was that while the traditional idea of an Islamic
umma governed by a strong and pious ruler had become
outmoded, the concept of securing equal loyalty for the
empire from different religious groups was too new and
untested.

The war of 1912–13, which led to the loss of the
remaining European territories, as well as Libya, once
again underlined the weakness of the Ottoman empire.
However, it could also be said that following the latest
setback the reduced empire had become religiously more
homogeneous. It was against this background that the
Kaiser's Germany encouraged the military leaders in Istanbul – known as the Young Turks – to liberate fellow Turks
from Russian bondage and extend their empire eastwards
to central Asia. It was thus that Turkey joined Germany in
the First World War in October 1914. The war ended four
years later with the Ottomans conceding defeat: an event
which signified the end of the last Islamic empire, a
traumatic experience for the world Muslim community.

For the next several years the situation in Turkey, the
heartland of the old Ottoman empire, remained turbulent.
In Istanbul Sultan Mehmet VI co-operated with the occu-

pation forces of the victorious Allies whereas the nationalist Turks, led by Mustafa Kemal, opposed them, and set up the Grand National Assembly in Ankara. Kemal's prestige rose sharply when he succeeded in expelling the occupying Greek forces from Turkey in August 1921. At his behest, in November 1922, the Grand National Assembly abolished the sultanate but retained the caliphate as a religious office. To justify this action Kemal referred to the precedent in the Abbasid period when the caliphs had lost all political authority and become symbolic figures of Islamic unity. This time around, however, the arrangement was to prove a stop-gap. In March 1924 Kemal asked the Grand National Assembly to 'cleanse and elevate the Islamic faith by rescuing it from the position of a political instrument, to which it has been accustomed for centuries'. The caliph was deposed, and the caliphate abolished, thus ending a 1,292-year-old tradition. This created a spiritual crisis in the Muslim world outside Turkey, which was to follow a militantly secular path under Kemal's leadership.

Muhammad Rashid Rida, a native of Greater Syria, was directly involved in the events that followed the dissolution of the Ottoman empire. In 1920 he became President of the Syrian National Congress which chose Prince Faisal ibn Hussein as King of Syria. Three years later he compiled his series of articles on the caliphate in *Al Manar* into a book entitled *The Caliphate or the Supreme Imamate*. This work established him as the founding theoretician of the Islamic state in its modern sense. In it he outlined the origins of the caliphate and examined the gulf that existed between the theory and practice of the caliphate, and went on to offer a blueprint for an Islamic state.[5]

The affairs of the Islamic state must be conducted within the framework of a constitution that is inspired by the Quran, the Hadith and the experiences of the Rightly Guided caliphs, Rida stated. Creative reasoning, ijtihad, must be employed to interpret these sources in drafting measures to promote public welfare. The head of the Islamic state – to be called the Caliph or Supreme Imam – must be a mujtahid. In his juridical role he is to be assisted by *ahl al hall wal aqd*, 'the people who loose and bind', a term which embraces various types of representatives of the community, including the ulama. They are to be the protectors of the Islamic character of the state. The caliph must consult them; and it is this consultation which makes his decisions religiously binding. Traditionally, 'the people who loose and bind' have been the community's representatives and electors of the caliphs. But nowadays they must also exercise the power to legislate, to find rational and systematic solutions to emerging problems. The Sharia is the dominant authority in legislation but, over the centuries, it has been complemented by a corpus of 'positive law', qanun, which is subordinate to it. In the final analysis the 'positive law' too must be in line with broad Islamic principles. A temporal authority must be established to conduct a system of sanctions and punishments to the law-breakers. (However, Rida was silent on the link between this authority and the Caliph/Supreme Imam.)

The Caliph/Supreme Imam must be chosen by the representatives of all Muslim sects (Sunni, Shia and Kharaji) from among a group of highly trained jurisconsults of unimpeachable renown. Rida's stress on jurisprudence stems from the fact that in modern times legislation is a crucial element of the state, and that the Caliph is expected to be the prime force behind the legislative process. As the head of state the Caliph is the leader of all Muslims, and must as such recognize the pluralism of the Islamic doctrine. The believers must obey the Caliph to the degree that his actions are in line with Islamic precepts and serve the public interest. When his decisions are perceived to contravene Islamic principles or public welfare, the community's representatives have the right to challenge them.

In Rida's view a Muslim is entitled to gain understanding of the Quran and the Hadith without the aid of any intermediary, past or present. Women should be treated on a par with men except in heading households or leading prayers or holding the office of the Caliph or Supreme Imam.

A systematic study of the theory and practice of the

caliphate coupled with updating of the caliphate concept in
the light of contemporary conditions was an important
milestone in the history of Islamic reform, and a symptom
of the innovative energy of Muslim thinkers in the first
quarter of the twentieth century. It is noteworthy that the
reformist line etched by Afghani–Abdu–Rida was double-
edged, poised as much against the scholastic tradition of
the fossilized jurisconsults, whom the reformers blamed for
Islam's decay, as it was against the western or westernized
detractors of Islam.

Rida was sufficiently realistic to regard the attainment of
the Islamic state of his vision as a long-term objective, and
quite willing meanwhile to settle for a 'caliphate of necessity'. His pragmatic approach was also reflected in the
implicit acceptance in his blueprint of the coexistence of
religious and political states, the Sharia and the 'positive
law'.

However, various factors brought about an end to this
duality, with the political aspect ceding its place to the
religious. First, the reformers gradually accepted the view
current among the ulama that the West's assault on Islam
was not only political but also ideological, and that western
secular ideas had penetrated Islamic thinking and debilitated it. Secondly, from the 1920s onwards it became
increasingly clear that the salafiya or any other reformist
idea could be realized only if it acquired the support of the
Muslim masses; and when the salafiya concept was exposed
to popular mobilization its religious dimension emerged as
the supreme element. Finally, with the abolition of the
caliphate in 1924, an acute crisis developed in the Islamic
world; and it pushed the religious aspect of Muslim life to
the fore.

While the reformers increasingly stressed confronting the
West, politically and culturally, they did not soft-pedal the
need for Islamic reform. Indeed, they felt an urge to cleanse
Islam of its non-Islamic accretions, and thus enable Muslims to reclaim the glory of the faith. In other words, they
led a movement which was two-tracked, where the emphasis came to be 'less on cleansing Islam from medieval

sufism or scholastic legalism and more on cleansing it from new heresies, Western secular ideas that had crept in under the guise of modernism; less on acquiring (or repossessing) for Islam the sources of Western strength, and more on ridding Islam of the seeds of Western decadence'.[6]

Unsurprisingly, the first country to spawn a popular Islamic revivalist movement was Egypt, politically and culturally the most important state in the Arab world, the historic nucleus of Islam. Before the Ottomans it had been the heart of the Islamic caliphate for two and a half centuries. As a protectorate of the British since 1882, however, it was subjected to ever-increasing waves of western thought and culture. The Islamist movement which grew and thrived on its soil was called Ikhwan al Muslimin, the Muslim Brotherhood.

4
THE MUSLIM BROTHERHOOD IN EGYPT AND SYRIA

Among the regular readers of Rashid Rida's *Al Manar* was Hassan al Banna (1904–49), a primary school teacher in Ismailiya, capital of the British-occupied Suez Canal Zone. He came from a pious family in the Nile delta town of Muhammadiya: his father, Ahmad al Banna, a graduate of Al Azhar University and author of books on the Hadiths and Islamic jurisprudence, was a religious teacher who led the prayers at the local mosque.

Banna grew up during particularly turbulent times. Following the First World War (during which Britain declared Egypt to be its protectorate) Egyptians revolted on a massive scale and won semi-independence in 1922. The first parliamentary election of 1923 saw the nationalist Wafd Party beat the Liberal Constitutionalists. In Turkey secular republican forces, led by Mustafa Kemal Ataturk, abolished the caliphate in 1924, an event which created a crisis in the Islamic world. Banna attributed the upheaval to the discord between the Wafd and the Liberal Constitutionalists, and 'the vociferous political debating' which had erupted after the 1919 revolution; 'the orientations to apostasy and nihilism' then engulfing the Muslim world; the attacks on tradition and orthodoxy, emboldened by 'the Kemalist Revolt' in Turkey, which had graduated into a movement for the intellectual and social emancipation of Egypt; and the non-Islamic, secularist and libertarian trends which had pervaded the academic and intellectual circles of Egypt. As a result of this turbulence, Banna argued, Egyptian youths were inheriting a 'corrupted religion'; and imbued with 'doubt and perplexity' they were tempted by apostasy.[1]

He responded to the prevailing conditions in moralistic and didactic terms. He sponsored discussions in public places, and went on to establish in 1928 the Muslim Brotherhood as a youth club with its main stress on moral and social reform through communication, information and propaganda. In retrospect the birth of the Muslim Brotherhood in Ismailiya seems logical. As the headquarters of the Suez Canal Company and the British troops in Egypt, Ismailiya was a powerful outpost of the West as well as a multi-dimensional threat to Egypt's political, economic and cultural identity.

It was only after Egyptians had mounted militant resistance to the 1936 Anglo-Egyptian Treaty, and Palestinian Arabs had launched an armed uprising in Palestine against the British Mandate and Zionist colonization in 1936–7, that the Muslim Brotherhood formally transformed itself into a political entity. This happened in 1939, and illustrated the thesis that radicalism thrives under the threat of an external enemy. Now the Muslim Brotherhood declared that: '(a) Islam is a comprehensive, self-evolving system; it is the ultimate path of life in all its spheres; (b) Islam emanates from, and is based on, two fundamental sources, the Quran, and the Prophetic Tradition; and (c) Islam is applicable to all times and places.'[2] In short, Islam was a total ideology, offering an all-powerful system to regulate every detail of the political, economic, social and cultural life of the believers.

The Muslim Brotherhood too was presented as an all-encompassing entity. Describing his movement as the inheritor and catalyst of the most active elements in Sunni traditionalist and reformist thinking, Banna stated that it was 'a Salafiya message, a Sunni way, a Sufi truth, a political organization, an athletic group, a scientific and cultural union, an economic enterprise and a social idea'.[3]

Along with this went a rapid expansion of the movement headquartered since 1933 in Cairo. In 1940 the Brotherhood had 500 branches, each one having its own centre, a mosque, a school and a club or home industry. Its schools ran religious classes, and imparted physical education (later military training) to its young members in order to prepare them for a jihad. The jihad was to be mounted not merely to liberate Egypt from alien control but also the whole of 'the Islamic homeland'. In this homeland was to be instituted 'a free Islamic government, practising the principles of Islam, applying its social system, propounding its solid fundamentals and transmitting its wise call to the people'. The objective was similar to what Afghani had propounded several decades ago. But he had lacked a vehicle to bring it about: a popular party of the believers.

The Brotherhood's growth occurred at a time when Egyptians were being humiliatingly made aware of their servitude to an alien power. In February 1942, while German troops were marching towards Egypt from Libya and King Farouq was considering appointing a new prime minister known to be anti-British, the British ambassador in Cairo ordered British tanks (normally stationed in the Suez Canal Zone) to surround the royal palace, and then gave Farouq the choice of abdicating or appointing the pro-British Wafd leader, Nahas Pasha, as prime minister. Farouq invited Nahas Pasha to form the government. While this secured the Allies' position in Egypt for the rest of the Second World War, it destroyed the monarch's prestige among his subjects.

Such events swelled the ranks of the Brotherhood, which drew its popular support from students, civil servants, artisans, petty traders and middling peasants. Brothers met for congregational prayers where they were exhorted by their leaders to observe religious duties and Islamize their personal lives. They were organized into cells of five – called families – and then upwards into clans, groups and battalions. Later the leadership was to set up secret cells.

After the Second World War the anti-British struggle escalated, and political violence became endemic in Egypt. King Farouq's popular standing suffered a further setback when, following the British withdrawal from Palestine in May 1948, the Egyptian army joined the Arab war effort against the newly formed state of Israel. It did badly, mainly due to the incompetence and corruption of its senior officers, the obsolescence of its (British-supplied) arms, and irregular and inadequate supplies of food and medicine. Muslim Brotherhood volunteers fought in the Arab–Israeli War and came into contact with nationalist Egyptian officers. While many officers picked up Brotherhood ideology, the Brothers underwent military training under the officers' supervision. Brotherhood leaders shared with the nationalist officers – functioning as the Free Officers' Organization – their frustrated anger at the injustice and decadence prevalent in Egypt, their disapproval of secular ideologies, particularly Marxism, which divided the nation, and their impatience with electoral politics. The recruitment of military officers into its ranks further strengthened the Brotherhood, which in 1946 claimed 500,000 active members and 500,000 sympathizers organized in 5,000 branches. It had by then coined a highly attractive slogan: 'The Quran is our constitution, the Prophet is our Guide; Death for the glory of Allah is our greatest ambition.'

The Brotherhood also benefited from the fact that the religious establishment, represented by Al Azhar University and its rector, sided firmly with the monarch. Al Azhar ulama considered any action against the ruler, indigenous or alien, as fitna, sedition, which contributed to creating chaos in society, which had to be avoided at all costs. So acute was their fear of chaos that in the past they had condoned foreign occupation. In 1798 Al Azhar ulama urged their followers to obey the French occupiers. 'It is incumbent on you not to provoke fitan [plural of fitna], not to obey trouble-makers, or listen to hypocrites or pursue evil,' they urged.[4] In 1914, following the declaration of martial law by the British occupiers, Al Azhar ulama stated: 'Praise be to God who cautioned the believers to avoid all fitan . . . Thus it is our duty to remain tranquil and silent and to advise others to do so, to avoid interfering in things which do not concern you.'[5] So the ulama's current servility to King Farouq was in line with their past behaviour. They showed no sign of distancing themselves from the ruler in the wake of the Egyptian defeat in the 1948 Arab–Israeli War.

By contrast the Muslim Brotherhood held the Egyptian political establishment solely responsible for the Arab débâcle in the war with Israel. It resorted to terroristic and subversive activities. Prime Minister Mahmud Fahmi Nokrashi Pasha retaliated by promulgating martial law and banning the Muslim Brotherhood in December 1948. Three weeks later he was assassinated by a Brother. This led to further repression of the organization by the state. Banna argued that since the Brotherhood had been disbanded the assassin could not be described as its member. On 12 February 1949 Banna was killed by secret service agents outside his office in Cairo.

Ideologically Banna was firmly in line with Afghani, Abdu and Rashid Rida's salafiya reformism. He was against taqlid, imitation of the ulama, and favoured maslah (choosing that ruling or interpretation which ensures greatest good) and ijtihad, independent reasoning, to be employed so that Islam could face the problems of the modern world. Where he differed with his reformist predecessors was on the means used to achieve an Islamic state. Afghani had limited himself in his pamphleteering to appealing to Muslim rulers and intellectuals to unite against the unbelievers. Abdu had focused his attention on religious reform and issuing fatwas, religious decrees; and Rashid Rida had used *Al Manar* to expound and propagate the salafiya ideology, and combined this with resorting to popular social and political actions to re-create the Islamic state. But it was Banna who had established a mass political party. Banna argued that the goal of re-creating the Islamic state could be realized within the existing constitutional framework. What the present regime had to do was to recognize the Sharia as the supreme source of law and replace the imported European codes which, by their rejection of the Sharia, had undermined the very foundations of the Islamic order.

These ideas were elucidated by Muhammad Ghazali, a Muslim Brotherhood ideologue, in his book *Our Beginning in Wisdom*, published in 1948. Ghazali argued that, like the French and Russian revolutionaries, true Muslims cannot separate their moral values from politics without depriving themselves of the possibility of promoting moral values. He insisted that the Sharia had to be the source of law in all aspects of life – be they social, political or economic. This was mandatory on the Islamic authority, because only then could the (social) Quranic injunctions on jihad, qisas (retribution) and zakat (alms) be enforced along with the (private) injunctions about prayers, fasting and pilgrimage. Ayatollah Ruhollah Khomeini was later to advance the same argument in his exhortations towards the creation of an Islamic state in Iran.

On the punishments prescribed in the Sharia, Ghazali agreed with Rashid Rida that amputation of thieves' hands and flogging of adulterers had to wait until a proper Islamic society had been established. He was critical of such practices in Saudi Arabia. 'We do not dispute that these prohibitions are part of Islam, but we find it strange that they are considered to be the whole of it,' he wrote. 'We wish to see the punishments enforced so that the rights and the security and the virtues may be preserved, but not that the hand of a petty thief be cut off while those punishments are waived . . . in the case of those who embezzle fantastic sums from the state treasury.[6] On women Ghazali took the traditional Islamic stance. He was for outlawing seductive clothing and appearance in women and their unchaperoned presence at picnics and outings. He favoured women's education as long as it was geared strictly towards preparing them for raising families.

When martial law was lifted in 1950 the ban on the Brotherhood was removed and it was allowed to function as a religious body. However, after the election a year later of Hassan Islam al Hudaybi – a senior judge who was opposed to violence and terrorism – the Brotherhood returned to the political arena. Responding to popular anti-British feelings, the government pressed Britain to withdraw its troops immediately from Egypt. When London stonewalled, Cairo unilaterally abrogated the 1936 Anglo-Egyptian Treaty (valid until 1956) in October 1951. The Brotherhood publicly offered its support to the Egyptian government, and declared a jihad against the British occupiers. With the Brothers now being trained and armed by their sympathizers in the army, the Brotherhood's leadership fell into militant hands. The organization played a significant role in the January 1952 riots in Cairo, an event which shook the monarchy and paved the way for an army coup six months later.

In their preparations for a coup against King Farouq the Free Officers assigned their Muslim Brotherhood cohorts back-up tasks. But these proved unnecessary: the coup on 23 July 1952 met with no resistance. When the officers, led by Brigadier Muhammad Neguib and Colonel Gamal Abdul Nasser, banned all political parties they exempted the Muslim Brotherhood on the grounds that it was a religious body. Of the eighteen members of the Revolutionary Command Council (RCC) which had assumed power, four had been close to the Brotherhood's hierarchy. These included Muhammad Anwar Sadat. One of the early acts of Neguib, the supreme military leader, was to visit Banna's tomb to pay his respects. The RCC offered the Brotherhood three seats in the cabinet, but Hudaybi declined the offer. When Nasser eased out Neguib and assumed supreme authority in late 1953, the military leaders began implementing land reform. This was opposed by the Brotherhood and a gulf developed between them and the regime. It dawned on the Brothers that the military rulers were by and large modernizers more interested in spreading secular education, giving equal rights to women and reforming landownership patterns than in applying the Sharia to all spheres of life. Militant Brothers revived the secret cells – also known as the Spiritual Order – to carry out assassinations and subversive acts. On 23 October 1954 Abdul Munim Abdul Rauf, a militant Brother, attempted to assassinate Nasser at a public rally in Alexandria. He failed. He and five other Brothers were executed, and more than 4,000 Brotherhood activists jailed. Several thousand Brothers went into self-imposed exile in Syria, Saudi Arabia, Jordan and Lebanon.

Two years later Nasser overcame the crisis caused by an

invasion of Egypt by Israel, Britain and France in a masterly fashion. His star rose, and the Brotherhood lost ground rapidly. Following the long-established tradition of backing the ruler, Al Azhar ulama offered whatever fatwas (religious verdicts) the Nasserist regime sought, whether the subject was land redistribution or nationalization of internal and external trade, or seizure of the property of political exiles.

In 1964, as part of a general amnesty, Nasser released the Brotherhood members with a view to co-opting them into a reformed political set-up as a counterforce to the communists who were also freed. But reconciliation between Nasser and the Brotherhood proved temporary. Many of its leaders were reportedly implicated in three plots to assassinate Nasser, allegedly inspired and financed by the Saudi monarch then engaged in a battle with Nasser for supremacy in North Yemen (following a republican coup there in September 1962) and elsewhere in the Arab East. As a result, following the arrest of 1,000 Brothers and the trial of 365, the top leaders were executed in August 1966. Among them was Sayyid Qutb (1906–66).

Sayyid Qutb was the leading ideologue of the Muslim Brotherhood. In his *Signposts on the Road*, published in the early 1950s, Qutb divided social systems into two categories: the Order of Islam and the Order of Jahiliya (Ignorance), which was decadent and ignorant, the type which had existed in Arabia before Prophet Muhammad had received the Word of God, when men revered not God but other men disguised as deities. Qutb argued that the Nasserist regime was a modern version of Jahiliya. This earned him the approval and respect of the young Brothers and the opprobrium of the political and religious establishment. He was arrested in 1954 during the clampdown on the Brotherhood. On his release ten years later the militant members of the (still clandestine) Muslim Brotherhood drafted him into the leadership. They wanted among other things to avenge the persecution of the Brotherhood in the mid-1950s. Qutb, by inclination a thinker, wished to avoid violence. But when his radical followers pressed for a jihad to be waged against the order he had himself labelled Jahiliya because of its betrayal of Islamic precepts, Qutb could find no way out.

During his trial he did not contest the official charge of sedition, and instead tried to explain his position ideologically. 'The bonds of ideology and belief are sturdier than those of patriotism based upon region, and this false distinction among Muslims on a regional basis is but one expression of crusading and Zionist imperialism which must be eradicated,' he argued.[7] In other words, watan (homeland) was not a land but the community of believers, umma. He argued that once the Brothers had declared someone to be jahil, infidel, they had the right to attack his person or property, a right granted in Islam. If in the process of performing this religious duty of waging a jihad against unbelievers, a Brother found himself on the path of sedition, so be it. The responsibility for creating such a situation lay with those who through their policies had created such circumstances in the first place.

Within a year of Qutb's death his thesis acquired a wider acceptance. This had to do with the Six-Day Arab–Israeli War of June 1967. The humiliating defeat that the Israelis inflicted on Egypt, totally destroying its air force and seizing the Sinai Peninsula, dealt a grievous blow to the semi-secular Arab socialism of Nasser, and created an environment conducive to the acceptance of the Brotherhood view that traditional Islamic beliefs had been neglected or suppressed by the Nasserist regime. A general belief prevailed among the populace that the Arabs had met defeat because they had turned away from the will of God. Even the monthly *Majallat al Azhar* (The Azhar Review), the mouthpiece of the revered university, which had been obsequious to Nasser, as it had been to rulers before him, stated that Egypt's humiliation had resulted from the fact that Muslims had discarded their glorious past and allowed themselves to be enticed by fleeting, superficial and exotic concepts. Arguing that the Arab–Israeli War was a conflict between Islam and Judaism, it called for intensified Islamic education of the masses as the most effective way of fighting Israel.[8] A common explanation for the Israeli victory was that it was due to Jews being truer to their faith than Arabs, who had been obsessed with building an Arab nation based on common language with equal rights for citizens of all religions. The defeat by Israel put secular pan-Arabists on the defensive and revived the confidence of the fundamentalists.

So severe was the shock of the defeat among the people that they badly needed solace, and they found it in religion. The government sensed this. The state-guided media reminded their readers and listeners of the great achievements and adversities of Islam and the actions of Prophet Muhammad and his companions. The military ranks were soon provided with a publication which set out the meaning and significance of jihad, and described the battles fought by Prophet Muhammad. Nasser's regime was quick to co-opt popular Islamic sensibility and identify it with Egypt's national interest and well-being. Not surprisingly, in April 1968 Nasser released several hundreds of the 1,000 Brothers he had imprisoned nearly three years previously.

The tidal wave of religiosity, which often took retreatist or sufi form, was given further impetus by the Israeli annexation of (Arab) East Jerusalem (which, with its Al Aqsa mosque and the Dome of the Rock, is the third holiest place in Islam) and the arson in July 1969 at Al Aqsa mosque.

Nasser's death in September 1970, followed by the accession to the presidency of Muhammad Anwar Sadat, raised the spirits of the Brotherhood. Sadat had first met Hassan al Banna in 1940, and attended several weekly lessons given by him at the Brotherhood headquarters in Cairo. He had maintained contacts with Brotherhood leaders during the 1940s. It was only after the Brothers had attempted to kill Nasser in 1954 that he had turned against their party. Sadat was well known for his personal piety, and Nasser often used him to project an Islamic image of the regime. For instance, Sadat was chosen as the general secretary of the Islamic Congress, established in 1965 to rally Muslim opinion abroad behind Egypt.

On assuming the presidency, Sadat came up with a slogan: 'Faith and Science'. He instructed the state-run radio and television to broadcast prayers five times a day. Promising that the Sharia would be the chief inspiration of future legislation, he released all Brotherhood prisoners, including Hudaybi. He deliberately cultivated the image of 'The Believer President'.

In May 1971 Sadat carried out a 'corrective' coup against the left-leaning Ali Sabri group in the ruling Arab Socialist Union, and actively encouraged Islamic sentiment and groups as a counterweight to the leftist influence. He directed General Abdul Munim Amin to establish about a thousand Islamic Associations in universities and factories with the sole objective of combating atheistic Marxism. He was keen to see that young Egyptians in search of an ideology turned to Islam rather than Marxism. Muslim Brotherhood exiles from Saudi Arabia and elsewhere began returning to Egypt, and strengthened Islamic forces at home.

The October 1973 Arab–Israeli War did much to improve Sadat's popular standing. He stressed the Islamic elements of the hostilities: these were mounted in the holy month of Ramadan, and were codenamed 'Badr' after Prophet Muhammad's first victory over pagan Meccans. The Egyptians gave their best performance on the battle-field so far. They crossed the Suez Canal and, despite repeated attempts by the Israelis, heavily armed with weapons airlifted from America, held on to most of their gains in the three-week-long conflict. Though in military terms the final outcome was a stand-off, the political pay-off for Sadat was enormous. The Sadat regime painted the result as a victory for Egypt and the Arabs. There is little doubt that the 1973 war, initiated by Egypt and Syria, helped restore Arab and Egyptian self-respect. Many Egyptians felt that Allah had accepted their collective penitence offered after the 1967 defeat and rewarded them with victory in the latest war.

Not surprisingly, the freedom allowed to the fundamentalists spawned the birth of groups more radical than the

Muslim Brotherhood. One such body was the Islamic Liberation Group. In June 1974 it mounted an armed attack on the Technical Military Academy in a Cairo suburb to capture its armoury before marching to the ruling party's headquarters in central Cairo – where Sadat was scheduled to give a speech – to overthrow the regime and establish an Islamic state. It failed. But its attack, which caused the death of thirty soldiers, was a sharp reminder to the government that Islamic militants functioning outside the Brotherhood's fold were active underground.

Sadat's declaration of a general amnesty in 1975, coupled with his decision a year later to allow a return to the multi-party system of the monarchical era, enabled the Brotherhood to reorganize its forces and reintegrate itself into Al Azhar University, the official centre of Islam, which had been purged of the Brotherhood elements by the Nasserist regime. But, because Sadat was apprehensive of the popular appeal of the Muslim Brotherhood, he frustrated its leaders' plan to have the organization recognized as a distinct 'tribune' by the authorities on the eve of the 1976 parliamentary poll. The Brothers therefore had no choice but to stand either as independents or as members of the ruling party. This suited Sadat, who was intent on dividing the Brotherhood and co-opting its moderate section into the political establishment.

The six Brothers elected to parliament on the ruling party's ticket, led by Salih Abu Rokait, were treated favourably by the government, and allowed to publish a monthly journal called *Al Daawa* (The Call). It was edited by Umar al Talmasani, an elderly lawyer who, as a veteran Brotherhood leader, had been given a long sentence in 1954 and was later allowed to emigrate to Saudi Arabia. Though the Daawa group shared Sadat's anti-communist and anti-Nasserist views, it opposed his policy of leading Egypt into the American camp and subscribing totally to the American-sponsored peace plan for the Middle East. The nine independent Brothers in parliament, led by Said Ramadan, enjoyed much wider popular support and were more radical than the Daawa group. They offered to co-operate with the government only on the basis of their programme of Islamic action.

Sadat's success in co-opting many of the Brotherhood leaders into the political system resulted in many militant Brothers leaving the organization and establishing radical groups clandestinely. Prominent among these were Mukfir-tiya (Denouncers of the Infidel), Jund Allah (Soldiers of God), Munnazamat al Jihad (The Jihad Organization) and Al Takfir wa Al Hijra (The Denunciation and the Migra-tion). All of these were violently opposed to the regime.

The members of Al Takfir wa Al Hijra played a leading role in ransacking and burning the nightclubs along Cairo's 'golden strip' during three days of widespread rioting in mid-January 1977 caused by the withdrawal of governmen-tal subsidies on daily necessities. It was led by Shukri Ahmad Mustafa, an agricultural engineer, who was arrested in 1965 as a Brotherhood activist. In jail he became disillusioned with the older Brothers whom he found frac-tious and weak.

After his release from jail Shukri Mustafa began recruit-ing members for his group. Though they called themselves Jamaat al Muslimin (The Muslim Society), the authorities were later to confer the title of Al Takfir wa Al Hijra on them to sum up their ideology and tactics. In his manu-script (which Mustafa refused to have printed to avoid the blasphemy of printing), entitled *Al Tawassumat* (The Searching Looks) Shukri Mustafa called on the faithful to escape the danger of shirk – ascribing another divinity to Allah – and avoid being tortured by infidels. Then they must spread 'the knowledge' throughout the land. Finally they must wage a jihad to establish an Islamic state. Mustafa argues that the destruction of atheists and their state could not be achieved while the faithful were living among them. Furthermore, he added, Prophet Muhammad required the believers to leave the blasphemous land. Only then would Allah's retribution fall upon the infidels. Since Mustafa considered Egyptian society infidel, it was incum-bent upon his followers to migrate and form a pure community along the lines of the Medinese polity of the Prophet.[9] Actually, many of Mustafa's followers took to living in the caves and mountains of Minia in Upper Egypt where, among other things, they underwent arms training. They were discovered by the security forces in September 1973, only to be pardoned by Sadat after the October War.

Since Mustafa's followers considered religious functionaries as infidel they boycotted prayers led by them, and prayed together in their own homes. They married among themselves, withdrew their children from state schools, and refused to be drafted into the military.

Some of the secret cells through which the organization functioned were assigned the task of attacking nightclubs, cinemas and bars. And that is what they did during the January 1977 rioting. The security forces picked up sixty members of the party. This incensed the younger adherents who demanded that those arrested should either be tried or released. When this did not happen, they forced the issue by kidnapping, on 3 July, Shaikh Muhammad Hussein al Dhahabi, a former minister of religious endowments and Al Azhar, for writing a newspaper article against their party. The government refused their demand, and they killed Dhahabi. The subsequent hunt by the security forces discovered Al Takfir wa Al Hijra members throughout the republic; 620 were arrested and 465 tried by military courts. Five, including Mustafa, were executed. Official investigations revealed that the organization had between 3,000 and 5,000 members belonging to all social classes and scattered throughout the country.

As it happened, in July 1977 a congress of Islamic Associations and Groups was held under the Al Azhar rector Shaikh Abdul Halim Mahmud in Cairo. The congress issued a comprehensive declaration.

All legislation and all judgment contrary to Islam is considered false . . . The faith of Muslims is only effective when submitted to the Divine Law [i.e. Sharia] and that alone. To demand the application of the Sharia is the duty of all Muslims. We accept no advice concerning moderation or delay in this matter. To postpone the application of Sharia is a sin and disobedience of God and his

Prophet. The legislature must proceed with the ratification of bills proposed to it.

Finally, the congress was 'pleased to note the President's declaration that he intends to purge the administration of all atheistic elements'.[10]

Soon after this congress Sadat ordered that those clauses of Egyptian law which were based on the Napoleonic Code be replaced with appropriate clauses from the Sharia. The State Council announced that a bill to punish those found drinking or committing adultery was being studied, and that a presidential decree specifying the death penalty for those who renounced Islam was to be submitted to parliament for approval.[11] On 10 August *Al Ahram* (The Pyramids), the official newspaper, said that a bill permitting amputation of a thief's hand was being drafted.

These statements pacified the Islamic groups, but upset the Copts, Egyptian Christians, who form about 10 per cent of the population. They felt that the apostasy bill was directed against them since they often converted to Islam to secure a quick divorce and then reverted back to Christianity. Led by their church the Copts undertook a four-day protest in early September 1977 and declared that they would not submit to the apostasy law if passed. Faced with such opposition Sadat dropped the idea.

Sadat was now caught between two contradictory forces in Egypt: orthodox Muslims attacked him for reneging on Islamizing legislation and liberal Muslims for encouraging traditional Islam. He tried to juggle his way out by offering contradictory concessions.

In his 9 November speech before parliament he combined his public offer to appear before the Israeli parliament in his search for Middle East peace with a blistering attack on the atheists whom he blamed for the riots of 18–19 January 1977. 'I will not permit any group . . . to spread atheism among our faithful people – our people in whose veins the faith flows,' he warned.[12] The warning was all the more ironic because radical fundamentalists were the major force behind these riots.

From then on Sadat busied himself with negotiating peace with Israel. Since such actions ran counter to Islamic sentiment at home and abroad it widened the gulf between his regime and the Islamic groups. This helped the Islamic movement as a whole to capitalize on the prevailing discontent and widen its base. 'The history of the Arab world is one of Islamic revival movements which appear in the aftermath of what is considered to be a great failure of the existing regime,' stated Saad Eddin Ibrahim, sociology professor at Cairo University. 'The present cycle began in 1974–5. Students looked with alarm at the apparent rapprochement with Israel, and generally with the West. There were also the socio-economic dislocation of society, the frustrations of the lower and middle classes.'[13]

An important manifestation of this phenomenon was the support gained by Islamic elements on university campuses. In the spring 1978 elections for the student union officials, the Islamists won 60 per cent of the posts. By then the Muslim Brotherhood and its offshoots had gained control of most of the 1,000 Islamic Associations established at Sadat's behest in the early 1970s.

The majority of present-day university students come from rural, petty-bourgeois families who have been the traditional backbone of the Muslim Brotherhood. Alienated by Sadat's recognition of Israel, and disgusted by the rising corruption, material and spiritual, engendered by the regime's open-door economic policy to attract foreign capital and give a boost to private enterprise, this section of society turned against the government. Sadat's economic policies widened the gap between the poor and the rich by causing sharp increases in food and rents, and by delivering a grievous blow to local industry with the imports of cheap foreign goods. Between 1964–5 and 1976 the share of the middle 30 per cent of the Egyptian population halved: from 40.2 per cent of the gross domestic product to 21.52 per cent. The corresponding figures for the lowest 60 per cent were 28.7 per cent and 19.93 per cent. In contrast the top 10 per cent nearly doubled their income: from 31.9 per cent to 58.55 per cent.[14] The new rich flaunted their affluence.

Cairo and Alexandria became the fleshpots of the Middle East, filling the vacuum caused by the war-ravaged Beirut. Along with western goods came western values of consumerism which scandalized the believers.

The impending signing of a peace treaty between Egypt and Israel in March 1979 so angered the Islamic students that they mounted anti-government demonstrations at Alexandria and Asyut universities: a daring step, since it made the demonstrators liable to life imprisonment. Their slogans summed up their grievances and aspirations: 'No peace with Israel'; 'No privilege for the rich'; 'An end to moral decadence'; and 'No separation between Islam and state'. They had no doubt been cheered by the victory of Islamic forces in Iran about a month earlier.

Sadat was quick to respond to the downfall of Muhammad Reza Pahlavi, the Shah of Iran, who was his personal friend. He urged the local Islamic leaders to reform the (official) Daawa group and increase the number of preachers on its staff. The ministry of higher education ordered the universities to make religious instruction compulsory, and the parliament's speaker promised that legislation based on the Sharia, which had been kept in abeyance since July 1977, would be passed and strictly enforced.

Al Daawa magazine, enjoying a healthy circulation of 80,000 copies a month, echoed the feelings of the protesting university students on the Egyptian–Israeli treaty. It greeted the accord with the headline: 'It is impossible to live at peace with the Jews.' The article drew heavily from the experiences of the Prophet, the Quran and Islamic history to illustrate its theme. Even the moderate Brothers, who published and read the journal, were disappointed by the failure of the Egyptian–Israeli treaty to resolve the crucial Palestinian problem. In contrast, under Sadat's prodding, Al Azhar produced a fatwa, religious verdict, in May 1979 to sanctify the President's act. 'The ulama of Al Azhar believe that the Egyptian–Israeli Treaty is in harmony with the Islamic law,' it stated. 'It was concluded from a position of strength after the battle of jihad and the victory realized by Egypt on 10th Ramadan 1393 A.H. (6

October A.D. 1973)' The statement then referred to the Hudabiya Treaty signed by Prophet Muhammad with the Quraish of Mecca in 628,[15] ignoring the fact that that treaty was a step towards Muhammad taking control of Mecca.

From then on the moderate Brotherhood, as represented by *Al Daawa*, began opposing Sadat on many other important issues. Its early support for his open-door policies meant to benefit private enterprise and attract foreign investment – seen as a welcome antidote to Nasser's propensity for nationalization and a strong public sector – turned into calls for state intervention in the management of the economy and redistribution of wealth. The Brotherhood denounced Sadat for selling Egypt's independence to America just as in the past it had attacked Nasser for kowtowing to the Soviets. It went on to argue that the so-called 'Communist threat' was concocted by western imperialism to keep the Third World countries tied to the West after they had acquired political independence. It continued to attack the government's economic policies, which had fostered a growing class of corrupt rentiers, property speculators, middlemen and importers of western goods. 'Who is protecting corruption in Egypt, the heart of Arabism and lighthouse of Islam?' asked *Al Daawa* in its July 1981 editorial. 'The stench is spreading and an explosion is feared.'[16]

Al Daawa's reference to corruption in high places was all the more apt since it appeared in the holy month of Ramadan. During that period Israel mounted several air raids on Palestinian targets in south Lebanon and central Beirut which left 386 Lebanese and Palestinians dead. All Arab states, except Egypt, rallied to the Palestinian–Lebanese side. Beyond voicing public disapproval of Israeli raids, and letting some Egyptian doctors fly to Beirut to tend the wounded, Sadat did nothing. This severely undermined his popular standing. On Eid al Fitr (1 August), encouraged by the Islamic Associations, over 100,000 faithful gathered for prayers in Abidin Square, outside the presidential palace in Cairo, and shouted anti-Sadat slogans. The criticism of the Egyptian–Israeli peace treaty became more vocal than before.

In late August the Israeli Prime Minister Menachem Begin reportedly warned Sadat that Israel would not honour its commitment in the treaty to vacating the Sinai Peninsula in April 1982 if open criticism of the treaty was tolerated in Egypt. On 3 September Sadat clamped down on the opposition, jailing nearly two thousand dissidents, most of them Islamic fundamentalists (including Umar Talmasani), and shutting down *Al Daawa*. He purged the military of 200 officers suspected of being pro-Brotherhood, and ordered that all independent religious societies as well as preachers must register themselves with the ministry of religious endowments. He also enjoined the 40,000 privately run mosques to register with the ministry. This meant the state extending its power over all preachers and mosques, and exercising full control over them, for the 1911 law, which established the Supreme Council of Al Azhar, had turned all ulama into state employees. This new Act authorized the government to dismiss an alim and even remove his name from Al Azhar records, thus rendering him ineligible for any job, religious or secular.

Sadat set up new disciplinary councils for students and civil servants. He swiftly quashed sporadic protest attempts made mainly by Islamic militants. He did all this at a time when the vast majority of believing Muslims held his regime in low esteem and harboured hatred for him.

On 6 October, four soldiers armed with automatic weapons and hand grenades attacked the review stand at the military parade in a Cairo suburb to celebrate the Egyptian performance in the October 1973 war. They killed Sadat and seven others. They were led by twenty-four-year-old Lieutenant Khalid Ahmad Shawki Islambouli whose older brother, Muhammad, was one of the 469 members of Al Takfir wa Al Hijra arrested in early September. Islambouli and his three colleagues belonged to Al Jihad Organization (Munazzamat al Jihad) led by Shaikh Umar Abdul Rahman, a blind professor at Asyut

University, Muhammad Abdul Salam Faraj, an Islamic ideologue, and Abbud Abdul Latif Zumur, a lieutenant-colonel in military intelligence.

Al Jihad leaders had visualized Sadat's assassination acting as a catalyst to transform Egyptian Muslims' simmering hatred of infidel Sadat's corrupt, oppressive rule into an uprising against the regime and for Al Jihad's armed attempt to bring about an Islamic revolution. In the event, ordinary Egyptians demonstrated their passive approval of the assassins' act by refraining from public mourning at the loss of their President,[17] nothing more. This disappointed Al Jihad leaders. However, armed confrontations occurred between Al Jihad militants and Egyptian security forces, most prominently in Asyut in Upper Egypt. There Al Jihad cadres stormed the local broadcasting station, several police stations and the headquarters of the security forces. Two days of fighting left 188 dead, including fifty-four security personnel. On 25 October *Al Ahram* reported that the Islamic groups had planned 'a bloody terrorist plot to impose a Khomeini-style regime in Egypt', and that this was to have been executed on 13 October, the day presidential elections were to be held. Hosni Mubarak, who had been sworn in as president on Sadat's death, was confirmed in office by popular vote. By late October he had imprisoned over three thousand Islamic extremists belonging chiefly to Al Jihad and Al Takfir wa Al Hijra.

During his trial Islambouli outlined his reasons for killing Sadat: the Egyptian President had made peace with Israel; he had persecuted 'the sons of Islam' by his wholesale arrest of them in early September; and the current laws of Egypt, being incompatible with the Sharia, imposed suffering on believing Muslims.

The authorities had first discovered Al Jihad in 1978 during Muslim–Copt riots. The organization was led by a ten-member committee headed by Shaikh Umar Abdul Rahman, whose fatwa on the legitimacy of Al Jihad's actions and policies were considered essential. Sometime in late 1980 he issued a fatwa which declared Sadat to be an infidel. This made him a legitimate target for assassination. In January–February 1981 Faraj and Zumur, head of the operational wing of the organization, set out to implement the plan to assassinate Sadat. It was Zumur who ensured that, unlike all others participating in the military parade on 6 October, Islambouli and his associates were equipped with live ammunition in their weapons.

Faraj, the organization's chief theoretician, was the author of two books: *Al Jihad: the Forgotten Pillar*, and *The Absent Obligation*. In these he outlined his theory and plan of action. His basic premises were that every true Muslim is obliged by his faith to struggle for the revival of the Islamic umma, and that the Muslim groups or leaders, who have turned away from the Sharia, are apostates. It is therefore sinful for a genuine Muslim to co-operate with an infidel ruler. Those who want to end the Order of Jahiliya (Ignorance) and revive the Islamic umma are obliged to wage a jihad against the infidel state. The only acceptable form of jihad is the armed struggle; anything less implies cowardice or foolishness. A true Muslim must first confront the internal infidel (i.e. the Egyptian state) and then the external infidel (i.e. the non-Muslim world at large). Straying from the course of jihad has led to the current sorry state of the Muslim world: divided, degraded and disdained. But this condition is destined to end as God has foreordained the history of Islam: the era of the Prophet followed by the eras of the caliphs, kings and dictators – and finally the replacement of dictators by a system similar to the one prevalent in the days of Prophet Muhammad. Leadership of the Islamic umma must be given to the strongest among the believers who also fears Allah. He must be chosen collectively and must then be obeyed.

Two concepts in Faraj's writing were new: jihad as the sixth obligation of a Muslim, and jihad as a perpetual movement to transform the non-Muslim world into the Islamic umma, something akin to Leon Trotsky's idea of permanent Marxist revolution. These concepts made Faraj the most radical fundamentalist thinker so far.

The eleven-year rule of Sadat was an important period

in the history of Islamic Fundamentalism in Egypt. It ceased to be a relentlessly persecuted movement as it had been during the Nasserite regime. While denying the Muslim Brotherhood a licence to function as a political party Sadat provided it with an environment in which its moderate wing could function in comparative freedom, acting as a reluctant ally of the government or at worst as its loyal opposition. On the other hand, the main thrust of Sadat's political, diplomatic and economic policies after the October 1973 war was so contrary to basic fundamentalist ideology and policies that, by co-operating with the government, albeit conditionally, the moderate fundamentalists lost much ground to their radical rivals.

Once Mubarak had overcome the immediate challenge to his regime he released the secular dissidents jailed by Sadat and engaged in dialogue with them. In contrast he intensified the drive to repress Islamic militants and their agitation. He was well served in this by the interior minister, Hassan Abu Bhasha. Overriding appeals from various quarters to spare the lives of Islambouli and his associates, Mubarak went ahead with their executions. His action was condemned by many in the Muslim world; and some radical fundamentalist groups called for the overthrow of his regime. An attempt was made by Islamic fundamentalists to assassinate him on 25 April 1982, but it failed. This led to the arrest of 140 Islamic militants who were accused of conspiring to install an Islamic regime. The government intensified its infiltration of the fundamentalist groups.

The measured, lacklustre style of Mubarak's leadership contrasted well with the flamboyance of Sadat, who was much given to theatricality. On the other hand, Mubarak made only cosmetic changes to his predecessor's open-door economic policy, alignment with the West and commitment to the Camp David peace process: policies which had proved to be a breeding ground for Islamic militants.

Mubarak used Al Azhar ulama not only to win legitimacy for his regime but also to re-educate the Islamist prisoners. These ulama tried to convince the extremists that their interpretation of Islam was wrong. Accepting this view and repenting for their past actions were deemed sufficient by the government to allow the imprisoned militants to go free. And many did.

To widen his popular base Mubarak allowed secular opposition an unprecedented degree of freedom. He let the conservative New Wafd Party contest the May 1984 parliamentary election, a privilege denied to it by Sadat. Since the New Wafd was for private enterprise, Mubarak's National Democratic Party presented itself as the defender of 'the socialist gains made by workers and peasants'! Next to no mention was made of Sadat in the election campaign. As before, poll results were forged. Still, the New Wafd won 15 per cent of the vote and fifty-eight seats in a house of 560 (with 450 elected seats), and replaced the Socialist Liberal Party as the major right-of-centre opposition force. Since the Election Law of June 1983, like its predecessor, disallowed parties based on religion or (Marxist) atheism, the Muslim Brotherhood was barred from contesting elections. In desperation the Brotherhood had allied with the New Wafd on the grounds that both of them had been opposed to the July 1952 Nasserist revolution. The New Wafd accommodated the Brotherhood by demanding that the Sharia should become the principal source of legislation. But it adopted only eighteen of the seventy candidates that the Brotherhood leadership offered. Of these, eight won. So, in essence, the strength of independent fundamentalists in parliament was about the same as in Sadat's days. Radical Islamic groups boycotted the elections as they had done in the past.

Yet there were differences. The protest against election-rigging was so vociferous that Hassan Abu Bhasha, the interior minister in charge of the poll, was moved to another ministry. Also, so fervent was Islamic sentiment at large that the opposition in parliament and the Islamic elements outside combined to demand full and immediate implementation of the Sharia. The movement gathered momentum in the spring of 1985, and was checked only by a ban by courts on pro-Sharia marches and demonstrations. The government found itself on the defensive. In public it argued that Egyptian law was 90 per cent Islamic, and that the Sharia was the basis for the Egyptian constitution. In private, however, it was unwilling to adopt the Sharia in full. It felt that such a step by the regimes in Sudan and Iran had led to unhealthy developments in those countries. Secondly, it was reluctant to alienate the Coptic minority. Finally, and most importantly, it feared that western investors and aid donors would be reluctant to do business with an Egypt functioning on Islamic lines. When pressured by opposition, the government promised to 'purify' the Egyptian law of its non-Islamic elements.

The fundamentalists accused the government of playing for time. In June 1985 Shaikh Hafiz Salaama, an eminent Islamist leader, called for a pro-Sharia march from his mosque in Cairo. Mubarak responded by having the mosque surrounded by a large contingent of the Central Security Police. Soon the authorities banned religious stickers on vehicles which had mushroomed over the past year and which, along with the sight of veiled women in the streets, were taken to be a visual and dramatic index of the rise of Islamic Fundamentalism.

At universities Mubarak's efforts to contain the fundamentalists' power by curtailing the organizing rights of the students and implanting secret police on the campuses failed. By early 1986 Islamic fundamentalists had gained control over all the university student unions and were actively pressuring university authorities to bring the curricula and textbooks into line with Islamic precepts and enforce sexual segregation.

Elsewhere, allied to the New Wafd, the Brotherhood had succeeded in dominating the ruling bodies of the influential syndicates of journalists, lawyers, doctors and engineers. Islamist journalists had established influence over two of the four opposition magazines which, among other things, published laudatory accounts of life in the Islamic Republic of Iran. Many construction and consumer goods firms owned by seven large Islamic holding companies with assets of billions of (American) dollars, financed by over a million Egyptians working in the Gulf, had become popular with small fundamentalist investors: they offered a share of profits in line with Islamic precepts, and not a fixed rate of return. These companies were said to be funding the Islamic organizations. The emergence of an independent economic base to sustain the Islamic groups was a new and important development in the history of fundamentalism in Egypt.

In late February 1986 some 17,000 conscripts of the Central Security Police rioted in five provinces including Cairo. The scale and diversity of rioting by one of the chief organs of state security jolted the regime. It took the army five days to quell the rebellion during which 115 people, including eighty-nine policemen, were killed. In a move reminiscent of the acts of Al Takfir wa Al Hijra adherents during the January 1977 rioting, the rebellious policemen destroyed bars, nightclubs, expensive hotels and apartment blocks – symbols of corruption and luxury – worth 500 million dollars. To the alarm of the authorities, half of the rioting policemen absconded with their weapons.

Islamic fervour seemed to be spreading among military cadets as well as non-commissioned and lower- and middle-ranking officers. Instead of watching films or playing games during their leisure the military cadets had taken to praying or discussing Islamic literature.[18]

A study of 303 Al Jihad members, jailed before Sadat's assassination, revealed that 4 per cent of them were military, police or intelligence officers.[19] This was not surprising. Given the traditional extended family system prevalent in Egypt, the members of the fundamentalist groups are bound to recruit some blood relatives employed in the security or intelligence services into their organizations. A fresh reminder that Al Jihad continued to be active in the military came in December 1986. Thirty of its members, including two majors, one captain and one lieutenant, were arrested for setting up combat training centres with a view to overthrowing the government.

The security police riots erupted at a time when Egypt was entering a period of acute economic crisis. All major sources of foreign income – oil, tourism and the remittances of Egyptian expatriates – were in decline. Oil prices had fallen by two-thirds in three months. Tourism was down by 40 per cent. The 3 million Egyptian workers in the Gulf states and Iraq, who in the past had contributed 4 billion dollars a year to Egypt's foreign revenue, were returning home in droves. The national debt stood at a staggering 32 billion dollars.

All this created an environment in which a growing number of ordinary citizens, suffering under the weight of inflation and deteriorating living conditions, shared the view of the fundamentalists summed up thus: since the capitalism of Sadat and Mubarak had failed in the way Nasser's socialism had, it was time to try the Islamic model. The Islamists argued that once Egypt had ended its dependence on the non-Muslim West and introduced an economic system based on Islam, it would solve the worsening socio-economic ills of society, including corruption.

Being out of power, the fundamentalists had the advantage of being able to make extravagant promises and paint a rosy picture of the model they offered. This was in stark contrast to President Mubarak's position. He presided over a sinking economy; he had undertaken half-hearted political liberalization; he had failed to offer any socio-economic ideology of his own; and his lack of strong direction had created a leadership vacuum at the top. He was in a quandary. Were he to suppress the fundamentalists violently (as Sadat had done towards the end of his rule) he would be accused of persecuting the sons of Islam and become a hate figure like his predecessor; on the other hand, were he to give free rein to the fundamentalists they would gain further ground and pose a real threat to his regime.

The parliamentary election of April 1987 demonstrated the growing strength of the fundamentalists. This time the Muslim Brotherhood allied with the Liberals and the Socialist Labour Party. The Alliance adopted a simplistic slogan: 'Islam – that is the solution.' As before, the election was rigged – 750 opposition supporters, chiefly fundamentalists, were arrested, ballot boxes were stuffed with the votes of the dead, absent and under-age for the ruling National Democratic Party, and the polling stations in many villages were closed several hours ahead of schedule to prevent legitimate voters from exercising their right. Yet the Brotherhood-led Alliance gained seventeen per cent of the popular vote and sixty parliamentary seats, displacing the New Wafd as the main opposition party.

With thirty-six of its members in the new chamber, the Muslim Brotherhood planned to dominate the Alliance's parliamentary activity, and reiterate its demands for the immediate application of the Sharia, the promotion of Islamic investment companies at the expense of conventional banks (which are seen as violating the Quran's injunction against usury), the termination of Egypt's strategic and economic links with the US, and the abrogation of the Camp David peace process. This would amount to questioning the very basis of the secular government.

Since there is no chance of the Mubarak regime fully adopting any of these policies the prospect is of sharpening differences between his government and the fundamentalists, and the creation of climate conducive to the growth of radical, clandestine groups which in mid-1987, according to Egyptian and foreign specialists, had a total membership of between 70,000 and 100,000.[20]

The emergence of the Muslim Brotherhood as the principal opposition in Egypt gave a fillip to the fundamentalists throughout the Arab world and Iran. After all, the Brotherhood is the oldest popular Islamist organization with formal and informal contacts with similar bodies in the Middle East and north Africa.

Indeed, until its dissolution in 1954, the Brotherhood in Cairo maintained an active international department through which it remained in touch with like-minded bodies abroad. During his visits to Jordan and Palestine between 1942 and 1945, Hassan al Banna set up Brotherhood branches in many towns. When the organization was first banned in Egypt in 1948 hundreds of its activists went into exile in other Arab states. The same thing happened in 1954. Consequently the Brotherhood exists in all Arab countries either overtly or covertly, sometimes under its proper name and other times not. In Algeria it is known as Ahl al Daawa (People of the Call), and in Tunisia as Hizb al Islami (The Islamic Party). In Jordan, where political parties are outlawed, it is registered as a charitable organization. In Saudi Arabia, whose rulers have been its chief financiers, a branch under the leadership of Shaikh Muhammad al Khattar, an eminent ideologue, is allowed to function. In other Gulf states, which also disallow political parties, the Brotherhood exists through its affiliate, Jamiyya al Islah al Ijtimai (The Society of Social Reform). In Syria it has proved to be the most persistent and violent clandestine opposition to the government in recent Middle East history.

Syria

The Muslim Brotherhood in Syria came into being in the mid-1930s when Syrian students of the Sharia returning from Egypt began forming branches in different cities under the title Shabab Muhammad (Young Men of Muhammad). The most important of these, established in 1935 in the northern city of Aleppo in 1935, became the organization's headquarters. The Brotherhood stood for an end to the French mandate (imposed in 1920), and for social and political reform along Islamic lines. In 1944 the headquarters was moved to Damascus, and Mustafa al Sibai was elected the General Supervisor. Born into a religious family, which provided preachers for the grand mosque in Homs, Sibai was a graduate of Al Azhar and a friend of Hassan al Banna. He ran the Syrian Brotherhood along the lines followed by Banna. Once the French departed in 1946, the organization concentrated on socio-economic issues, always stressing its opposition to secularism and Marxism. It drew the bulk of its support from urban petty traders and craftsmen; they and their families comprised about one-sixth of the Syrian population. Unlike its Egyptian counterpart, it lacked rural middle-class backing. The creation of Israel and the defeat of the Arab forces in 1948 gave a boost to the Brotherhood, and politicized it.

Its fortunes improved further when, in the wake of the ban on the Egyptian Brotherhood, in 1954 many Egyptian activists took refuge in Syria. For the first time the Syrian organization's programme clearly called for 'the establishment of a virtuous polity which would carry out the rules and teachings of Islam'.[21] However, when Syria joined Egypt in early 1958 to form the United Arab Republic (UAR) and the ban on political parties in Egypt was extended to Syria, Sibai formally dissolved the Brotherhood. But it functioned underground. Growing disaffection with Nasser's presidency of the UAR helped the Brotherhood to expand its base. The result of the election held in December 1961, a few months after Syria's secession from the UAR, proved this. The Brotherhood won ten seats, nearly half as many as the older, more established National Bloc.

However, the parliament was dissolved, and the Brotherhood and other parties were banned in March 1963 following a military coup by the Arab Baath Socialist Party. This organization had been founded in 1943 by Michel Aflaq, a Christian, and Salah Bitar, a Sunni Muslim, with the leading slogan of 'Unity, Freedom, Socialism'. Describing Islam as civilization, Aflaq, the party theoretician, defined it as the embodiment of Arabism. If cultural and civilizational aspects of Islam (and not its religious and legal aspects) were emphasized, then Islamic and Arab identities merged imperceptibly, he concluded. This concept appealed to the intellectuals and power-wielders in such heterogeneous societies as Syria and Iraq, for it provided a bridge between Kurd and Arab, Sunni and Shia, Ismaili and Druze, and Alawi and Christian. Not surprisingly, the Baath Party in Syria proved popular with underprivileged classes and sectarian or religious minorities. Among the latter were the Alawis, settled as peasants mainly in the mountainous region around the Mediterranean port of Latakia, who had been the favourite military recruits of the French during their rule from 1920 to 1946. Alawis were only 12 per cent of the Syrian population, Druzes 3 per cent, and Christians 14 per cent. Sunnis, who comprised 69 per cent of the total, almost monopolized urban trade, industry and the professions. Thus the sectarian divide was reinforced by socio-economic differences.

Though the political hue of their governments has varied widely, formal Baathist control of power in Syria has remained uninterrupted since March 1963. Baathist rule can be divided into three phases: from 1963 to 1968; from 1968 to 1970; and from 1971 onwards.

During the first phase power was shared by military officers of Alawi, Druze or Sunni persuasion who had village or small-town background. They carried out land reform and nationalized industry and (wholesale) foreign trade. Along with this went a swift infiltration of the civil service by men with rural backgrounds allied to the military officers. These developments undermined the economic and political interests of industrialists, financiers and wholesale merchants as well as small traders, craftsmen and professionals, who were by and large Sunni and favoured the outlawed Muslim Brotherhood. Syrian clerics were so poorly paid by the government that they had to have a trade or job to survive. Since most of them were petty traders or artisans they had suffered economically due to the Baathists' socialist policies.

Encouraged by the popular urban discontent due to the economic downturn in early 1964, the Muslim Brotherhood stepped up its activities. In April, following anti-government rioting in Hama, a stronghold of Sunni orthodoxy, the muezzin of the famous Al Sultan mosque issued the crusading cry: 'Islam or Baath'. This brought the security forces to the neighbourhood. When they responded to the firing directed at them from the mosque with shelling they damaged one of the mosque's minarets. This led to widespread strikes in major cities. It was only after the government had formed workers' militias, consisting of its proletarian supporters, and they had resorted to meting out summary justice to the Muslim Brothers, that the unco-ordinated protest petered out.

The second round between the Brotherhood and the Baathists came in early May 1967 following a bitter attack on the government by Shaikh Muhammad Hassan Habanka, the chief alim of Damascus, on the basis of an article in *Jaish al Shaab* (The People's Army), the army's official journal. The article was entitled 'The Means of Creating the New Arab Man', and the offending sentence read: 'God, religion, feudalism, capitalism and colonialism, and all the values that prevailed under the old society are no more than mummies in the museum of history, and absolute belief in man's ability should be treated as the only new value.'[22] Demonstrations against the government ensued and were accompanied by a merchants' strike in Damascus. Once again the government rearmed the work-ers' militia, which played a major role in ending the traders' shutdown in the capital. It arrested the protesting leaders as well as the author of the offending article. After a summary trial he was sentenced to life imprisonment. To underline its Islamic credentials the government undertook an ambitious programme of mosque-building. In the next three years it constructed more mosques than had been done in the previous thirty.

What enabled the radical Baathists, who had been in power since February 1966, to withstand the threat from the Brotherhood was the active support of the militant peasants, both Sunni and non-Sunni, in the countryside and the armed workers' militia in cities, and, most import-antly, the continued loyalty of the army. Since the 1963 coup, the officer corps was continually purged of urban Sunni officers and staffed with Alawi and Druze ones with rural backgrounds, who were hostile to the interests of the (Sunni) urban bourgeoisie, whether petty, middle or top. By 1968 Alawi officers had become the pre-eminent force in the military.

The Arab defeat of June 1967 split the Brotherhood into two factions: the Damascus-based moderates guided by

Issam al Attar, operating from exile in West Germany, and the radicals based in the northern cities of Homs, Hama and Aleppo, headed by Marwan Hadid, who advocated a jihad against the Baathist rule. Hadid and young militants travelled to Jordan where they received commando training from Al Fatah, a constituent of the Palestine Liberation Organization, at a Palestinian camp. Their action marked the militarization of the Brotherhood, a process which was to gather momentum in the 1970s.

The second phase of Baathist rule (1968–70) saw differences between two leading Alawi generals, Salih Jadid and Hafiz al Assad, reach breaking point. Leading the radical, political wing of the party, Jadid proposed a people's war against Israel. He was opposed by the pragmatist Assad, the defence minister, who headed the moderate, military wing of the Baath. In this struggle Attar, the Brotherhood leader, backed Assad.

Assad assumed supreme authority in November 1970 in a bloodless coup, and ushered in the third phase of Baathist rule. He tried to placate those sections of urban society who had been alienated by the radical, secular policies of the past seven years. So far the Baathist regime had favoured the military, peasantry, industrial workers, and sectarian and religious minorities – and not the poorly paid ulama or the petty traders and artisans of the bazaars. Assad eased import controls on consumer goods and encouraged small and medium-sized private enterprises, thus placating merchants and small manufacturers, the traditional backbone of the Muslim Brotherhood.

But, being an Alawi, Assad was vulnerable on religious grounds. Islamists argued that since Alawis were neither Muslim nor People of the Book (Christian or Jew), they were infidels and idolators, who worshipped Ali. Assad tried diligently to project his image as a faithful Muslim by participating in prayers and other religious ceremonies in various mosques throughout the country, and by declaring publicly that he, an Alawi, prayed regularly and fasted during Ramadan. He was keen to counter the widely prevalent belief among Sunni ulama and lay persons that

Alawis worshipped Ali and were therefore heathens. Assad resorted to peppering his public speeches with Quranic verses. He replaced the secular oath for government officials, 'I swear on my honour and beliefs', with the traditional, 'I swear by Allah the Great.'

Yet the Brotherhood continued to believe that the Baathists were intent on leading Syria away from its Islamic heritage. It found fresh evidence in the new constitution adopted by the People's Assembly in January 1973. The constitution sanctified the leading position of the Baath Party and described the Syrian Arab Republic as a 'democratic, popular, socialist state'. An influential group of pro-Brotherhood ulama attacked the constitution as being 'secular and atheistic', and demanded the insertion of an article declaring Islam to be the state religion. Anti-government riots and boycotts followed. Assad compromised by directing the Assembly to specify that the head of the state must be Muslim, and the Assembly complied. At the same time the government arrested and tortured the ulama held responsible for the riots.

Not satisfied with this concession, the ulama called for nationwide demonstrations. These were held, and turned violent. Later the ulama instructed their followers to abstain in the referendum on the constitution. Consequently the Sunni regions of the country registered a low voter turnout. Sporadic agitation continued. Skirmishes between anti-government demonstrators and the security forces in Aleppo, Homs and Hama on the eve of Prophet Muhammad's birthday in April left twenty dead and sixty injured. But, unlike his predecessors, Assad combined repression with co-option. He offered state honours and higher salaries to the ulama and cultivated close links with them.

Assad made adroit use of the October 1973 war against Israel to reassert the Islamic credentials of his regime. 'Badr', the code word used for the Arab offensive on 6 October, was significant: it was the battle of Badr which had established the supremacy of Prophet Muhammad's early followers over the unbelievers. In his radio broadcasts during the war Assad described the conflict as a jihad against 'the enemies of Islam', and referred to the Syrian forces as the 'soldiers of Allah'. This was in marked contrast to what had happened during the 1967 conflict when radical Baathist officials had maintained a secular interpretation of the war. Another point of departure was Assad's sacking of many Alawi officers for poor performance in the 1973 conflict and replacing them with non-Alawi officers. This action improved Assad's standing among Sunni officers and troops as well as civilians.

In February 1974 Assad visited King Faisal of Saudi Arabia in Riyadh, and then travelled to Mecca for a short hajj, pilgrimage. This finally established him as a true believer. He combined such steps with official attempts to bolster the Alawi community's claim to be genuinely Muslim with pronouncements from non-Alawi ulama to that effect. A fatwa by Musa Sadr, a leading Shia alim of Lebanon, that Alawis were part of the Shia community went a long way in legitimizing the Alawi claim of being true believers.

Under the circumstances the Brotherhood's hostility towards the regime lessened. It confined its criticism of Assad to his loss of the Golan Heights to Israel in the 1973 war and his participation in the peace process initiated by the American secretary of state, Henry Kissinger.

However, this state of affairs was short-lived. In June 1976 Assad intervened militarily in the year-old Lebanese civil war on the side of Maronite Christians against the alliance of Lebanese Muslims and Palestinians. This shocked and alienated large segments of Syrian society. It angered the Brotherhood, which had already been critical of Assad's growing dependence on Soviet arms and advisers, government corruption and high inflation. The Brotherhood, now led by Adnan Saad al Din (a one-time member of the Egyptian Brotherhood), accused Assad of acting as an agent of Maronite, Israeli and American interests. The main thrust of the Brotherhood's attack on the regime, however, was that military power was what counted and that it was concentrated in the hands of Assad's Alawi kinsmen while Sunnis were given important positions only in the civilian sector. As it was, there were two parallel power structures in Syria, both of them headed by Assad. In the structure that encompassed the cabinet, parliament and the Baathist hierarchy, there were many Sunnis. But real power rested with President Assad and his five close aides: the chiefs of air force intelligence, army intelligence and internal security; and the heads of two special military forces: the Defence Brigades and the Special Units. The Brotherhood routinely described the Assad regime as 'sectarian' and composed of 'false Muslims'. Its paper, *Al Nidhar* (The Struggle), depicted the 'Islamic struggle' as being 'between the suppressed Muslim majority [i.e. Sunnis] and the infidel Nusairi [i.e. Alawi] minority, whose adherents have made Islam their traditional enemy'.[23]

Soon after Assad's intervention in the Lebanese civil war, the Brotherhood decided to wage a jihad against his regime. The jihad went through two phases before collapsing: from July 1976 to May 1979, and from June 1979 to August 1980.

During the first phase of the jihad the Brotherhood's military units – called Combat Vanguard of Fighters – carried out assassinations of Baathist officials, Alawi leaders, security agents and informers in order to highlight the minority status of the regime, and goad the government to increase repression and thereby alienate large sections of society. The government used its internal security apparatus and the Defence Brigades to catch the assassins and their accomplices. An attack in February 1978 by dissident army officers on Rifaat Assad, the president's younger brother who headed the 36,000-strong Defence Brigades, indicated that the Brotherhood enjoyed support in the officer corps. This alarmed President Assad, who relied increasingly on the much-hated Defence Brigades as well as on the Special Units headed by Ali Haidar, an Alawi kinsman. While the majority of Sunnis came to (passively) resent the government's repression, Alawis drew together and backed Assad solidly, afraid that his overthrow would lead to their massacre by Sunni militants as heathens who had for several years persecuted true believers.

The Brotherhood's military units were manned by the young sons of its traditional members. Unlike their fathers they were university-educated and often professionally qualified. Their activities attracted a large number of recruits to the Brotherhood and other smaller Islamic groups. In Aleppo, for instance, the Brotherhood membership in 1975 was less than 800. But three years later the membership was estimated to be between 5,000 and 7,000.[24] The national total was widely put at 30,000. (In contrast, the Baath Party membership stood at over 200,000.) Despite the phenomenal growth in their size the Islamic organizations maintained extreme secrecy about their membership and structure, and their leaders remained shadowy figures.

In the second phase of the jihad the Brotherhood's military units combined attacks on police stations, Baath Party offices, army units and government buildings with large-scale demonstrations and strikes. They heralded this phase with a daring assault on the Aleppo Artillery School on 16 June 1979. Aided by a (Sunni) duty officer, the Brotherhood militants fired machine-guns and lobbed hand grenades at an assembly of some 200 Alawi cadets, killing eighty-three of them. This incident engendered a climate of crisis and fear in the country. In a major sweep the authorities arrested 300 Brotherhood activists, and mounted a major anti-Brotherhood campaign in the state-controlled media, describing them as 'gangsters funded by the Iraqis, Israelis, Americans and Lebanese Maronites', and reiterating that the government was safeguarding 'the true interests of Islam'. But there was no let-up in the violent activities of the Brotherhood, whose victims now included not only Syrian military and intelligence personnel but also Soviet military and civilian advisers, and pro-government Sunni ulama.

These acts occurred against the background of rising discontent among the urban petty bourgeoisie due to high inflation, housing shortage and maldistribution of daily necessities in an atmosphere rife with stories of corruption among civilian and military leaders, and administrative inefficiency and bungling. The Sunnis among this class nursed particular grievances. Their share of jobs in the police, intelligence, military officer corps, the presidential entourage and the Baathist hierarchy was nowhere near the two-thirds mark to which their proportion in the population entitled them. The Brotherhood's charges of despotism and corruption against the regime were all the more effective when they were presented as violations of Islamic norms of morality and behaviour.

Assad realized that intensifying repression would not do, and that the crisis needed to be tackled politically. He called a special congress of the Baath Party in late December, and encouraged the 700 delegates to speak their minds freely. They reportedly did so. A report passed by the congress stated that the party was suffering from 'indifference . . . lack of enthusiasm and party spirit; opportunism; misunderstanding of democracy; and growth of inherited illnesses of society'.[25] While endorsing such governmental decisions as overhauling the wage scales in the public and private sectors to keep pace with inflation, the congress appointed a special Inspection and Control Commission to ensure that no party member used his position for personal gain. Two-thirds of the twenty-one-member National Command of the party were replaced, with many seats going to such prominent Sunni leaders as Hikmat Shahabi, army chief of staff. A new thirty-seven-member cabinet included a substantial number of Sunnis. The governors of Aleppo, Homs and Hama (the main centres of Brotherhood agitation) were dismissed as were twenty-one top officials of large public sector enterprises.

But the Brotherhood leaders were unmoved by these actions. While the Baath Party congress was in progress in Damascus they were busily forging an alliance with the remaining opposition forces in Aleppo, the second largest city, and organizing strikes and demonstrations in different parts of the city. Matters came to a head in early March when the merchants of Aleppo, protesting against price controls, declared an immediate general strike. At about the same time, following a fatal shooting by a traffic policeman of a Brotherhood leader in Hama, the third largest city, the local residents demonstrated for free elections, a liberalized economy and a jihad for 'saving the pure faith from the filth of its enemies'.[26] Soon the national syndicates of lawyers, engineers, doctors and academics issued statements demanding the lifting of the state of emergency (which had been in force since March 1963), the release of political prisoners and an end to sectarianism.

This was the most serious challenge yet to Assad's regime. He saw in the massive demonstrations and strikes mounted by the Brotherhood-led coalition of opposition forces the making of an Islamic revolutionary movement along Iranian lines. Worried that applying sheer force against the popular agitation might prove counter-productive, he tried to defuse the situation. He addressed the merchants' grievances, which had got the anti-government movement going, by sharply increasing their import quotas of consumer goods. Secondly, he tried to draw a line between the Brotherhood's militants and its ordinary members. 'The Muslim Brothers in Syria are not all with the assassins,' he said on 23 March 1980. 'The great majority of them condemn murder and are opposed to killers. This majority believes that they should work for the sake of religion and not for any other objective. We have absolutely no difference with them . . . We encourage anybody who works for religion and upholds religious values.'[27] Thirdly, he released 200 political prisoners, sacked several unpopular provincial governors, and dismissed twenty-five directors of state sector companies for corruption or incompetence. His opponents saw these moves as a sign of Assad's weakness. To enfeeble him further they decided to maintain the pressure. The merchants of Aleppo and Hama kept their shops shut.

Assad finally decided to act with an iron hand. On 6 April he despatched 11,000 troops of the Special Units under their commander, Ali Haidar, to Aleppo. They cordoned off the city, undertook house-to-house searches, and marched off thousands of residents to hastily built detention centres. They killed or executed several hundred people. Similar treatment was accorded to the citizens of Hama. On 9 April Assad dissolved the executive councils of the professional syndicates. A spate of arrests of the leading protestors resulted in some 5,000 Syrians ending up in jail. With this, the protest which had once threatened to destabilize the regime petered out.

The Syrian president coupled the clamp-down with promises to release all political prisoners and respect the rule of law. When this did not happen, Aleppo and Hama experienced renewed demonstrations and strikes on a smaller scale in May and June, which were followed by a repressive reaction from the authorities.

The seesaw affair between Assad and the opposition, which now comprised both religious and secular elements, came to an abrupt halt on 25 June. On that day an unsuccessful assassination attempt was made on Assad in Damascus.

The government now went all out to smash the Brotherhood. Over the next several days the security forces executed more than 100 imprisoned Brothers. When political prisoners in Palmyra (Tadhmur) attempted a jail break, the Defence Brigade soldiers massacred between 250 and 300 of them.[28] On 7 July 1980 parliament passed a bill which made membership of, or even association with, the Muslim Brotherhood a capital offence. Armed with this law the security forces resorted to setting up street courts in the strongholds of the Brotherhood, and meting out instant justice to those unable to clear themselves of contacts with the Brotherhood. On 11 August all eighty inhabitants of a house in the old city of Aleppo, from which a shot had been fired at the security forces, were pulled out of their apartments and executed instantly.[29] In a way this massacre was a retribution for the June 1979 massacre of eighty-three Alawi cadets. It made the backers of the Brotherhood, the Sunni bourgeoisie of Aleppo, conclude that the fighting was unequal and that the state's will and capacity to unleash terror was far higher than the Brotherhood's. Also the Sunni shopkeepers, having for over a year suffered economic recession as a result of the civil war ethos generated by the Artillery School massacre, were unwilling to continue the resistance. With this the Islamic rebellion virtually collapsed.

In short, in the early stages Islamic resistance grew when government repression produced martyrs, and the cycle of opposition's terrorism and the regime's violence escalated. But when the state pressed into action the full armoury of its awesome coercive machine – causing popular disarray, fear and consternation – Islamic opposition declined sharply.

Having suffered defeat at the hands of a draconian state, the Muslim Brotherhood leaders reassessed their tactics and strategy. They decided to ally with smaller Islamic organizations: the Society of Abu Dharr, the Islamic Liberation Party, the Northern Circle, and the moderate faction of the Brotherhood led by Issam al Attar. Out of this arose, in October 1980, the Islamic Front of Syria. It was led by Shaikh Muhammad Bayununi of the Society of Abu Dharr, Adnan Saad al Din of the Brotherhood, and Said Hawa, a leading Islamist ideologue, of the Northern Circle.

In its programme, called 'The Declaration and Programme of the Islamic Revolution in Syria', issued in November, the Islamic Front tried to present itself as an alternative to the Baathist regime.[30] It also attempted to drive a wedge between the Alawi leaders and the masses, and to reassure the leftist and secular opposition forces. In so doing the Front came up with a programme which, as a compendium of Islamic concepts and liberal democracy, was an extraordinarily liberal interpretation of Islamic theory and practice intended to accommodate Islamists of different hues as well as the interests of various socio-economic classes and ethnic minorities.

Instead of threatening to decimate the Alawis, as some militant Brothers had tried to do, the Declaration appealed to the 'Wise Men' among them Alawis to 'shake off' the guardianship of Hafiz al Assad and his brother Rifaat in order to 'prevent the tragedy [of civil war] from reaching its sad end'. It condemned martial law, arbitrary decrees and inhuman police practices, and demanded the release of all political prisoners, freedom to think, publish, assemble, protest, oppose and form political parties and trade unions, and the preservation of the rights of minorities. It stood for the separation of legislative, executive and judicial powers, the independence of the judiciary, and a government subordinate to the rule of law and resting on shura, popular consultation. In the economic field the Declaration advocated peasant proprietorship and the elimination of middlemen and state officials who 'suck [peasants'] blood in the name of the state, party and socialism'. It demanded the transfer of public sector industries to workers. It recommended 'freedom to private capital' to export, import and manufacture within the limits of 'a studied plan approved by the shura, consultative assembly'. The Declaration committed itself to promoting social justice and the Sharia. It got around the conflict between Arab nationalism and Islamic umma by committing itself to Arab nationalism and unity within the wider context of Islamic solidarity. It opted for neutrality in foreign affairs and expressed uncompromising opposition to Israel and Zionism. Finally, and most importantly, the Declaration accepted Faraj's view of jihad as a compulsory obligation in Islam, and reasserted the Islamic Front's commitment to wage a jihad to transform the present 'sectarian regime' into an Islamic one.

On one hand the Islamic Front's programme bore the imprint of the thoughts of Rashid Rida, Banna, Qutb and Faraj; on the other there were marked differences between it and the programme adopted by Egypt's Muslim Brotherhood. This illustrated an important point made by Qutb:

The Islamic system is not restricted solely to a replica of the first Islamic society, but is every social form governed by the total Islamic view of life. The Islamic system has room for scores of models which are compatible with the natural growth of a society and the new needs of the contemporary age as long as the total Islamic idea dominates these models in its expansive external perimeter.[31]

The very emergence of an Islamic Front, composed of one major and several minor parties with a common programme, set the Syrian fundamentalist movement apart from its Egyptian counterpart. There was a singular absence in Syria of millennarian and messianic groups like Egypt's Al Takfir wa Al Hijra. In general the Syrian movement was more ideologically flexible and pragmatic than the Egyptian. It was also free of the complicated doctrinal arguments which plague the Egyptian Islamic scene. These differences stem primarily from the diverse nature of the two societies. Egypt is a homogeneous society with a long tradition of centralized rule, Syria a heterogeneous one lacking a strong central authority.

Ironically, while being less doctrinaire than the Egyptian Brothers, the Syrian fundamentalists conducted a long, bitter jihad against Assad's secular regime which was fiercer and more lasting than any other such struggle in the Middle East. This was partly because Assad (like Nasser in Egypt) was allied with the Soviet Union, a Marxist atheist state, and partly because at the centre of power stood Alawis, a closely knit minority which had risen by subverting the traditional rulers: Sunni feudals, merchants and industrialists. The heterodox beliefs and practices of the Alawis came in handy to the displaced ruling class which backed, politically and financially, the Muslim Brotherhood – monopolized by Sunnis – to overthrow the Assad regime under the cloak of Islam. The aspirations of this class were well reflected in the Islamic Front's programme. In the universally Sunni Egypt there was no heretic sect whose members dominated state authority; and the Egyptian bourgeoisie, which had been stripped of its economic and political power by Nasser, had been quickly rehabilitated by Sadat. Unlike in Egypt, the Syrian Brotherhood never struck roots in the countryside. Yet there were strong similarities between the social background of the fundamentalist militants – those who planned or carried out violent acts in the two states. A study of 1,384 Syrian fundamentalists imprisoned between 1976 and 1981 showed 27.7 per cent to be college or university students and 13.3

per cent professionals, the corresponding figures for the Egyptians being 40 per cent and 6 per cent.[32]

Once fundamentalist leaders in Syria had forged the Islamic Front, hammered out a common programme and charter, and reorganized their cadres, they resumed the jihad in August 1981. The Combat Vanguard of Fighters now operated as commando units equipped with light arms and shoulder-held rockets. In November a massive car bomb near a school in Damascus killed more than 200 people. Though the Islamic Front did not claim responsibility, the government blamed it, and tried to create revulsion against the Brothers by showing the dismembered, mangled and charred bodies of the victims on television. In January 1982 reports of a failed coup by some air force officers showed that all was not well with the regime.

In early February a unit of the mainly Alawi Third Armoured Division, posted near Hama, was lured into an ambush by a group of armed Brothers. This was the signal for insurgency in the city. For several days the Islamic Front activists successfully resisted the security forces. This was the best organized fundamentalist insurrection yet. The Islamic Front leaders, operating from Iraq, repeatedly broadcast appeals to the people in Syria, particularly in the capital, to declare 'a civil mutiny' against the regime, and close 'stores, shops, schools, universities, institutes, factories and all public establishments'.[33] Assad despatched 12,000 soldiers to Hama, a city of 200,000. After cordoning it off they used helicopter gunships, tanks and artillery to defeat the insurgents. It took them two weeks to gain full control. In the process some sections of the old city were flattened, and between 5,000 and 10,000 people – including about 1,000 soldiers – were killed. Unlike in March 1980, the rebellion did not spread to other cities, either due to the severity of repression or the lack of groundwork done by the fundamentalists, or both. The Brothers were certainly less numerous now than two years before. The July 1980 law, making Brotherhood membership a capital offence, had probably reduced the national membership from a peak of 30,000 to 5,000.[34] The failure of the Sunni merchants of Damascus to follow the Islamic Front's call for 'a civil mutiny' was not surprising. Over the years their leaders had established contacts with influential civilian and military personalities, and they were therefore equivocal about the overthrow of the regime. Also, the capital had been one of the main beneficiaries of governmental policies, and the merchants had participated in the prosperity which had resulted. Finally, they functioned among citizenry which had been overawed by the ruthlessness of Assad in exterminating whosoever raised arms against the government. The events at Hama established clearly that Assad could not be overturned so long as the structure, composition and the ideological orientation of the military remained unchanged.

Unusually for Syria, the crushing of the Hama insurrection was celebrated in the form of a huge, pro-government rally in Damascus, and followed by another rally on 8 March 1982, the anniversary of the 1963 Baathist takeover, when Assad led a public march – an unprecedented act. 'They [Muslim Brothers] are butchering children, women and old people in the name of Islam,' he said. 'They extend their hand to the foreigner and his agents and to the pro-US puppet regimes on our borders . . . to receive funds and arms to doublecross their homeland and kill fellow citizens . . . They are apostates. We are the ones who defend Islam, religion and the homeland.'[35]

Assad's words acquired greater significance three months later when Israel invaded Lebanon. The Syrian troops stationed in Lebanon became partially involved in the fighting; and the Syrian air force suffered many losses. These dramatic developments diverted popular attention away from Islamic resistance and rebellion, and towards the government's attempts to frustrate Israeli designs in Lebanon.

This weakened the Islamic movement, which had already been plagued by splits in the leadership. Attar had dissociated himself from the adventurest policy of jihad. Differences within the movement on the 1979 Islamic revolution in Iran and the Gulf War became irreconcilable. The Syrian fundamentalists, who had welcomed the Iranian revolution, were disappointed to see Ayatollah Khomeini's regime forge an alliance with Assad in its pursuit of war with Iraq led by President Saddam Hussein. The Brotherhood had for some years maintained warm relations with Iraq. In its sustained campaign against Assad it had received financial, military and logistical assistance from Saddam Hussein and Jordan's King Hussein. As the leading constituent of the Islamic Front, the Brotherhood wanted the Front to embrace its pro-Iraqi policy. This divided the Islamic Front into two camps: the compromisers led by Saad al Din, and the purists headed by Adnan Uqla, who was the chief of the Muslim Brotherhood's Combat Vanguard of Fighters. The purists held that Saddam Hussein was an anti-Islamic ruler since he had invaded the Islamic regime of Khomeini, and there was no question of co-operation with him. The compromisers were prepared to co-operate with anybody and everybody willing to help them overthrow the hated Assad regime.

This was the main reason why Saad al Din led the Islamic Front, in March 1982, into a coalition with seventeen other opposition parties and groups to form the National Alliance for the Liberation of Syria, which was sponsored by Iraq and Jordan. The Alliance called for a constitutional parliamentary regime, Islam as the state religion and the Sharia as the main inspiration for legislation and reform. Later, Saad al Din held meetings with American officials in Amman. Saad al Din's actions were condemned by Uqla and his followers, who were by and large young, puritanical and idealistic. In late April 1982 Uqla was expelled from the Islamic Front. He then transformed the Combat Vanguard of Fighters into a political party. The net effect of the internecine fighting among the fundamentalists was a dramatic drop in their violent activities.

For a brief period in late 1983 Islamist leaders saw their political opportunities rising. In November Hafiz al Assad suffered a severe heart attack, and the country witnessed an unseemly battle for the succession in which Rifaat Assad played a prominent part. But the president survived.

Having regained full control over the state machinery, civil and military, by the following spring, he sent his younger brother into exile. Through erudite moves President Assad frustrated US–Israeli plans to impose Maronite Christian hegemony in Lebanon and consecrate friendly relations between Israel and Lebanon through a peace treaty. The rising armed resistance by the Lebanese against the Israeli occupation, in which Syria played a key role, led to the Israeli withdrawal from Lebanon by June 1985. These developments raised Assad's status at home and in the region.

Earlier his regime had received a shot in the arm when Colonel Muammar al Qadhafi, leader of Libya, offered the merger of his country with Syria. This was readily accepted by Assad. The two heads of state signed a formal agreement on 10 September 1980. Allowing for the popular indifference to such impulsive moves by the leaders, this step had the effect of softening the anti-regime stance of Syria's Sunni establishment, since Libya was a Sunni state with Islamic credentials.

Having overthrown King Muhammad Idris of Libya on 1 September 1969, the Free Officers set up a republican regime. They promulgated a constitution and a set of laws which, they said, were based on the humanistic values of Libya's Islamic Arab heritage. Qadhafi, the Free Officers' leader, argued that the Sanusiya sufi order, which had sanctified the unIslamic institution of hereditary monarchy, was a mystical perversion of Islam. The new regime's decrees included a ban on alcohol, the closure of nightclubs as well as churches, and the appointment of the Grand Mufti to offer official interpretations of the Sharia. These measures endeared the republican officers to orthodox ulama who had been shunted to the sidelines by King Idris and his ancestors.

But relations between the ulama and the government became strained as Qadhafi advocated a flexible approach to Islam, and argued that in Islam there was room for more than one ijtihad. He strengthened his plea for flexibility by citing the example of Prophet Muhammad: while continuing to receive divine revelations in Medina he had issued a constitutional manifesto there.

Though not a trained cleric, Qadhafi undertook an interpretation and expansion of the Quranic verse on shura, consultation, and produced a book in 1975, entitled *The Green Book: The Solution to the Problem of Democracy – People's Power*. In it he made a plea for the people to exercise control over their lives by direct participation in democratic institutions. Out of this arose the concept of popular congresses and popular committees. A vast gathering of these bodies on 2 March 1977 affirmed the absolute authority of the people, and renamed the country as the Socialist People's Libyan Arab Jamahiriya, the term jamahiriya meaning populist republic.

The second volume of *The Green Book*, subtitled *The Solution to the Economic Problem – Socialism*, published in early 1978, was a guide to economic freedom through a 'new socialism' which, Qadhafi asserted, was different from the socialism of the East or West. He defined socialism as an absolute value, like truth. At home Qadhafi adopted the concept that 'land belongs to no one' on the basis of a hadith of Prophet Muhammad. 'Whoever owns land, let him cultivate it,' the Prophet is reported to have said. 'If he cannot, or is physically unable to do so, then let him grant it to his Muslim brother. But let him not lease it out to him.'[36] In May 1978 the government issued a decree which limited the size of landholdings, and applied it to all persons and institutions including religious endowments, a step which alienated the ulama.

In mid-1979 came the third and final volume of *The Green Book*, subtitled *The Social Foundations of the Third Universal Theory*. The term 'Third Universal Theory' implied that Qadhafi was offering an alternative to capitalism and Marxism. In this book Qadhafi articulated the concept of the social law being based on urf, social custom, and din, faith. By urf he meant ethnic identity or nationalism. 'The sole mover of human history is the social and ethnic factor,' he stated. 'The social link forms the basic relationships among the primary units of human societies, from the family to the tribe, then the nation, which is the fundamental factor of history.'[37] According to Qadhafi, ethnic identity was the cement that held large groups together. The only rival to this common social factor was religion, which was capable of dividing an otherwise unified people as well as unifying different ethnic groups. In case of competition between social and religious factors, the social factor would prevail. The only way to resolve this conflict, present or potential, was to adopt the concept of 'To every people, their own religion', Qadhafi argued.

Whatever the merit of Qadhafi's thesis it is not a variant of Islamic fundamentalism, where religion reigns supreme and where the ultimate aim is to forge a single umma of Muslims throughout the world. No wonder that by the early 1980s most fundamentalist thinkers came to regard Qadhafi as a maverick at best or a heretic at worst.

Yet certain views and actions of Qadhafi found favour with the Iranian clerics who gained power in early 1979: his vehement condemnation of monarchy as unIslamic, and his revolutionary activism at home and abroad which inter alia brought him into confrontation with American imperialism.

5

SAUDI ARABIA: THE OLDEST FUNDAMENTALIST STATE

The collapse of the Ottoman empire followed by the abolition of the caliphate by Mustafa Kemal Ataturk in March 1924 created a leadership vacuum in the world Muslim community. Among those who tried to fill it was Sharif Hussein ibn Ali al Hashim of the Hashimi dynasty which had governed Hijaz, containing Mecca and Medina, since the tenth century and which claimed lineage from Prophet Muhammad. During the First World War the British had successfully encouraged Sharif Hussein to rebel against his Ottoman overlords, and after the war placed his two sons on the thrones of Iraq and Transjordan. The Hashimi–British alliance was regarded as anti-Islamic by non-Arab Muslims as well as by many Arab leaders. Sharif Hussein's claim to the caliphate therefore received scant support outside Hijaz. In certain cases it even aroused outright hostility. Among those who took umbrage at Sharif Hussein's declaration was Abdul Aziz ibn Abdul Rahman al Saud (1879–1953) – also known as Ibn Saud – whose forces controlled the territories surrounding Hijaz.

Abdul Aziz symbolized a high point in the varying fortunes of the House of Saud. After its defeat by the Ottomans in 1819 it had recaptured Riyadh only to be sent into exile in 1891 by the Rashidi tribal chief, Muhammad ibn Rashid, acting as a client of the Ottomans. In 1902 Abdul Aziz had ventured out of Kuwait and regained Riyadh. From there he had mounted a series of campaigns to gain control of Najd and defeat Muhammad ibn Rashid. He then extended his domain to the eastern territory of Hasa, inhabited by Shia tribes, in 1913. But his plans to

attack Sharif Hussein's Hijaz were disrupted by the outbreak of the First World War.

The central Arabian region of Najd was sparsely inhabited, with half of its population being nomadic tribes who
were none the less related to those settled in villages and
towns. Though nominal Muslims, these tribes had taken to
resolving their disputes through customary tribal law rather
than the Sharia, and reverted to performing pre-Islamic
rituals. The tribes had also taken to distinguishing themselves as noble, inferior or despicable. (The Saudi family
belonged to the Musalikh branch of the Ruwalla section of
the Anza tribe, considered a noble tribe.) Abdul Aziz
resolved to transform the fractured, hierarchical Najdi
community into a unified Islamic umma by replacing
loyalty to the tribe with loyalty to Islam and its leader, the
Imam: a replay of what had occurred in Arabia during the
days of Prophet Muhammad. Abdul Aziz used Wahhabism
as his ideological tool to achieve this end. At the same time,
by reiterating the Arab and Islamic heritage of the Saudi
dynasty and its frequent intermarriage with the descendants of the much-revered Muhammad ibn Abdul
Wahhab, he justified its assumption of the Imamate.

Unitarianism and socio-religious equality of the believers
were the hallmarks of Wahhabism, and as a Wahhabi
leader Abdul Aziz stressed these. He abolished the protection tax which the inferior and despised tribes used to pay
to the noble ones, thereby underlining the egalitarian
nature of Wahhabism and winning fierce loyalty from the
lower tribes. Having done this, Abdul Aziz decreed that all
tribes must pay him zakat, the Islamic tax – an order which
firmly established him as the Imam even though the
nominal title stayed with his father, Abdul Rahman, until
the latter's death in 1928.

Considering themselves as 'the truly guided Islamic
community', the Wahhabis set out to attack polytheists,
unbelievers and hypocrites (i.e. those who claimed to be
Muslim but whose behaviour was unIslamic). Any deviation from the Sharia was labelled by them as innovation,
and therefore unIslamic. Any Muslim who disagreed with

the Wahhabi interpretation of Islam was regarded by them as unbelieving apostate who deserved severe punishment.

Wahhabis believed intensely in the division of the world into Dar al Islam and its counterpart, Dar al Harb (The Realm of War between believers and non-believers), and in the concept of hijra, migration. They viewed the departure of Muhammad ibn Abdul Wahhab in 1744 from Uyaina to Diriya in the same light as they did Prophet Muhammad's migration from Mecca to Medina – and called it Al Hijra.

Abdul Aziz sponsored the fresh converts' 'hijra' to Wahhabism which was both physical and religio-spiritual. It meant having to give up nomadic life and 'migrating' from customary tribal law to the Sharia and from the traditional tribal bonds to membership in the Islamic Brotherhood, called the Ikhwan.

He set up Ikhwan colonies, called hijar, soon after his conquest of Hasa in 1913. Each settlement included agricultural land, grazing pastures and reliable water supplies. Yet most of them failed to become self-sufficient and had to be subsidized by Abdul Aziz. In due course they became the religious, political, military, administrative and educational centres of Wahhabism, and enabled Abdul Aziz to achieve something that no other power or leader has so far done: impose a centralized rule over the forty major tribes inhabiting Najd. In order to lessen inter-tribal conflict Abdul Aziz ordered that no tribe should leave its territory without his permission. He kept many tribal chiefs in the capital, Riyadh, under surveillance under the guise of educating them in Wahhabism.

Life in an Ikhwan colony, with an average population of 2,000, was highly organized and centred round the mosque. The ulama played an important role as did the muttawin, religious police, who were trained in Riyadh. The tasks of the religious police were to impart the Wahhabi doctrine to the faithful and punish those found smoking, singing or dancing, wearing gold or silk, or failing to perform the Islamic rituals. An Ikhwan colony was run jointly by an emir and a governor. The emir, elected by the local consultative assembly, was responsible to the Imam in

Riyadh. The governor, who dealt with the Sharia, was responsible to the Shaikh al Islam, the head of the ulama, also based in Riyadh.

Abdul Aziz combined ideological zeal with pragmatism. He made it a point to marry into the family of the subjugated tribal chief, thus consolidating his control of the conquered territory without in any way undermining the internal structure of the defeated tribe. In the process he acquired seventeen wives and sired fifty-four sons and 215 daughters. Thus the religious unity of the new and expanding Dar al Islam – now encompassing 200 Ikhwan settlements with many thousands of soldiers – was reinforced with filial connections.

Like the first converts to Islam in the mid-seventh century, the Ikhwan were fired with crusading zeal to spread the Wahhabi version of Islam to the farthest corners of the Arabian Peninsula and beyond. By 1920 their colonies had become the primary source of soldiery to Abdul Aziz. They proved to be excellent fighters; they were highly mobile, and, being members of nomadic tribes, they were extraordinarily tenacious and hardy. On top of this, they were motivated by religious fervour. While fighting they used such Islamic war cries as: 'The Riders of Unity!', 'The People of Unity!', and 'The Winds of Paradise are blown/Where are you, the Dissenter?!' If they won and lived, they felt proud to have been instruments in effecting a victory of virtue over sin. If they met death, they believed, it transformed them into martyrs and thus guaranteed them a place in paradise. After all, Taqi al Din ibn Taimiya, one of the major inspirers of Abdul Wahhab, had stated: 'Death of the martyr for the unification of all people in the cause of God and His word is the happiest, best, easiest and most virtuous of all deaths.'[1] Finally, since the Ikhwan were engaged in Islamic jihad, they were religiously entitled to four-fifths of the booty, with only one-fifth going to the state.

In 1920 Abdul Aziz conquered Asir province south of Hijaz, a fertile region. The next year he dealt a final blow to his rival, Muhammad ibn Rashid, captured Hail, and proclaimed himself Sultan, Commander, a secular title. After he had added more territories to his domain in 1922, he became Sultan of Najd and its Dependencies. He couched every campaign in Islamic terms, as a struggle to punish either religious dissenters or those who had strayed from true Islam. Only then could his forces take the booty as their legitimate reward.

Abdul Aziz wanted to seize Hijaz in order to control the lucrative traffic of Muslim pilgrims to Mecca and Medina. At the same time he was intent on clothing his actions in Islamic terms. By declaring himself caliph Sharif Hussein provided Abdul Aziz with the kind of pretext he was looking for. At about the same time the British decided to punish Sharif Hussein for his continued refusal to sign an Anglo-Hijazi treaty by cutting off their subsidies to him: a development which emboldened Abdul Aziz to implement his plans. He condemned Sharif Hussein for the sacrilegious act of claiming to be the caliph, for the corrupt ways in which he managed Mecca and Medina, and the desecration he caused to the holy places by letting Christians enter them. During the 1924 hajj season Abdul Aziz sponsored a conference of the ulama and lay notables, which was presided over by his father, Abdul Rahman, the nominal Imam. It called on the (Wahhabi) Ikhwan to act on behalf of the Islamic umma and overthrow the false caliph Sharif Hussein. Messages to this effect were sent to the leaders of Muslim communities throughout the world for their endorsement. Given the trepidation which most foreign Muslim leaders felt about the prospect of Wahhabis gaining administrative control of Mecca and Medina, very few responded. But the exercise served Abdul Aziz's purpose. He had created an Islamic aura around his impending military action, and by so doing actively discouraged the British, the ultimate underwriters of Sharif Hussein's power, from siding with him.

In early October the Ikhwan led by Abdul Aziz laid siege around Mecca. To avoid bloodshed and destruction the local ulama and traders prevailed upon Sharif Hussein to abdicate in favour of his son, Ali, and leave Mecca. For his part Abdul Aziz promised that there would be no repetition of the violent 1803 takeover of Mecca by the Wahhabis. Ali fled. And Abdul Aziz occupied Mecca. A year later Medina surrendered to the Ikhwan.

'I have no wish to be the master of Hijaz,' Abdul Aziz wrote to the heads of various governments in Muslim countries. 'It is a mandate that has been entrusted to me until the Hijazis have chosen a governor who can consider himself servant of the Muslim world and who will work under the watchful eye of the Muslim people.'[2] Obviously, Abdul Aziz had learned from the experience of his forefathers that, unlike other parts of the Arabian Peninsula, the fate of Hijaz mattered enormously to the leaders of foreign Muslims, and that it would be foolhardy to ignore this fact. At the same time there was no doubt in his mind as to whom the Hijazis would 'choose' as their governor.

In early 1926 Abdul Aziz proclaimed himself King of Hijaz, the title used earlier by Sharif Hussein; it was intended to reassure foreign Muslims who would have protested vehemently had Abdul Aziz declared himself Imam of Hijaz. He was aware of the need to reassure foreign Muslim communities that Mecca and Medina would remain open to all Muslim sects. In order to impress the pilgrims with the welcome changes he had implemented, he prescribed capital punishment for any local Hijazi trying to swindle pilgrims or extort protection money from them – a common practice during the Hashimi rule. He allowed Hijazi courts to follow the Hanafi school of law, as they had done before his conquest, and not the Hanbali school which prevailed elsewhere in Abdul Aziz's domain.

While these steps went some way to reassure local Hijazis and foreign pilgrims, they caused a rift between Abdul Aziz and his Ikhwan followers who, now settled in 222 colonies, numbered more than 150,000 men.[3]

The fast growth of Ikhwan settlements, both in number and size, meant a greater demand on the treasury of Abdul Aziz. Only the booty gained from a succession of victorious campaigns in the early 1920s allowed Abdul Aziz to overcome the problem. Administering Hijaz was an expensive business; and a tax on tobacco had been a major contributor to the state revenue during the Hashimi rule. Abdul Aziz's decision to continue the tobacco tax met with stiff opposition from Wahhabi ulama. They argued that since smoking tobacco was unIslamic (and punishable in Najd) levying tax on it was unIslamic. Abdul Aziz reluctantly accepted their ruling. But, soon, pleading insufficient funds, he refused to pay salaries or give gifts to the Ikhwan. This created disaffection among them.

In late 1926 two militant Ikhwan leaders – Faisal al Dawish of Artawiya colony (and Mutair tribe) and Ibn Humaid Sultan ibn Bijad of Ghatghat colony (and Utaiba tribe) – convened a conference. It criticized Abdul Aziz for levying unIslamic taxes, failing to impose the Wahhabi doctrine on the Shias of Hasa, and using telephones, telegraphs, cars and planes in whose working magic, and therefore the devil, was involved.

Abdul Aziz responded by convening a conference in January 1927. He abolished all the non-Islamic laws of Hijaz, and ordered that all Shias attend classes in Wahhabism and stop celebrating publicly their festival of mourning – Ashura. The ulama attending the conference ruled that levying unIslamic taxes was not sufficient ground for the faithful to disobey the Imam.

These moves only postponed a confrontation between Abdul Aziz and the Ikhwan which seemed inevitable, and which had many precedents in Islamic history – replete with examples of temporal and spiritual forces allying to achieve certain aims and then parting bitterly, with the temporal force emerging as the victor.

In practical terms, having conquered 80 per cent of the over one million square miles of the Arabian Peninsula with a population of 1.3 million, there was virtually no more territory left for Abdul Aziz to capture. So he had little use for a militant force of 150,000 Ikhwan fanatically committed to the tenets of Wahhabism. Having declared himself King of Najd and its Dependencies in January 1927, Abdul Aziz sought international recognition. He was keen to secure it from Britain, the single most important foreign power in the Arabian Peninsula. The result was the 1927 Treaty of Jidda. London recognized Abdul Aziz as king of Hijaz and Najd and its Dependencies. In return Abdul Aziz accepted Britain as the 'protector' of the Arab principalities in the Gulf and Oman, and the integrity of Transjordan and Iraq under British mandate. This meant having to rein in the Ikhwan to whom fixed, western-style borders were meaningless, and whose fervour to spread the Wahhabi creed to the rest of the world remained undiminished.

Their continued raids on the territories outside Abdul Aziz's domain strained relations between the Ikhwan and their ruler. When the British insisted on restitution for the Ikhwan raids, Abdul Aziz resorted to confiscating the booty that the Ikhwan were entitled to on such occasions (had their actions been sanctified by the Iman or ulama). In early 1929, after failing to cross into British-controlled Iraq, the Ikhwan spent their aggressive energies on the tribes on their side of the border. This enraged Abdul Aziz. He ordered the disbanding of the Ikhwan. His decree was ignored. He secured a ruling from the ulama that attacking the Ikhwan was now legitimate, and began to enlarge his army with recruits from the tribes and townsmen. He led an army of 30,000, equipped with motorized weapons supplied by the British, to confront 8,000 Ikhwan headed by Faisal al Dawish and Sultan ibn Bijad at Sabila in March 1929, and defeated them.

However, the Ikhwans' final demise did not occur until December. They found themselves sandwiched between the advancing forces of Abdul Aziz and the British contingents in Kuwait. Large-scale desertions reduced their ranks. Finally they surrendered to the British, who passed them on to Abdul Aziz. He punished them mercilessly to ensure that no such revolt would ever occur again.

So, what finally decimated the Ikhwan was the acceptance by Abdul Aziz, the one-time Imam of the Islamic umma, of fixed, western-style frontiers, and his crushing attack on them with the active assistance of the non-Islamic

British. Obviously, between waging an eternal jihad against Dar al Harb, the non-Muslim world, and building a power base in one country, Abdul Aziz chose the latter.

In September 1932 Abdul Aziz combined his two domains into one and named it Kingdom of Saudi Arabia, proclaiming himself King of Saudi Arabia. The national flag carrying the Islamic shahada, central precept, and the crossed swords of Muhammad ibn Abdul Wahhab and the House of Saud aptly symbolized the new political entity.

Having established a state (in the modern sense of the word), the House of Saud has used Islam to legitimize its dynastic rule. Saudi Arabia is unique. It was created out of a series of Islamic campaigns in modern times, and its character as a fundamentalist polity has remained unchanged since its inception in 1932. It is thus the oldest politically independent Islamic fundamentalist state in the world.

Fundamental Islam and the Modern State

Strictly speaking, kingship and hereditary power have no Islamic sanction. This is obvious from the early history of Islam. The caliph was chosen by consultation among either traditional community elders or an electoral college appointed by the reigning caliph. Contrary to this practice, the Imams of the House of Saud had taken to naming their successors, and establishing dynastic rule.

When Abdul Aziz and his successors were subjected to this criticism they replied that the Quran was the constitution of Saudi Arabia, and since the king was as much subject to Quranic dictates as any other believer, monarchy was legitimate in Islam.

There was yet another Islamic principle which was flouted by the House of Saud: a Quranic verse requires that the ruler must consult the people in governing them.[4] To be sure, when Abdul Aziz acquired the title of King of Hijaz, he announced the establishment of a twenty-four-member Consultative Assembly consisting of ulama, lay notables and merchants. It played an insignificant role for a while, and then disappeared unceremoniously. Since then none of Abdul Aziz's successors has even publicly endorsed the principle of a Consultative Assembly, much less appointed one or allowed citizens to elect it.

The possession of Mecca and Medina enabled Abdul Aziz to emphasize his role as the Custodian of the Holy Places and the Patron of Hajj, and paint the House of Saud in deeply Islamic colours. Actually Abdul Aziz's status was far more complex and weighty. Not only was he the head of state, the commander in chief and the head of the royal family but also the leader of all tribal chiefs (shaikh al mashaikh). As the Custodian of the Holy Places, he acquired the status of the protector of the faith.

However, Abdul Aziz founded his kingdom at a time of economic crisis caused by a severe drop in the number of pilgrims (because of a world-wide depression) and therefore in the pilgrimage tax payable to the government. It was against this background that he granted an oil concession to Standard Oil Company of California in 1933 for £50,000, paid in gold, as advance against future royalties on actual oil production. Exploration began immediately in Hasa, and modest commercial extraction followed five years later.

Oil production was interrupted by the Second World War, but once the war was over, it jumped from 50,000 to 900,000 barrels per day in 1951. The subsequent boom in the economy overstretched the rudimentary institutions of the state supervised by Abdul Aziz and some of his close relatives. Yet it was not until October 1953 – a month before his death – that King Abdul Aziz issued a decree establishing a council of ministers as an advisory body.

Five more years passed before the new ruler, King Saud ibn Abdul Aziz, gave executive and legislative powers to the ministers. He did so only because by then the country's administration, lacking any budget or even an accounting system, had come to a virtual halt, and Crown Prince Faisal ibn Abdul Aziz had been put in overall charge of state affairs.

In 1960 a draft constitution, declaring Islam to be the state religion, describing private property and capital as 'fundamental values of natural wealth', and specifying the creation of a National Assembly of ninety to 120 members – two-thirds elected and the rest nominated by the monarch – was presented to King Saud for approval. He rejected the document, stating, 'The Quran is the oldest and the most efficient of the world's constitutions.'[5]

But the overthrow of religious monarchy in neighbouring North Yemen on 27 September 1962 made the Saudi royal family anxious. On 6 November Crown Prince Faisal issued a ten-point programme covering the constitutional, religious, judicial, social and economic aspects of the state. It declared its commitment to the improvement of 'the lot of the average citizen' through intensified economic development and the implementation of 'social legislation'. It promised the issuance of a 'Basic Law' (i.e. constitution), based on the Quran and the Hadiths, which would provide a citizen with his fundamental rights including 'the right to freely express his opinion within the limits of Islamic belief and public policy'. It also pledged to reform the existing Committees for Propagation of Virtue and Prevention of Vice in accordance with the Sharia, and establish a Supreme Judicial Council of twenty members to reconcile the legal problems of modern society with the Sharia. (A quarter of a century later the constitution had not even been drafted, much less issued. It was only in mid-1975 that the promised Supreme Judicial Council was formed.)

In the kingdom religious hierarchy is interwoven with secular authority at all levels. Locally, the religious establishment – the imam, the ulama and the qadi (religious judge) – works in conjunction with the government administrator along the lines followed earlier in Ikhwan colonies. The muttawin, religious police, execute the local imam's decisions. They ensure that Islamic practices are observed, that businesses close during prayer times, that women in the street are clad in modest, Islamic dresses, that no alcohol is consumed publicly, and that during Ramadan there is no infringement of the ban on food and drink between sunrise and sunset. They also instruct the faithful at educational institutions, and outside, on the observance of Islamic edicts. At the national level the king is assisted in religious and judicial matters by the minister of religion/justice, traditionally a descendant of Muhammad ibn Abdul Wahhab, and the chief qadi, religious judge.

In 1970 the Office of the Grand Mufti (also called Shaikh al Islam), head of Sharia courts, was replaced by a Ministry of Justice. Following the previous practice, the new ministry was headed by a respected alim from the family of Abdul Wahhab, known as Aal Shaikh. Whereas the Grand Mufti had been an independent religious authority, the justice minister, being a member of the cabinet, was required to follow the monarch's instructions. This change put the final seal on the subordination of the ulama to the political authority of the Saudi king, a situation reminiscent of the Ottoman court. In the mid-eighteenth century, though, the founders of the Saudi dynasty and the Wahhabi doctrine were equally dependent on each other. The balance had shifted perceptibly in favour of the House of Saud during the rule of Abdul Aziz. Indeed, once Abdul Aziz had (gradually) replaced Hanafi jurists in Hijaz with Hanbalis, the ulama as a body came to rely exclusively on the state for their livelihood and status. With this Saudi Arabia fell in line with most other Sunni countries where the ulama are dependent on the state for their upkeep.

In Saudi Arabia, however, the ulama enjoy more power and prestige than in any other Sunni state. They are the key element in bestowing legitimacy on the Saudi regime. This became clear during the crisis in the early 1960s when King Saud ibn Abdul Aziz proved extraordinarily inept and spendthrift. In late March 1964 a dozen senior ulama issued a ruling that while Saud should remain king, Crown Prince Faisal ibn Abdul Aziz should supervise all internal and external affairs without consulting King Saud. Faisal, son of an Aal Shaikh mother, was well known for his piety and asceticism, and fiscal responsibility. The next day seventy senior princes, representing all six branches of the House of Saud, endorsed the ulama's ruling. But Saud refused to act as a figurehead, and called on the ulama to reconsider their decision. On 29 October 1964 a conclave of all senior ulama invoked the Sharia principle of 'public interest', and ruled that King Saud should step down and that Faisal should assume the highest office. About a hundred senior princes backed the ulama. In the face of such an alliance of the religious establishment and the overwhelming majority of the royal household, Saud had no choice but to abdicate. He did so on 2 November, and left the country. Faisal ruled until March 1975, when he was assassinated by a disgruntled junior prince.

One of the important functions of the senior ulama is to advise on the drafting of royal orders, called nizams, which regulate Saudi society in those areas where fiqh (traditional religious jurisprudence) is either absent or insufficient or radically out of tune with the modern age. The Saudi government views the issuing of such regulations as part of its administrative effort to implement the Sharia rather than expanding or altering it. Such a legislative practice is firmly rooted in the history of Islam, and goes back at least nine centuries. The Ottomans had a distinct term for such laws: qanun. The earliest example of qanun in the Saudi kingdom was the Commercial Code decreed by Abdul Aziz in 1931. During King Saud's rule came a revision of the Commercial Code along the lines of the western-influenced Ottoman Commercial Code – and the promulgation of the laws on nationality, forgery, bribery and mining. Among the important laws King Faisal decreed were those on labour and workmen, social insurance and the civil service.

Such actions are permitted in the Hanbali school of Islamic law. While it demands strict application of the Quran and the Hadiths it is quite flexible in the areas not covered by these scriptures. Also Hanbali jurists never closed their doors to ijtihad, independent reasoning, for those areas where the Quran and the Hadiths are vague. Furthermore, the jurists are allowed to choose a ruling from other recognized schools where their own school is silent or confused on a particular subject. Finally, the Hanbali school accepts the general Islamic principle of 'public interest' or 'welfare of society' which, for instance, was invoked by the ulama to demand the deposition of King Saud.

When it comes to coping with the day-to-day problems of staying within what is legitimate in Islam in the face of new situations and modern inventions, Saudi rulers apply the general criterion of 'welfare of society'. It was on this basis that Abdul Aziz found telephones, telegraph, cars and aeroplanes acceptable. But most Ikhwan leaders had different views: they saw these contraptions as the works of the devil. Yielding to their pressure Abdul Aziz postponed using these inventions, but not for long.

But Ikhwan leaders were not the only ones to oppose modern technology. Certain senior ulama did too. When it came to radio, Shaikh Abdullah ibn Hussein al Aal Shaikh, the chief qadi of Hijaz, believed that it was Satan himself who carried messages through the air and that the operators at various radio stations in the kingdom worshipped Satan. Abdul Aziz arranged for the Quran to be read at Riyadh radio station for Shaikh Abdullah ibn Hussein to hear it in Mecca, thus proving that Satan was not involved: it was unthinkable that Satan would carry the Word of God even a single inch forward. From then on radio became Allah's own miracle.

As petroleum exploration and extraction got under way there was an increasing presence of American and other western oil technicians in the kingdom. Abu Bahz, a former Ikhwan leader, criticized King Abdul Aziz for this and argued that the monarch was helping non-believers to gain profit from Muslims. Abdul Aziz called Abu Bahz and a group of leading ulama to his court in Riyadh. He showed himself to be well-versed in the life and traditions of Prophet Muhammad, and referred to several instances where the Prophet had engaged non-Muslims, singly or jointly, for specific jobs. 'Am I right or wrong?' he reportedly asked. Those present replied that he was right. 'Am I breaking the Sharia law, therefore, when I follow in the footsteps of the Prophet, and employ foreign experts to work for me . . . under my direction to increase the material resources of the land, and to extract for our benefit the metals, oil and water placed by Allah beneath our land intended for our use?' Abdul Aziz inquired. The unanimous view was that the monarch had not broken the Sharia.[6] Elsewhere he argued that as Christians the Americans and British were People of the Book, and therefore preferable to idolators and back-sliders.

Abdul Aziz took issue with the ulama on photography. Islam forbids man's intervention in creating human forms – that is, all graphic arts which involve human shapes and forms. Abdul Aziz argued that photography, being merely juxtaposition of light and shade created by Allah, was quite distinct from the pictorial arts. So photography was allowed in Saudi Arabia. It was on this foundation that King Faisal tried to introduce television in 1965. He faced stiff opposition from conservative ulama. So he introduced it stealthily, always insisting that television broadcasts – consisting exclusively of prayers, readings of the Quran and religious discussions – were being 'tested' to assess the virtues and vices of the medium.

While Abdul Aziz and his successors had periodically to cajole the ulama to accept modern technology and rapid economic development, they fully agreed with the ulama that Saudi Arabians should not abandon their traditional ways of living and thinking for western ones. This was particularly true of Abdul Aziz, who did not consider Europeans or Americans more civilized than Saudi Arabians. Since Saudi Arabia had undergone neither western colonization nor governance by a local westernized élite, which regarded the West as being the pace-setter in all endeavours of life, Saudi monarchs genuinely believed that as a social–moral system Islam was superior to any other.

As the oil industry expanded, and with it the size of the foreign population, both Muslim and non-Muslim, and as Saudis themselves travelled abroad increasingly or undertook higher education at western universities, Saudi Arabia began to lose something of its rigid, austere face. This worried the ulama and the monarch. In the autumn of 1967 King Faisal issued a proclamation which warned the country's youth against laxity in behaviour and dress, and ordered that civil servants must cease working at prayer times and congregate for prayers on the premises, that school children must be segregated sexually at nine, and that all females aged nine or more must wear a veil. The proclamation had the enthusiastic backing of the ulama.

The ulama were well paid and well respected. They stayed in touch with the community by acting as counsellors on personal problems, mediating in disputes and helping citizens in their dealings with the bureaucracy. They ran the judicial system where the Sharia's hadd punishments were in force: flogging for drinking alcohol, cutting off hands for stealing, and death by stoning for adultery committed by married adults. The Sharia courts, presided by the ulama, were generally considered fair by the public. The ulama managed the affluent religious endowments which included not only numerous hostels endowed for use by poor pilgrims but also the influential Imam Ibn Saud Islamic University in Riyadh. They were in charge of organizing the hajj, a six-day-long ritual, which in the mid-1960s attracted up to one million Muslims from home and abroad. They ran the Committees for Propagation of Virtue and Prevention of Vice and their executive arm of the muttawin, religious police. Armed with batons the muttawin compelled shops to close at prayer times, destroyed dolls in stores (since they violated the Islamic ban on the representation of the human form, an activity likely to lead to idolatry), raided houses suspected of containing alcoholic drinks, and beat the exposed calves of European women.

In Saudi Arabia the role of women is defined strictly, according to the Quran; and these restrictions apply to all women, whether Muslim or not. The position of women derives from the premise that the family is the cornerstone of Muslim society, and that an Islamic state must create an environment where men are not tempted to indulge in extra-marital sex and thus undermine the foundation of family life. From this stems the prohibition on women driving motor vehicles or travelling alone or working alongside men to whom they are not related. A general view prevails among the ulama and others that Islam indeed upgraded the position of women in the Arabia of the seventh century by conferring upon them the rights of marriage, divorce and inheritance. Since men are, broadly speaking, emotionally stable and intellectually superior – so the argument runs – they are entitled to lead society in general and the family in particular. Woman's primary role is as wife and mother, and so her education should be directed mainly along these lines.

There was resistance to women's education *per se* in Saudi Arabia from the ulama. Faisal and his (one and only) wife Iffat bint Ahmad al Thunayan introduced girls' education in 1960. The Quran, argued Faisal, enjoins learning on every believing Muslim, whether male or female. Despite this it took a few years before the idea of female education was formally accepted by the ulama.

Faisal enjoyed high standing among the ulama before and after he became king. Through his mother he claimed lineage from Abdul Wahhab, the progenitor of Wahhabism. He lived a spartan life, and his piety was legendary. He increased the salaries of the ulama and at the same time strengthened state control over them. By introducing price controls, and authorizing generous grants for educational and health facilities, he widened his popular support.

The October 1973 Arab–Israeli War added further to his prestige. By giving an enthusiastic lead in imposing an Arab oil embargo on the countries backing Israel, Faisal scored a double hit. He showed that he was an Arab nationalist and simultaneously helped to secure a quadrupling of the oil price. Whereas the First Five-Year Plan (1970–75) had cost 8 billion dollars, the Second Plan (1975–80) amounted to 142 billion dollars. More than 80 per cent of the First Plan funds were earmarked for building or expanding the infrastructure of roads, communications and power plants. These ambitious plans could only be realized by importing a vast pool of foreign workers from other Arab countries and elsewhere. The presence of a large number of single, unmarried men created a host of social and other problems.

Saudi society itself underwent profound social change. The oil boom led to a rapid and dramatic expansion of urban centres, and an equally rapid disappearance of villages and nomadic tribes. In the mid-1970s nomads formed only 10 per cent of the indigenous national population of 4.3 million. Urbanization and commercialization undermined tribal loyalties, a process which had been accelerated by such governmental actions as the nationalization of water supplies and active discouragement of tribal attachment to specific grazing lands and certain water wells.

On the other hand, the oil boom acted as cement to hold the vastly inflated royal family together. There were now over 4,000 princes, one half of them direct descendants of Abdul Aziz, and the other half of his five brothers and cousins. Between them they held most of the top civilian and military positions. In a sense the inflated royal family paralleled the single ruling party in many secular Third World countries.

Yet there were always some malcontents. One senior prince, Talal, had in August 1962 defected to Egypt, then led by Nasser, an enemy of King Faisal, and formed the Liberation Front of Arabia. Later, after he had relented, he was welcomed back into the royal fold. In August 1965 another prince, Khalid ibn Musaid, led his followers in an attack on Riyadh television station. He and his close associates were killed by the security police. It transpired later that Prince Khalid ibn Musaid was the leader of the revived Ikhwan movement and that he had opposed Faisal's modernization plans in private before mounting his dramatic assault on the television station. Some ten years later, on 25 March 1975, his younger brother, Faisal ibn Musaid, assassinated King Faisal. The twenty-eight-year-old prince had personal and political reasons for his action. There was the killing of his brother to be avenged. There was also the element of inter-tribal feuding since the mother of these two princes was from Rashidi tribe, a traditional rival to the House of Saud. Faisal ibn Musaid was engaged to a daughter of King Saud, in whose deposition Crown

Prince Faisal had played a crucial role. The later discovery that the young prince had received military training at one of the Palestinian camps in Lebanon meant that he was a political radical of some kind.

Beyond the portals of royalty there existed opposition to the monarch from secular quarters: Arab nationalists operating either as Nasserists or Baathists, and Marxists. In the 1970s these opposition groups, functioning clandestinely, declined partly due to the success the Saudi government had in buying off expatriate opponents. Their place was taken by the fundamentalist groups. The revival of the Ikhwan was part of that process. It was to mature in the late 1970s in the form of a dramatic assault on the legitimacy of the Saudi monarchy.

Crown Prince Khalid's accession to the throne in March 1975 came at a time when the Saudi economy was entering a period of boom. The over-heated economy and the concomitant socio-religious problems caused differences within the ruling élite. One group led by King Khalid and Prince Abdullah, head of the National Guard, advocated a slower pace of industrialization and closer adherence to the Wahhabi doctrine; the other group, headed by Crown Prince Fahd and Prince Sultan, the defence minister, wanted a faster pace of industrialization accompanied by greater religio-cultural liberalization and closer ties with America.

Saudi Arabia was generous in its purchase of US treasury bonds to prop up the ailing American dollar. It reinforced its intelligence links with Washington. Saudi contacts with the West had grown to the extent that the number of Saudi students at universities in the West, particularly in America, was far higher than the 14,500 at home.[7] The vigorous implementation of the economic and military plans – including the construction of three military cities – led to a rapid rise in the American presence in the kingdom. In early 1977 the number of civilian and military American personnel was 30,000: five times the figure in 1971.[8] In their day-to-day business they often dealt with Saudi ministers and top civil servants who were themselves

American-educated and enamoured of the American lifestyle.

The rapid spending of billions of dollars had its own logic. Corruption and kickbacks on contracts in the public and private sectors reached unprecedented proportions, and fostered billionaire princes. Along with this went a decline in public morality. The unIslamic behaviour of many princes and their close associates, and the prospering businessmen, within the privacy of their palaces – involving drinking, gambling and fornication – became grist to the gossip mills at home and abroad. There were also growing mutterings against the excessive presence of Americans in the oil industry, military and the National Guard.

Soon after his accession King Khalid ibn Abdul Aziz considered establishing a Consultative Council, but nothing came of it. In mid-1978 Crown Prince Fahd opposed the notion of representative government on the ground that elections would not confer leadership on the country's most qualified people: the young Saudis who had received university education at home or in the West. 'We have invested heavily in educating these young men, and now we want to collect a dividend on our investment,' he told *Time* magazine. 'But if we were to have elections . . . the winners would be rich businessmen.'[9]

But the overthrow of the dictatorial Muhammad Reza Pahlavi of Iran by a popular Islamic republican movement led by Ayatollah Khomeini in February 1979 alarmed the Saudi royal family. The Iranian media, particularly radio, often attacked the unIslamic lifestyle of many members of the House of Saud. King Khalid responded by ordering that no prince should vacation abroad during Ramadan, a device frequently used by the royals and their families to avoid the rigours of fasting between sunrise and sunset. At least one princess was publicly beheaded for adultery. The revitalized Committees for Propagation of Virtue and Prevention of Vice closed all beauty parlours and hairdressing salons and forbade women to try on garments on the premises of clothing stores. Yielding to their pressure the government banned all non-Islamic services, including confirmation classes at foreign schools in the kingdom. The sale of crosses, even as jewellery, was prohibited. Ever since the rule of Abdul Aziz there had existed a ban on the building of any church or temple of a non-Islamic faith.

During the hajj season in October–November the Saudi authorities awaited the arrival of the Iranian pilgrims, imbued with revolutionary fervour, with trepidation. But the hajj passed off peacefully. It was on 1 Muharram (20 November 1979), the New Year's Day – which also marked the beginning of the Islamic fifteenth century – that the House of Saud was severely shaken.

At 5.20 A.M. on that day some 400 well-armed Islamic militants, calling themselves the Ikhwan, took over Islam's holiest shrine, the Grand Mosque in Mecca. Their military leader was forty-year-old Juhaiman ibn Saif al Utaiba, and their religious leader twenty-seven-year-old Muhammad ibn Abdullah al Qahtani, brother-in-law of Juhaiman.

Juhaiman was born around 1939 in the Utaiba colony of Sajir in the west-central province of Qasim, and was a grandson of an Ikhwan militant who died in the battle of Sabila in 1929 fighting Abdul Aziz. He grew up when the memory of that battle was fresh among the Arabian tribes. In his late teens he joined the National Guard, and rose to become a corporal. However, military discipline seemed to frustrate his fierce piety and his vocal opposition to the presence of non-Muslim westerners in the kingdom's institutions (including the National Guard) and elsewhere. In 1972 he left the force after fifteen years' service. He enrolled at the Islamic University of Medina, an institution set up in 1961 by leading Egyptian Muslim Brothers after they had convinced the Saudi king that President Nasser was misusing Al Azhar and that an alternative centre of Islamic learning was sorely needed. At this university Juhaiman became a student of Shaikh Abdul Aziz ibn Baz, the rector since 1969, who was later to become the head of the Council of the Ulama. Shaikh Ibn Baz advocated a return to the letter of the Quran and the Hadiths, and decried innovation of any kind. Juhaiman imbibed Ibn Baz's teachings and applied them to the actions of the Saudi dynasty only to conclude that the Saudi rulers had deviated from the true path of Islam. Juhaiman's uncompromising stance towards the House of Saud created friction between him and Ibn Baz, and led to his expulsion in 1974.

Accompanied by ten of his followers Juhaiman retired to his native Qasim and began to preach along the lines of Shaikh Abdul Wahhab in the mid-eighteenth century. Juhaiman was a charismatic figure, courageous and a natural leader. He was also a popular poet and writer on Islam. He set up cells in numerous beduin settlements in Qasim. His followers were inspired by militant piety, a recurring theme in Islam through the centuries. In 1976 he and his close followers moved to Riyadh. There he published a pamphlet, *Rules of Allegiance and Obedience: the Misconduct of Rulers*. In it he attacked the Saudi rulers for their deviation from the Sharia, their greed and corruption, misuse of the laws for their own benefit, and for mixing with atheists and unbelievers.

In the summer of 1978 the government arrested Juhaiman and ninety-eight of his followers in Riyadh. Shaikh Ibn Baz was called from Medina to interview them. He concluded that what they had been propagating was not treasonable. Their six-week-long detention ended when they promised not to undertake subversive actions or propaganda.

They were kept under surveillance. But Juhaiman and his close associates gave the slip to the intelligence agents. Juhaiman took to clandestine preaching and developed the idea of mahdi – the one guided by God – which he allied to the traditional Wahhabi doctrine. The concept of mahdi, one who will restore the faith and usher in a golden age while claiming divine sanction, is not as sharply defined in Sunni tradition as it is in Judaism, Christianity and Shia Islam. Among Sunnis the prevalent concept is that of mujaddid, renewer of faith. The idea is rooted in the hadith revealed by Abu Huraira, a companion of Prophet Muhammad, and recorded by Abu Daoud.[10] As a renewer of the faith, the mujaddid appears every (Islamic) century to defend the sunna (tradition) from bida (innovation). So the belief goes. A mujaddid is not a messiah, a mahdi; and he may be recognized only after his death. For instance, many Muslims regard Hassan al Banna as a mujaddid. In contrast, a mahdi claims divine sanction and is recognized by the people as a messiah during his lifetime. One of the earliest references to al Mahdi al Muntazir, the Awaited Messiah, appears in *Muqqadimma* by Abdul Rahman ibn Khaldun, (1332–1406) an eminent Arab historian.

There will arise a difference at the death of a caliph, and a man of Medina will go forth, fleeing to Mecca. Then some of the people of Mecca will come to him, and make him go out against his will, and they will swear allegiance between the rukn [courtyard of the Grand Mosque] and the maqam Ibrahim [building beside the Kaaba containing a stone with Prophet Abraham's footprint]. And an army will be sent against him from Syria, but [it] will be swallowed up in the earth in the desert between Mecca and Medina.[11]

What Juhaiman al Utaiba did was to study the traditions about the mahdi meticulously and publish them in August 1979 in his *The Call of the Ikhwan*. In his brother-in-law, Muhammad ibn Abdullah al Qahtani, a former student of the Islamic University of Riyadh, he had found the mahdi with the name of the Prophet, and a surname which was a derivative of Qahtan, the legendary ancestor of Arabs. To this material he tagged the notion widely held among Sunnis that a mujaddid appears once every century. The new Islamic century was to begin on 20 November/1 Muharram, and on that day he and his close aides expected King Khalid to be present at the Grand Mosque in Mecca to offer his dawn prayers. Given his military expertise, his wish to avenge the death of his Ikhwan grandfather, his fierce piety, his charisma and the tradition of tribal retribution, Juhaiman al Utaiba was an ideal figure to lead an insurrection against the House of Saud.

During the hajj season Juhaiman al Utaiba sent messages to his followers in the country to converge on the Grand Mosque in Mecca on the eve of the New Year's Day. They did so, making sure to smuggle arms and hide them in the cellars and retreats of the vast mosque.

Though King Khalid was not to be found in the Grand Mosque offering dawn prayers on the fateful day, Juhaiman al Utaiba and Muhammad al Qahtani went ahead with their plans. After their followers had closed all forty-eight gates of the mosque Juhaiman al Utaiba delivered a speech in which he set out his ideology. It was mandatory for true Muslims to follow Prophet Muhammad's example of revelation, propagation and military struggle, he began. In the present circumstances genuine Muslims must overthrow their present Saudi rulers: they are deficient in Islamic attributes and had been forced upon the populace; and in any case in Islam there is no place for kings or dynasties. A legitimate Muslim ruler must govern according to the Sharia, must be a devout Muslim, originate from the Quraish tribe, and must be chosen by the Islamic umma. None of these attributes applied to the Saudi monarchs. Islam must be grounded in the Quran and the Hadiths, and not on taqlid, blind emulation of the interpretations offered by the ulama, as was the practice in contemporary Arabia. Believers must detach themselves from the present system by rejecting all official positions, he urged. The mahdi will come from the House of the Prophet, through the lineage of the Imam Hussein ibn Ali, to counter impiety and taqlid, and to bring peace and justice to the believers. It is the duty of all true Muslims to establish an umma which protects Islam from the unbelievers and refrains from courting non-Muslim aliens.[12] In short, Juhaiman al Utaiba issued a call for the overthrow of the Saudi monarchy and severance of ties with the unbelieving West. As for Qahtani, Juhaiman claimed mahdiship on his behalf, and referred to the tradition: 'The Mahdi and his men will seek shelter and protection in the Holy Mosque because they are persecuted everywhere until they have no recourse but the Holy Mosque.' The gathering of many thousands of worshippers was stunned by this event and by the speed with which the armed militants had taken charge of the vast mosque, the courtyard of which had a capacity of a quarter of a million people.

It was significant that the revived Ikhwan led by Juhaiman al Utaiba and Qahtani challenged the deviation of King Khalid from true Islam and his alliance with the Americans just as the original Ikhwan had fought King Abdul Aziz for straying from the true faith and allying himself with the British.

King Khalid called the Council of the Ulama to seek its ruling on the storming of the Grand Mosque. The Council was quick to point to the Quranic verse: 'Do not fight them near the Holy Mosque until they fight you inside it, and if they fight you [inside], you must kill them for that is the punishment of the unbelievers.'[13]

Repossession of the Grand Mosque proved to be a tortuous and bloody operation for the government. It had to deploy 10,000 security personnel of its own as well as thousands of Pakistani troops and a contingent of French anti-terrorist experts, and wage a fortnight-long battle to restore order. In the process 127 troops were killed, as were twenty-five pilgrims and 117 Ikhwan members, including Muhammad al Qahtani. Of the 170 militants arrested, sixty-seven were beheaded. Of these, twenty-six were non-Saudi Arabs. The uprising in the Grand Mosque and its bloody end severely damaged the prestige of the House of Saud, the custodians of the holy shrine.

There was a news blackout in Saudi Arabia as long as the crisis lasted. Later, however, the government made it a point to decapitate the sixty-seven culprits in the public squares of different cities to impress on the people the severity of their crime and its determination to carry out the executions. A study of the demographic and tribal background of the Saudi Ikhwan militants had disturbing implications for the authorities. In the main the radicals came from Najd, the power base of the Saudi dynasty. Many of the militants were Utaibas, members of the tribe to which Sultan ibn Bijad, an Ikhwan leader who in 1929 confronted King Abdul Aziz, belonged. Obviously, tribal loyalties ran deep, and so did inter-tribal feuding. The Ikhwan ranks also contained a substantial number of theological students, both Saudi and non-Saudi. Among those whose 'errors' Juhaiman al Utaiba claimed to have corrected were the Muslim Brothers from Egypt, the Ansars from Sudan, and the members of the Society of Social Reform in Kuwait. It was hard for observers inside Saudi Arabia or outside to gauge the feelings of ordinary Saudis to the uprising. Later, as the severity of the crisis became known, considerable sympathy for the rebels was detected among students, junior ulama and the lower- and middle-middle classes in cities and towns, and among those tribal chiefs who were opposed to the governmental policies of settling the nomads and centralizing authority. Often, it was noted by observers, criticism against the insurgents was directed not at their action but at the target they had chosen: Islam's holiest shrine. The graffito discovered in the toilets of Riyadh University many months later probably summed up the popular feeling: 'Juhaiman, our martyr, why didn't you storm the palaces? The struggle is only beginning.'[14]

Undoubtedly the Mecca uprising was the severest shock that the Saudi dynasty had received in the half century since the 1929 Ikhwan rebellion. It was accustomed to attacks from the proponents of such alien ideologies as liberalism, nationalism and Marxism, and knew how to tackle them. But a frontal and bloody assault from the followers of fundamental Islam, on which the Saudi dynasty based its own legitimacy, was new and carried extraordinarily dangerous implications. Its ideological response was to denounce the insurgents as Kharajis, the anarchic seceders of early Islam, notorious for their terroristic tactics which led to the death, among others, of Imam Ali. Its political–administrative response contained the usual mix of repression and reform. The government arrested about 7,000 sympathizers of the Ikhwan, and imposed stricter controls on the freedom of movement of expatriate workers. If nothing else, the Mecca insurgency made the ruling family freshly aware of the deep bitterness of inter-tribal feuding, and thus lessened its trust in the military and the National Guard, the successor to the White Guard established by Abdul Aziz in 1932 with a sprinkling of former Ikhwan fighters. This led to plans to engage three Pakistani brigades, dressed in Saudi military uniforms, as the special royal guard.[15] Being mercenary and without any roots in Saudi society, the Pakistani troops were regarded by the ruling élite as highly reliable. King Khalid reshuffled the top seventeen military and civilian posts. He tried to reassure the populace that some sort of political reform was being seriously considered. His appointment of a committee to produce a draft constitution was followed by an announcement by Crown Prince Fahd that a Consultative Council of sixty to seventy nominated members would be established 'in the near future'.[16] Also the government whittled down its rhetoric about rapid economic and technological development being the most effective way of safeguarding Islam.

In March 1982 Crown Prince Fahd declared that a Consultative Council would come into being 'shortly'. In June, following King Khalid's death, Fahd acceded to the throne. But the Consultative Council remained a mere idea. Nor was there any sign of a constitution being prepared.

Meanwhile, following the Mecca insurrection, there have been increasingly overt signs of rising fundamentalism in Saudi Arabia. The number and size of the Jamaat al Daawa, Society of the Call, has risen sharply. Its members are identifiable by their full beards and very short hair; instead of the conventional white robe, which extends to the ankles, and a rope over the headcloth, they wear a short white robe up to the knees, and a cap and a cloth over their heads. To them the conventional dress is a sign of affluence and vanity. The Society of the Call enjoys much support in the science and technology faculties of universities. Its members refuse to enrol at western universities for further studies – a step which they believe the government encourages in order to erode their Islamic fervour. The preponderance of such Islamists in the science and technology faculties is not accidental. As one such student put it: 'We cannot strengthen ourselves under these weak regimes by simply reading the Quran and [Islamic] history, but by studying science, to use western technology against the West.'[17] The idea of imbibing western technology without western social values, first articulated by Afghani, is apparently catching on. There is nothing subversive about such a view. The Society of the Call does not threaten the Saudi regime, and functions openly. However, there is little doubt that it provides a recruiting ground for more militant and violent organizations in the kingdom.

One of the major weaknesses of the present Saudi system is that the ruling family has so far refused to co-opt, institutionally, the members of the rising technocracy into the decision-making apparatus of the state. Its other weakness is that it continues to ignore Shias and their notables and clergy. Though only 8 per cent of Saudi Arabia's citizenry, Shias are concentrated in the oil-rich province of Hasa.[18]

The Shia problem erupted dramatically when, encouraged by the climate created by the Mecca uprising, the 400,000-strong Shia community broke the long-established ban on the celebration of their festival of mourning, Ashura, on 29 November 1979. To the alarm of the authorities, the Ashura processions turned into pro-Khomeini demonstrations in eight important towns of the oil region. The government pressed into action 20,000 security men to break them up. But sporadic demonstrations and pitched battles between government forces and Shia militants continued for about two months, and led to the death of fifty-seven security personnel and ninety-nine Shias. About 6,000 people were arrested.[19] During these events the existence of the Shia-dominated Islamic Revolutionary Organization of the Arabian Peninsula came to light.

Ever since Hasa fell to Abdul Aziz, its Shia inhabitants have periodically protested against the government either on sectarian or socio-economic grounds without obtaining any redress. When in 1926 Muhammad al Habshi, a Shia leader, established a local council to air grievances Abdul Aziz immediately banned it. Later Abdul Aziz decreed that Shias should familiarize themselves with the Wahhabi doctrine, an order much resented by Shias. The governors of Hasa, drawn traditionally from the Jiluwi clan of the House of Saud (to which King Khalid belonged), have always discriminated against Shias by barring them from the teaching profession and depriving them of such benefits as government loans and grants.

Discovery of oil in Hasa turned the province into an area of crucial significance. The oil workers – about one-third Saudi Shia and another third foreigners – resented the astronomical salaries paid to the American employees of the Arabian American Oil Company and their own poor working conditions. Brief labour stoppages in 1944 and 1949 were followed by a two-week-long strike in October 1953. King Abdul Aziz broke the last stoppage with an iron hand. Oil workers were in the forefront of the Arab oil boycotts of June 1967 and October 1973 against the West. The Shias among them were particularly excited when an anti-American Shia regime came to power in Iran under Ayatollah Khomeini. It hardened their resentment of the Saudi government's discrimination against them in the sharing of the benefits stemming from the oil wealth produced by them.

In the wake of the Shia riots of November–December 1979 the Saudi authorities accelerated the pace of economic development in Hasa, and made half-hearted attempts to co-opt Shia leaders into the political–administrative system. But these attempts have been only partially successful. As a group Shias are apprehensive about becoming absorbed into the Wahhabi mainstream; and individually they have been reluctant to avail themselves of the governmental loans and subsidies offered to them.

Despite the severe repression suffered by the Islamic Revolutionary Organization of the Arabian Peninsula, with its leader Said Saffran forced into exile in Iran, it continued to operate clandestinely. Its adherents made it a point to contact Iranian pilgrims during the hajj – when nearly 1.5 million foreign Muslims congregate in Mecca and Medina – an activity which made the Saudi authorities nervous. Saffran founded a journal in Iran, and from there he broadcast revolutionary Islamic commentaries against the Saudi royal family: a source of anger and embarrassment in Riyadh. In the past the broadsides that the Saudi royals faced had originated from such secular sources as Nasser's Egypt, Baathist Syria or Iraq. The present attacks from an Islamic camp, albeit of a different hue, deeply puzzled and disturbed the House of Saud which had, particularly over the past decade, carved out an unrivalled position for itself in the Muslim world, and which had all along prided itself on following genuinely Islamic policies at home and abroad.

Saudi Arabia's Islamic Foreign Policy

It has been a cardinal policy of Saudi monarchs to stress their roles as the custodians of the holy places, patrons of the hajj, and supporters of Islamic causes throughout the world.

Due to the absence of European imperial colonialism in Arabia the idea of nationalism never took root there. The partition by the British and the French of the Arab part of the Ottoman empire left the Arabian Peninsula virtually untouched. The people and territories that Abdul Aziz brought under his control did not constitute a nation-state. It was only under the leadership of Faisal – first during King Saud's reign and then under his own – that the infrastructure of a modern state began to emerge. In a general sense the foreign policy of a state is based on the notion of national interest. But by constantly stressing Islam, a universalist ideology, Saudi Arabia has tended to de-emphasize nationalism.

In any case, during the days of Saud and Faisal the concept of an 'Arab nation' – one Arab nation divided into twenty-two states – was being fostered by Nasser. In so far as Prophet Muhammad was an Arab from Arabia and it was through him, and in Arabic, that the Word of Allah was revealed to humanity, King Faisal and his followers took pride in being Arab. But to them articulating and fostering the idea of the Arab nation as a separate entity, apart from the Islamic umma, was unforgivable. Faisal expressed this view forcefully to counter the attacks made on him and his kingdom, as being corrupt and reactionary, by Nasser. Faisal contended that Arab nationalism was a Trojan horse to smuggle into the Arab world such alien doctrines as socialism.

As it happened, in May 1962 Nasser transformed the National Union, Egypt's ruling party, into the Arab Socialist Union with a national charter which adopted Arab socialism as its doctrine. This was the time of the hajj. At Faisal's behest a group of senior ulama in Saudi Arabia issued a statement condemning socialism as being inimical to Islam. Faisal himself stated: 'We believe neither in socialism or in communism, nor in any doctrine outside Islam. We only believe in Islam.'[20]

Soon Faisal set up the World Muslim League in Geneva. Its function was to hold seminars and conferences on Islam, and act as a mouthpiece of Saudi Arabia in its interpretation of Islam. 'The Islamic world forms one collectivity united by Islamic doctrines,' stated the World Muslim League charter. 'In order for the collectivity to be a reality, it is necessary that allegiance will be to the Islamic doctrine and the interests of the Muslim umma in its totality above the allegiance to nationalism or other isms.'[21] Faisal employed many exiled Muslim Brothers at the World Muslim League headquarters.

Though this was a move in the right direction by Faisal, it had little impact on the Arab heartland of Islam. Here Nasser's pan-Arabist socialist ideology continued to engage popular imagination and following. In late 1965 King Faisal tried to launch an official trans-Islamic body, to be named the Islamic Alliance, with the backing of Muhammad Reza Pahlavi of Iran and King Hussein of Jordan. The project failed to get off the ground.

However, the defeat of Nasser's Egypt in the June 1967 Arab–Israeli War – and the loss to Israel of Arab Jerusalem containing Al Aqsa mosque, Islam's third holiest shrine – changed the scene dramatically. Many Arabs believed that they had been defeated because they had deviated from their faith. The secular states of Egypt and Syria, humiliated by the setback, accepted subsidies from Saudi Arabia and the other oil-rich Islamic monarchies to rebuild their armed forces and economies. Yet all this was not enough to enable King Faisal to realize the Islamic Alliance he had mooted earlier.

Oddly, the action of a deranged Australian Christian came to Faisal's rescue. In July 1969 the Australian tried to set fire to Al Aqsa. He failed. But the arson attempt sent shock waves throughout the Muslim world. At Faisal's behest an Islamic summit conference, attended by twenty-five Muslim countries, was convened in Rabat, Morocco, in September. Faisal declared a jihad against Israel and vowed to liberate Al Aqsa from the Israelis. Nasser sent his vice-president, Anwar Sadat, to the conference. It was decided to set up a permanent secretariat. Out of this emerged the Islamic Conference Organization, the first official pan-Islamic institution of inter-governmental co-operation among Islamic regimes, with its headquarters in Jidda: a body funded mainly by Saudi Arabia. Since then there has been a proliferation of transnational Islamic organizations financed chiefly by Saudi Arabia: the Islamic Development Bank, the International Islamic News Agency, the International Centre for Research in Islamic Economics, and the Institute for Muslim Minority Affairs. All of these are based in Saudi Arabia.

As Saudi oil revenue rocketed in the 1970s Riyadh's influence rose sharply in the Muslim world outside. Saudi Arabia became one of the leading aid donors. But it limited its financial assistance to Muslim countries, and that too to those which accepted its policies. First and foremost, the recipient country must wage a struggle against Marxism and the Soviet Union since atheistic Marxism is, according to Riyadh, the deadliest enemy of Islam. Second, the recipient Muslim state must join the jihad against Israel and Zionism. Indeed, these two points were seen at least by King Faisal as interrelated: he genuinely believed that Zionism had been propped up by communists as part of their world-wide conspiracy. Thirdly, the Muslim state must agree to enforce the Sharia, howsoever gradually, along the lines already being pursued in Saudi Arabia.

The early years of Sadat's presidency in Egypt fitted the

Saudi prescription well. No wonder Sadat received generous aid from King Faisal. But later when Sadat went out
on his own and signed a separate peace treaty with Israel
in March 1979, he was stigmatized by the Saudi regime.

In any event there is an inherent contradiction in the
Saudi alliance with the US, which is the strategic partner
and principal underwriter, economic and political, of Israel.
This exposes the regime to attacks from secular leftists and
radical Islamic fundamentalists who argue that the Saudi-
led jihad against Israel and Zionism is an exercise in
hypocrisy.

The November 1979 American hostage crisis in Iran and
the Soviet military intervention in Afghanistan in December raised tensions in the region and brought pressure on
Riyadh from Washington to lease military bases to the US.
Aware that such an overt alliance with the US would
damage Saudi standing in the Muslim world, King Khalid
took to advocating non-alignment in international affairs.
Addressing the third Islamic summit in Taif, Saudi Arabia,
in January 1981, he said, 'Our loyalty must be neither to
an eastern bloc nor to a western bloc. The security of the
Islamic nation will not be assured by joining a military
alliance, nor by taking refuge under the umbrella of a
superpower.'[22] There was nothing original in this. Indeed,
Sayyid Qutb of the Egyptian Muslim Brotherhood had
expressed similar sentiments a generation before. 'There
are two huge blocs: the communist bloc in the East and the
capitalist bloc in the West,' he wrote. 'Each disseminates
deceptive propaganda throughout the world claiming that
there are only two alternative views in the world, communism and capitalism, and that other nations have no
alternative but to ally themselves with one bloc or the
other.'[23] The only difference is that while Qutb never held
power Khalid did. Yet the Saudi monarch's statement in
favour of non-alignment was rhetorical. Saudi Arabia is too
closely tied to the West, especially America, militarily,
economically, diplomatically and intelligence-wise to envis-
age seriously a truly non-aligned stance for itself.

In any case Saudi Arabia is a major financier of several

movements to overthrow leftist regimes allied with Moscow. It pours large sums into the coffers of Afghan guerrillas fighting the Marxist regime in Kabul. Pakistan, a neighbour of Afghanistan and a close friend of America, has become a substantial recipient of Saudi aid, and consequently a political and military ally of Riyadh. In Asia, Saudi funds have flown into Bangladesh, Malaysia, Indonesia and the Maldive islands. For many years Riyadh has been backing the Eritrean insurgents against the Marxist regime in Ethiopia. And in non-Arab Africa Saudi funds have gone to Cameroon, Chad, Gabon, Mali, Niger, Nigeria and Uganda.

It is widely believed that Riyadh has been the major financial backer of the Muslim Brotherhood in various countries as well as the Jamaat-e Islami in Pakistan. In addition Saudi Arabia channels moneys through its ministries for such diverse activities as sponsoring foreign scholars to study at Saudi universities, production of radio and television programmes on Islam, the teaching of Arabic in non-Arab states, and building of mosques and Islamic schools and colleges abroad. Saudi Arabia also funds conferences and seminars on Islam and Islamic subjects, and distribution of Islamic materials.

For a decade, from the founding of the Islamic Conference Organization in 1969 to the Iranian revolution in early 1979, Saudi Arabia had a clear run in its campaign to project itself as the leader of the Islamic world, and present its capitalist policies at home and friendship with America abroad as the desirable Islamic model for other Muslim countries to emulate.

But since 1979 both its leadership role and the model it offers have been seriously challenged by the fundamentalist regime of Khomeini. This has taken some of the shine off Riyadh and put it on the defensive. Still, Iran has considerable difficulty in displacing Saudi Arabia from its leading position. The main reason is sectarian: Iran is an overwhelmingly Shia country whereas the Muslim world as a whole is predominantly Sunni.

6

IRAN: REVOLUTIONARY
FUNDAMENTALISM IN POWER

Though a minority, Shias have enjoyed periods of supremacy in Islamic history – a Shia king subjugating the Sunni
Abbasids in 932, and a Shia caliphate, the Fatimids,
emerging in Cairo in 969. The setback suffered by Shias as
a result of the overthrow of the Fatimid caliphate in 1171
by Salah al Din Ayubi, a Sunni general, proved temporary.
The destruction in 1258 of the Abbasid caliphate by the
Mongol leader Hulagu Khan created a political–ideological
vacuum in which Shiaism and sufism thrived. Allama
Jamal al Din ibn Yusuf al Hilli (1250–1325), a Shia thinker,
rehabilitated the concept and practice of ijtihad; and this
vastly invigorated Shiaism.

Unsettled conditions in west Asia led to the rise of
various sufi orders. One of them was Safavi, founded by
Shaikh Safi al Din al Ishaq (d. 1334) around Ardebil in the
Azeri-speaking region of Iran. This was a Sunni order and
remained so for at least a century.

Towards the close of the fourteenth century Iran was
absorbed into the empire of Timur Lang (1336–1405)
which extended from the Oxus river in Afghanistan to the
eastern shores of the Mediterranean. With the death of
Shah Rukh, a Sunni, in 1447, the empire disintegrated.
The consequent power vacuum aroused the temporal ambi-
tions of the Safavids. Aided by militant tribesmen, who
combined their sufi beliefs with veneration for Imam Ali,
Shah Ismail, the Safavid chief, captured Tabriz in the
highlands of Azerbaijan in 1501. Within seven years Shah
Ismail extended his domain from Herat, Afghanistan, to
Baghdad.

Once in power, the Safavids adopted Twelver Shiaism to

appeal to the heterodox sentiments of the populace, particularly tribesmen, and to differentiate themselves from the competing Sunni Ottoman Turks who wanted to incorporate Iran into their empire.

The Safavids declared Twelver Shiaism to be the state religion, something neither Fatimids nor Buyids had done in the past. This meant Shia jurisprudence, theology and philosophy had to be systematized. In order to achieve this, and indoctrinate their subjects with Shiaism, the Safavids imported orthodox ulama from southern Iraq, Syria and Lebanon. By so doing they conferred status and wealth on the ulama. In return the ulama allowed the temporal ruler to extend his authority in order to ensure 'order and tranquillity'. They declared the Safavids to be the descendants of the seventh Imam, Musa al Kazim. This implied that Shah Ismail ruled on behalf of the Hidden Imam. Unsurprisingly, Shah Ismail and his successor Shah Tahmasp tried to present themselves as the 'Allah's shadow on the Earth'. In this capacity they were expected by the ulama to enforce the Sharia. Given the occultation of the Hidden Imam, the Shah had to rely on ijtihad, reasoned interpretation, offered by senior mujtahids. In his enthusiasm to spread Shiaism, Shah Ismail ordered all preachers to lead the Friday prayers in the name of the Twelve Imams and curse the first three Sunni caliphs – Abu Bakr, Umar ibn Khattab and Uthman ibn Affan – for usurping the rightful place of Imam Ali. This ideological uniformity aided Shah Ismail to secure territorial unity – so also did the competition and confrontation with the Sunni Ottoman empire. Due to periodic wars the borders of the Ottoman and the Safavid empires moved back and forth. In 1638 the Ottomans seized Iraq from the Safavids. This was after Shah Abbas, whose rule, from 1587 to 1629, formed the peak of the Safavid dynasty.

In the late 1710s Shah Sultan Hussein tried to convert the Sunni tribes in Afghanistan to Shiaism. They rebelled. In 1722 they invaded and occupied Isfahan, the Safavid capital, and tried to reimpose Sunnism on Iran, which was by now predominantly Shia, an endeavour in which they

failed. Most of the senior Shia ulama left Isfahan for the
Shia holy cities of Najaf and Karbala in Ottoman Iraq.
Even though the Afghan rule lasted only eight years the
practice of senior Shia ulama residing in Iraq continued,
and later proved to be a source of strength for the ulama in
their confrontations with the Iranian monarchy.

The Afshars, who succeeded the Afghans, tried to modify
Shiaism in such a way as to make it acceptable to Sunni
opinion. Nadir Shah Afshar (1736–1747) banned public
cursing of the first three caliphs. He renamed Shiaism as
Jaafari school after Imam Jaafar al Sadiq, the main codifier
of Shia jurisprudence. But these moves proved inadequate
to lessen the inter-sectarian gap. The divide between
Shiaism and Sunnism had become much too sharp and
wide. The differences spanned doctrine, ritual, law, theology and religious organization.

Shia ulama argued that Prophet Muhammad had named
Ali as his successor when he said, 'He for whom I am the
master should have Ali as his master.' Following Muhammad's death Muslims needed to be ruled by infallible
leaders who, possessed of profound knowledge of the Quran
and the Sunna, would lead the community in the right
direction. Only those who were close to Prophet Muhammad could have possessed such knowledge and infallibility,
the latter stemming from isma, immaculateness. Ali was
one such Companion of the Prophet. After Imam Ali only
the descendants of Ali and Fatima (a daughter of the
Prophet) were entitled to rule the Muslim umma. According to Shias, therefore, the Imams are infallible, and the
leadership of the Muslim umma must lie within the House
of the Prophet. Sunnis, on the other hand, adhere more to
principles than personalities. They argue that Prophet
Muhammad deliberately left the question of succession
open, leaving it to the community to decide it after his
death. The manner in which this selection was made by
those who 'loose and bind' gave rise to the concept of ijma,
consensus, of the notables. Later this was to evolve into
consensus of the ulama, trained religious scholars, a group
which emerged in the medieval age. Unlike Shias, Sunnis

regard the caliphs as fallible interpreters of the Quran and the Hadiths.

Shias insist that the ruler must be just, and refer to the Quranic verse: 'Lord said, "Behold, I make you a leader for the people." Said he [Abraham], "And of my seed?" Lord said, "My covenant shall not reach the evildoers."'[1] Conversely, say Shia ulama, if the ruler is unjust he must be overthrown.

According to Shias the Quran bears a pledge of sovereignty of the earth to the oppressed. To prove it they refer to the following Quranic verses: 'Surely the earth is God's and He bequeaths it to whom He will among His servants';[2] 'For We have written in the Psalms, after the Remembrance, "The earth shall be the inheritance of My righteous servants"';[3] and 'Yet We desired to be gracious to those that were abased in the land, and to make them leaders, and to make them the inheritors.'[4] Rooted in this pledge to reward the lowly and the suffering are the concepts of the return of the Hidden Imam, the arrival of the Mahdi, and the rehabilitation of society. In other words, according to Shias, Islamic history is moving towards a fixed goal, and the forces of injustice will ultimately be defeated. This acts as a spur towards radical activism. In contrast, Sunnis view Islamic history essentially as a drift away from the ideal umma which existed under the rule of the four Rightly Guided Caliphs.

The Shia ethos is different from the Sunni. Shia emotionalism finds outlets in mourning Imams Ali, Hassan and Hussein, and in the heart-rending entreaties offered at their shrines. Shias believe that through asceticism and suffering one can remove the ill-effects of sin. Small wonder that the Imams' biographies are full of incidents in which they underwent humiliations and suffering even when they had the power to defeat their adversaries. Humiliations, persecution and martyrdom are the staples of these biographies. The annual enactment of the passion plays about the martyrdom of Imam Hussein and the self-flagellation by the faithful provide outlets for expiating guilt and pain originally felt by Kufa's inhabitants for having abandoned

Imam Hussein after inviting him to their city to take charge. Sunnism proper has no such outlets for its followers. Only sufi orders within Sunnism offer the believers anything emotional or heart-warming.

Sunnis and Shias differ on how to organize religion and religious activities. Sunnis regard religious activities as the exclusive domain of the (Muslim) state. As and when the ulama act as judges or preachers or educators they do so under the aegis of the state. There is no question of the ulama organizing religion on their own. This is not the case among Shias, as we shall see in a study of Iran.

The Shia ulama based in Iraq became increasingly literalist, interested more in transmitting religious knowledge than in encouraging interpretative reasoning, ijtihad. They came to be called Akhbaris, the word akhbar meaning report, another term for hadith. It was not until the early 1780s that the literalist tradition began to wane under the forceful opposition of the prestigious Aqa Muhammad Baqir Behbehani (died 1793). He argued that a living mujtahid, a practitioner of ijtihad, was needed to interpret the basic foundations of the faith, and that every believer must choose a mujtahid as a source of emulation: marja-e taqlid. This school was called Usuli, the word usul meaning root or origin. The Usulis based their case on the premise that since mujtahids derived their authority from the Hidden Imam they were entitled to interpret the Sharia. By the early nineteenth century the Usulis had prevailed over the Akhbaris. 'The need to follow the rulings of a living mujtahid, who was less fallible than any temporal ruler, gave a basis for power in the hands of the mujtahids that was far greater than that of the Sunni ulama,' notes Nikki R. Keddie, an American specialist on Iran.[5] Thus mujtahids acquired a basis for making political decisions, impinging on Islamic principles, independently of temporal rulers. From this arose the independence exercised by the Shia ulama during Iran's subsequent history.

Iran was now governed by the Qajars. Though they were Shia they lacked the spiritual power of their Safavid predecessors. Having defeated the Zand ruler in 1779, Aqa

Muhammad Khan Qajar had conquered most of Iran by 1790. He was succeeded seven years later by his nephew, Fath Ali Shah, who proved to be a patron of the ulama.

Under Fath Ali Shah's benign rule the ulama consolidated their position. They administered vast religious endowments, waqfs, and received 10 per cent of the income as commission. Since they were regarded as the trustees of the Hidden Imam they also collected the Islamic taxes – khums and zakat. Though khums was originally one-fifth of the booty that the believers took from the conquered non-believers to be handed over to the ruler of the Islamic umma, Shias interpreted it as a general income tax. The ulama used these funds to run educational, social and charitable institutions as well as theological colleges. They conducted Sharia courts which dealt with personal and family matters. In the process of enforcing court decisions, they resorted to leading private armies composed of their religious students and the fugitives they had sheltered. They enjoyed higher esteem among the believers than the local Friday prayer leaders and judges – dealing with crimes according to the customary law – appointed by the Qajar king. Moreover, they felt uniquely independent since their spiritual superiors, living in Najaf and Karbala, were outside the jurisdiction of the Qajars. Parallel to this ran the concept of religious sanctuary, bast. Since the ulama claimed that mosques, religious shrines and their homes were in principle territories of the Hidden Imam, the Qajar government had no right to enter them. As such these places came to provide sanctuary to all sorts of fugitives. More importantly, this tradition helped to make mosques physical centres of opposition to unjust Iranian monarchs.

As the nineteenth century progressed the mujtahids took to naming the most revered colleague as the marja-e mutlaq (absolute source) whose guidance they agreed to accept. All told, therefore, these developments gave the ulama much muscle, political, spiritual and ideological, and went a long way in spawning unity among them, and imparting coherence to their teachings. Curiously enough, the practice of choosing the marja-e mutlaq, and the presence of senior ulama leadership outside Iran, meant that Iranian society developed a Church–State divide along the lines witnessed earlier in Christian Europe. This was unlike the state of affairs in Sunni countries.

The emergence of an independent socio-economic base gave the ulama potential for independent action. They exercised this power to protest against the erosion of Islamic tradition in society and against the economic and political penetration of Iran by European powers, particularly Britain and Tsarist Russia. The 1891–2 Tobacco Protest was a good example. The ulama allied with secular intellectuals and nationalists to protest against the concessions given by Nasir al Din Shah (1848–96) to Britain for a monopoly over the production and sale of tobacco. Jamal al Din Afghani played a leading role in persuading the marja-e mutlaq, Hajj Mirza Hussein Shirazi, to issue a religious verdict on the subject. 'In the name of Allah, the Merciful, the Compassionate, today the use of tobacco in any form is war against the Imam of the Age[6],' declared Shirazi. The ulama wanted to block European penetration by strengthening Islam and resisting the Shah's autocracy.

By giving a vigorous lead to a popular protest which succeeded, the ulama showed that they were an important and vital political force. This episode was to prove to be the forerunner of something bigger: the Constitutional Revolution.

The constitutional movement was backed by propertied classes as well as by religious and intellectual leaders. The former, consisting of landowners, administrators, merchants and artisans, wanted Iran to be free of European domination so that they could develop their own potential, unfettered by the Shah's practice of giving economic concessions to Europeans. Religious leaders felt, rightly, that reduction in the monarch's authority would increase their power in manipulating tribal chiefs, feudal aristocrats and clerics.

Though the ulama were in a majority in the assembly convened in October 1906 to produce a constitution, they failed to act as a bloc. Their training had not equipped them with a political theory, and they did not have a constitutional model in mind. As such they merely reacted to the initiative taken by the secularists to use the Belgian constitution as the model.

The ulama were divided broadly into purists and pragmatists. The purists argued that in the absence of the Hidden Imam – popularly known as Imam al Zaman (Imam of the Present) or Vali-e Asr (Ruler of the Age) – the present government of the Tyrant should be replaced by a constitutionalist government of the Wise Mujtahids. The pragmatists, forming a large majority among the ulama, agreed with the purists' sentiment but found it impossible to implement it.

Among the pragmatists were moderates and radicals. The moderates wanted to check the monarch's arbitrariness along the lines laid out in such European constitutions as that of Belgium. The radicals, led by Shaikh Fazlollah Nuri, wanted to limit the ruler's power within an Islamic framework.

On sovereignty, the radicals argued that since sovereignty had been delegated by Allah to the Hidden Imam, and then on to mujtahids, it did not rest with the people. Their view was opposed by moderate clerics as well as secular constitutionalists. They lost. 'Sovereignty is a trust confided (as a Divine gift) by the People to the person of the King,' stated Article 35.

The final document, called the Fundamental Laws, modelled on the Belgian constitution, was a compromise between moderate and radical views, with the radical clergy winning a few points. With certain modifications this constitution remained in force until the 1979 revolution.

It was framed within an Islamic context. Article 1 declared Jaafari or Twelver Shiaism to be the state religion. Only a Jaafari Shia could become the king, a minister or a judge. Article 39 enjoined upon the monarch to 'promote the Jaafari doctrine' and 'to seek help of the holy spirits of the Saints of Islam to render service to the advancement of Iran'. Article 18 specified free education provided it did not contravene the Sharia. Article 27 confirmed the right of Sharia courts to exist.

The following year came the longer Supplementary Fundamental Laws, which outlined a bill of rights for citizens, and a parliamentary form of government, with power concentrated in the legislature at the expense of the executive. Significantly, Article 2 specified that no bill passed by the Majlis, parliament, was valid until a committee of five mujtahids – elected by the Majlis from a list of twenty submitted by the ulama – had judged it to be in conformity with Islam. So, although the committee of the mujtahids possessed veto power, it could not act as a creative body in its own right as the radical clergy, led by Nuri, had wanted. In practice, however, this article was never implemented. The Qajars ignored it, and so did the Pahlavis.

Interestingly, some senior ulama resident in Iraq backed the constitution, seeing in it a chance for the Majlis to aid the enforcement of the Sharia. One of them, Shaikh Ismail Mahallati, described the constitution as a reasonable compromise between the unattainable objective of installing the government of the infallible Imam and the unacceptable tyranny of absolute monarchy.

In 1909 Muhammad Ali Shah mounted a royalist counter-revolution against the 1906–7 constitution. This was foiled, and the Shah was forced to abdicate in favour of his twelve-year-old son, Ahmad. But in order to forestall the occupation of Tehran by Russian troops the Regent dissolved the Majlis in November 1911. This marked the end of the Constitutional Revolution, but not of the constitution.

Throughout this six-year period, from December 1905 to November 1911, the ulama were actively involved in politics, something they were not to repeat until the late 1970s. They were moved as much by an urge to expand their socio-political domain at the expense of the secular authority as by economic gain. Many of the senior clerics were related to wealthy merchants who found their ambition to establish large-scale commercial or industrial enterprises thwarted by the Shah's preference for Europeans in the economic development of Iran.

Disregarding Tehran's neutrality in the First World War, the forces of Tsarist Russia, Britain and Ottoman Turkey invaded Iran. The October 1917 Bolshevik Revolution in Russia deprived the Shah of his major foreign patron. Two years later Britain foisted a treaty on the Iranian regime which amounted to Iran becoming a virtual protectorate of London. But, responding to the patriotic sentiment of the people, the Majlis refused to ratify it.

Iran was by now an important oil-producing state with British capital and expertise playing a leading role. Britain thought it essential to have a strong administration in Iran so as to facilitate oil extraction among other things. It instigated Colonel Reza Khan of the Cossack Brigade to depose the current government and install himself as war minister. Having done so in February 1921, Reza Khan consolidated his position by suppressing internal rebellions. He appointed himself prime minister and aspired to become the Shah. He took to cultivating the clerical leadership. In April 1924 he visited Qom, a shrine city where the recently exiled senior Shia ulama from Iraq had taken up residence. 'Since my personal aim and method from the beginning has been, and is, to preserve and guard the majesty of Islam and the independence of Iran . . . I and all other people in the army have from the very beginning regarded preservation and protection of the dignity of Islam to be one of the greatest duties,' he declared.[7] Some months later senior mujtahids publicly supported Reza Khan's government. This enabled Reza Khan to win backing for his move to depose the Qajar ruler, Ahmad Shah, in December 1925, and appoint himself regent. Four months later he crowned himself king. By then, following the law passed in the spring of 1925, which required all Iranians to acquire a birth certificate and a surname, Reza Khan had chosen for his family the name of an ancient Iranian language, Pahlavi, a symbolic act which at the very least showed his preference for pre-Islamic Iran.

Having ascended the throne Reza Pahlavi Shah set out

to curtail the powers of the ulama. His government passed a civil code which brought Sharia courts under state control and increased the authority of the state's religious endowments department. Then came the Uniformity of Dress Law in 1928: it required all males to wear western-style dress and a round peaked cap. The Law of Sharia Courts of 1930 restricted courts to marriage, divorce, guardianship and deciding only the innocence or guilt of the accused. The Law Concerning the Registration of Documents and Property of 1932 ended the right of the Sharia court to act as the registrar of documents: something that had been a substantial source of income to the ulama. The 1934 Law of Waqfs boosted the powers of the waqfs department of the ministry of education. It was authorized to take over all the religious endowments with no or unknown administrators, and supervise others by approving or disapproving their budgets. Since the endowments were the prime source of income for the ulama this law curtailed their economic power and independence considerably. In 1934 the Shah ordered that all public places be opened to women. The next year he outlawed the veil – particularly the chador, an all-embracing shroud, commonly used by Iranian women. The ulama opposed this vehemently since the veil is, according to them, sanctified by the Quran. The appropriate verse in the Quran states, 'And say to the believing women, that they cast down their eyes and guard their private parts . . . and let them cast their veils over their bosoms, and not reveal their adornment save to their husbands, or their fathers, or their husbands' fathers, or their sons, or their sisters' sons, or their women . . . or their children who have not yet attained knowledge of women's private parts.'[8]

The Shah also decreed that all men must replace round peaked caps with European felt hats. This interfered with the Islamic way of praying which required the believer to touch the ground with his forehead in the course of the prayer. In 1936 he sought to prohibit the popular mourning of the death in Najaf of Shaikh Mirza Hussein Naini, revered as marja-e mutlaq by Iranian Shias. Three years later he forbade self-flagellation in public on the anniversary of the death of Imam Hussein. He then sought to ban the public performance of Shia passion plays preceding the mourning, and the pilgrimage to Mecca. To get his way with the Majlis he rigged elections. The result was dramatic. Whereas in the Sixth Majlis (1926–8) 40 per cent of the deputies were clergy, in the Eleventh Majlis (1936–8) there was not a single well-known cleric. The overall impact of Reza Shah's policies was summed up by Nikki R. Keddie thus: 'The upper and new middle classes became increasingly westernized and scarcely understood the traditional or religious culture of their compatriots. On the other hand, peasants and urban bazaar classes continued to follow the ulama, however politically cowed the ulama were . . . These classes associated "the way things should be" more with Islam than with the West.'[9]

When Reza Shah was forced to abdicate in favour of his twenty-three-year-old son, Muhammad Reza, in September 1941 by the British and Soviet forces, the ulama were prominent among those who celebrated his departure. They had endured fifteen years of relentless pressure from the Shah which had considerably reduced their power and prestige.

Muhammad Reza Pahlavi Shah was too young and inexperienced to rule autocratically even if he wanted to. His kingdom was occupied by foreign powers, and his government beset with acute problems stemming from the Second World War. Yielding to clerical pressures he annulled his father's bans on Shia passion plays and pilgrimage to Mecca. He even instructed government offices to observe the Islamic prohibitions during the fasting month of Ramadan, a small but highly significant step. He knew that he lacked the active support of any segment of society. He therefore tried to win the sympathy of the ulama, a group which was in daily touch with the masses.

No wonder, when in January 1948 a group of fifteen mujtahids issued a religious decree that women must wear a veil while shopping, all that the government did was to appeal to Ayatollah Muhammad Musavi Behbahani, the capital's clerical leader, to help stop attacks on unveiled women by zealots.

Both Behbahani and Ayatollah Muhammad Hussein Borujerdi, the marja-e mutlaq, were moderate. That is, they stressed that the clergy must stay away from day-to-day politics. Their view was opposed by Ayatollah Abol Qasim Kashani, a militant cleric, who had after the Second World War formed a political party, Mujahedin-e Islam, Combatants of Islam. It drew its strength from small traders, theological students and older leaders of bazaar merchant families. It demanded the cancellation of all secular laws passed by Reza Shah, the application of the Sharia (as stated in the 1906–7 constitution), reintroduction of the veil for women and, interestingly, protection for Iranian industries.

Kashani was arrested in the wake of an unsuccessful assassination attempt on the Shah by a press photographer on 4 February 1949. The attacker was killed on the spot. But because his identity papers showed him to be working for the *Parcham-e Islam* (Flag of Islam), a religious publication, the Shah hit out at militant Islamic forces. At his behest the Majlis passed a law restricting political activity. The moderate ulama leaders rallied round the ruler. A conference of 2,000 clerics called by Borujerdi in Qom on 20–21 February decided against political activism by the clergy, and threatened to derecognize any cleric who defied the directive.

However, this did not deter several senior ulama from issuing religious decrees in favour of nationalization of the British-owned Anglo-Iranian Oil Company (AIOC), a subject that dominated the elections to the Sixteenth Majlis, held from July 1949 to February 1950. In backing nationalization Kashani argued that he was following the example of Shirazi of the Tobacco Protest fame. Supporting Kashani, the prestigious Ayatollah Muhammad Taqi Khonsari quoted the Prophet's hadith: 'He who upon waking does not concern himself with the affairs of Muslims is not himself a Muslim.' Such statements had a profound impact on young Islamic militants. On 7 March 1951

Khalil Tahmasibi, a member of the clandestine Fedayin-e Islam (Self-sacrificers of Islam) assassinated the pro-British Premier General Ali Razmara.

Soon the Majlis passed a Bill for the takeover of the AIOC. On 1 May 1951 the Shah gave his assent to the oil nationalization bill, and appointed Muhammad Mussadiq, leader of the National Front, prime minister.

Kashani and his followers were prominent among those who agitated in favour of nationalization and Mussadiq. Kashani was moved as much by anti-imperialist feelings as by an Islamic vision of the fusion of politics and religion. 'Islamic doctrines apply to social life, patriotism, administration of justice and opposition to injustice and despotism,' he said. 'Islam warns its adherents not to submit to foreign yoke. This is the reason why the imperialists are trying to confuse the minds of the people by drawing a distinction between religion and government and politics.'[10] A quarter of a century later similar sentiments were to be expressed by another ayatollah – Ruhollah Khomeini – and fuel the forces of Islamic revolution.

As the western boycott of Iranian oil began to hurt Iran, causing a severe economic crisis, the alliance between Kashani and Mussadiq became strained. Kashani, a Majlis deputy, split with Mussadiq in March 1953. But the remaining eight clerics in the Majlis continued to back Mussadiq. Kashani's move made him acceptable to the Fedayin-e Islam, which believed that Mussadiq had fallen under western and leftist influences.

Formed in 1945 by a young theological student, Sayyid Navab Safavi (alias Sayyid Mujtaba Mirlohi), the Fedayin went beyond the customary call for the application of the Sharia as provided in the constitution, and demanded a ban on tobacco, alcohol, cinema, opium, gambling and even wearing of foreign dress. It advocated the reintroduction of the veil for women, and such Sharia prescriptions of punishment as cutting off a hand for stealing. It demanded comprehensive land reform, nationalization of industry and various social welfare measures. It drew its following from the lower sections of the bazaari community: porters, shop

assistants, hawkers and pedlars. The Fedayin used assassination as a political weapon. Their first target, in March
1945, was Ahmad Kasravi, a leading secularist lawyer and
historian. Their second victim, in November 1948, was
Abdul Hussein Hazhir, (royal) court minister, considered
to be an agent of British imperialism. Then came the
assassination of General Razmara, which goaded the Majlis
to nationalize oil.

Mussadiq came to rely increasingly on the support of the
pro-Moscow Tudeh (i.e. Masses) Party to withstand the
pressures from the British and American governments
backing the oil companies' embargo against Iranian oil.
This alienated him from the moderate ulama led by Behbahani and Borujerdi. In fact Behbahani is reported to
have helped gather crowds from the bazaar in south Tehran
against the Mussadiq government on 19 August 1953 in
the counter-coup to restore the Shah and topple Mussadiq,
the main conspirators being the US Central Intelligence
Agency and pro-Shah army officers.

After his restitution the Shah tried to project himself as a
saviour of Islam. Along with his wife, Soraya, he took to
visiting the holy shrines in Qom, Mashhad and Karbala.
They made a pilgrimage to Mecca. The Shah offered easy
access to Borujerdi and Behbahani, with the latter's activities prominently reported in the state-controlled media.
The government increased religious instruction in schools.
In return clerical leaders refrained from commenting on the
Shah's secular decisions. For instance, they said nothing
about the iniquitous agreement that the Shah signed with
the western oil consortium in August 1954, which the
Fedayin strongly condemned. Following an unsuccessful
attempt by a Fedayin member in November 1955 to kill
Premier Hussein Ala, the Shah crushed the organization.

While the ulama had lost control of the judicial and
educational systems, they were still powerful enough to
deserve respect from and be consulted by the monarch, and
cohesive enough to formulate and advocate a point of view
on certain aspects of the Iranian polity. One such issue was

women's right to vote. Borujerdi repeated his opposition to it in early 1959.

When the government submitted a draft bill on land reform to the Majlis in December 1959, Borujerdi described it as being against the Sharia and the constitution. He was specifically worried that the takeover, or break-up, of the religious endowments' estates – which paid for the upkeep and running of mosques and religious schools, and the financing of Shia ceremonials during Muharram – would destroy the ulama's economic independence. His protest was effective. The agrarian reform bill of May 1960 included many exemptions, including one to religious endowments. Moreover, the emasculated act fell into disuse almost immediately.

With John Kennedy becoming the American President in January 1961, pressure grew on the Shah to implement wide-ranging reform and appoint Ali Amini, a rich Iranian aristocrat and a friend of Kennedy, as prime minister. The Shah complied in May 1961. On Amini's advice the Shah dissolved the Majlis and took to ruling by decree to introduce reform.

This happened at a time when the ulama were feeling leaderless in the wake of Borujerdi's death in March 1961 after sixteen years of being the marja-e mutlaq. Ayatollah Muhsin Hakim, based in Najaf, became the new marja-e mutlaq. As an Arab by birth living in Iraq, Hakim lacked an intimate knowledge of Iranian affairs. This suited the Shah, but not the Iranian ulama who were divided roughly into three categories: conservative, centrist and radical.

The conservatives wholeheartedly supported Borujerdi's line of staying out of politics. After his death this policy was upheld by the triumvirate of Ayatollahs Muhammad Reza Golpaygani, Shahab al Din Marashi-Najafi and Muhammad Kazim Shariatmadari, the most senior clerics of Qom. They opposed the idea of the state takeover of land above a certain ceiling, a crucial part of the agrarian reform. They saw in it an attack on private property, a right sanctified by the Sharia, and therefore inviolable. The centrists disagreed with Borujerdi's directive of keeping away from politics, but did little in practice to defy it. They tended to concentrate on the educational and social aspects of Shia institutions. Their best-known spokesmen were Ayatollahs Murtaza Motahhari and Muhammad Husseini Beheshti, both of them based in Tehran. They were in touch with Ayatollah Mahmud Taleqani, a leader of the radicals, who also lived in the capital. On land reform he argued that of the private, state, waqf and waste lands, the last category should be given to the landless for reclamation to help them end their destitution. As a group the radicals stood for popular participation in the parliamentary process and limiting the Shah's powers, vastly increased due to the dissolution of the Majlis.

In Qom the radical viewpoint was now being articulated by Hojatalislam Khomeini, a comparatively junior cleric, who came into prominence after Borujerdi's death. He openly criticized the Shah for violating the constitution by failing to call new elections within a month of the dissolution of the Majlis.

In January 1962 the government approved a new agrarian reform bill which extended and strengthened the previous one, but left the waqfs' exemption intact. The implementation began immediately. Six months later, unable to secure a reduction in the military budget from the Shah, Amini resigned. His successor, Assadollah Alam, came up with the idea of multi-layered democracy, starting with elections for local councils. Unlike previous electoral decrees the new one did not specify that the candidates had to be male and Muslim. Detecting in this a ploy to enfranchise women, the ulama denounced the new decree.[11]

The Shah responded by mounting a frontal assault on the ulama, describing them as reactionary and opponents of the Islamic concept of equality. From then on until his downfall in early 1979 the Shah remained mortally opposed to the ulama. In early January 1963 he launched a six-point White Revolution. Besides the agrarian reform, it included forest nationalization, the sale of public sector factories to pay compensation to agricultural landlords, votes for women, profit-sharing in industry and the eradication of illiteracy.

Instead of decreeing Majlis elections the Shah ordered a referendum on the White Revolution on 25 January. The result was a 99.9 per cent 'Yes' vote. In early March the pro-regime *Ittilaat* (Information) published a series of editorials arguing that the state's reforms were in conformity with the Sharia. Describing Islam and other monotheistic religions as 'eternal', it added, 'By the same token, religion is a matter apart from politics. Politics is an everyday term, religion an eternal one.'[12]

Such statements were anathema to radical clergy, particularly Khomeini, and inflamed the situation. Anti-Shah demonstrations were held in Qom, Tehran, Tabriz and Mashhad. Paratroopers and Savak (political police) agents attacked theological colleges in Qom and Tabriz. Unofficial estimates of those killed by the security forces were put at 'hundreds'. Khomeini was arrested but released shortly after.

Tension rose sharply in late May as the month of Muharram approached. On 3 June (10 Muharram), in his address to the faithful, Khomeini attacked the Shah personally. 'You miserable wretch, isn't it time for you to think and reflect a little, to ponder where all this is leading you?' he asked hetorically. 'The ulama and Islam are some form of Black Reaction! And you have carried out some form of White Revolution in the midst of this Black Reaction!' He then referred to a number of ulama in Tehran being taken to Savak offices and ordered 'not to say anything bad about the Shah, not to attack Israel, and not to say that Islam is endangered'. But, he continued, 'All our differences with the government comprise exactly these three [points]. Does the Savak mean that the Shah is Israeli?'[13]

The next day copies of Khomeini's speech appeared on the walls of Fatima's shrine and the adjoining Faiziya theological college in Qom. Thousands gathered to read and discuss it. This speech established Khomeini as a fearless leader with strong convictions ready to attack the dreaded Shah's policies and personality in public. Overnight, it turned him into a national hero among the religious masses who despised the royal autocracy but dared not express their feelings or views.

Khomeini was arrested in the early hours of 5 June (or 15 Khurdad, an Iranian month). This led to massive anti-government demonstrations in Qom and other cities. The anti-Shah feelings that had been accumulating over the past decade erupted with unprecedented violence. The Shah himself took control of the government and the riot control operations. He declared martial law in the riot-torn cities, and pressed tanks and troops into action with orders to 'shoot to kill'. Even so it took the troops two days to crush the uprising, which was sanctified by some leading ulama with a call to jihad against the unIslamic government of the Shah. Up to 10,000 demonstrators were killed in half a dozen cities.[14]

Having beaten the opposition the Shah relaxed his iron grip a little. He placed Khomeini under house arrest. He ordered Majlis elections in September. When Khomeini called for their boycott he was again put in jail, where he stayed until April 1964.

Soon popular attention was focused on the issues of a 200 million dollar loan from the US for the purchase of weapons and the granting of diplomatic immunity to American citizens, military or civilian, engaged in military projects in Iran. These bills stirred up old memories of the days of the capitulations to European powers. A staunch supporter of Iranian independence, Khomeini was fiercely against Iran becoming a dependency of America, or any other power. His vitriolic denunciations of these bills earned him deportation to Turkey in November 1964. After a year in the Turkish city of Bursa he moved to Najaf in Iraq.

There Khomeini spent his time in prayers, teaching and counselling his followers. He utilized the annual pilgrimage to Mecca (in January–February 1971) to address open letters to the Muslims of Iran and elsewhere through his Najaf-based emissaries. Referring to the Shah's scheduled celebrations in October of 2,500 years of unbroken monarchy in Iran, Khomeini warned: 'Anyone who organizes or participates in these festivals is a traitor to Islam and the Iranian nation.'[15]

Khomeini found the regal ceremonies in Persepolis, once the capital of the Achemenian dynasty, on 25 October 1971 a perfect occasion on which to attack the institution of monarchy openly and unambiguously. 'Tradition relates that the Prophet said that the title of the King of Kings, which is [today] borne by the monarchs of Iran, is the most hated of all titles in the sight of God,' Khomeini said. 'Islam is fundamentally opposed to the whole notion of monarchy . . . Monarchy is one of the most shameful and disgraceful reactionary manifestations.'[16]

Monarchy was one of the subjects that Khomeini had tackled systematically in a series of lectures which he gave to his students in 1970, and which were published the following year under the title: *Hukumat-e Islami: Vilayat-e Faqih* (Islamic Government: Rule of the Religious Jurist). In it Khomeini argues that the ulama should go beyond the traditional prescribing of do's and don'ts for the believers, and waiting passively for the return of the Hidden Imam. They must commit themselves to ousting corrupt officials and repressive governments, and replacing them with regimes led by Islamic jurists. He exhorts the theological students of Najaf, Qom and Mashhad to 'instigate and stimulate the masses'. Khomeini urges the subordination of political power to Islamic precepts, criteria and objectives, calls on the ulama to bring about an Islamic state and participate in its legislative, executive and judicial organs, and offers a programme of action to establish an Islamic state.

In his book Khomeini describes the movement to reduce Islam to a mere system of ritual and worship as a deviation from the true faith: a development much encouraged by the imperialist West to weaken Muslims and their states. Since Islam is above all a divine law, Khomeini argues, it needs to be applied as a form of state. Only a government can properly collect the Islamic taxes of khums and zakat, and spend them honestly on the needy members of the community – as well as enforce Islamic injunctions about the duties of the believer and punishment of the transgressor. 'It is a logical necessity that there must be a government which undertakes to put the [Islamic] rules into practice and to apply all [Islamic] measures absolutely,' he writes.[17]

An Islamic government requires an Islamic ruler. All Muslims agree that an Islamic ruler must be a Just Faqih, Religious Jurist. He must know the Sharia thoroughly, and must be absolutely just in its application. According to Shias, their Imams possessed these qualifications. Indeed, being infallible and superior human beings, they were more than Just Faqihs.

In the absence of an Imam – who has been missing for the past eleven centuries – Muslims must find an alternative in order to avoid living in anarchy or under an alien, atheistic government, Khomeini argues. Though lacking the infallibility and personal superiority of an Imam, a Just Faqih is qualified to head an Islamic state. He is to be assisted by jurisprudents at various levels of legislative, executive and judicial bodies. The function of a popularly elected parliament is to resolve the conflicts that are likely to arise in the implementation of Islamic doctrines. The actual administration is to be carried out by civil servants who are familiar with the laws pertinent to their specific jobs. However, judicial functions are to be performed only by the jurisprudents who are steeped in the knowledge of the Sharia. Such jurisprudents are also to oversee the actions of the legislative and executive branches. The overall supervision and guidance of parliament and the judiciary is to rest with the Just Faqih, who must also ensure that the executive does not exceed its powers. Finally, since the overriding purpose of the Islamic government is to meet the needs of its citizens, the jurisprudents must ensure that wealth does not get concentrated in the coffers of a few through their exploitation of people and/or natural resources.

At its simplest, the Vilayat-e Faqih is the rule of the divine law as interpreted and applied by the Just Faqih. Since he does not rule according to his own will, the system is not dictatorial. And, as the position of the Just Faqih is not hereditary, the system is certainly not monarchical.

Since Khomeini visualizes the people as a political force, the system can be described as republican, but within an Islamic context. 'The great reformist movements in history did not possess power at their inception,' he writes. 'The cadres of the [reformist] movement would draw the attention of the people to oppression and awaken them to the dangers of submitting to the rule of the tyrants, then the people become the active force which sweeps away all the obstacles in their way.'[18]

What makes Khomeini's thesis attractive to many Muslims is that it is simple, direct and free from non-Islamic influences. It is derived from the first principles of Islam, and avoids convoluted, hair-splitting religious arguments which leave most religious laymen baffled. Moreover, as Sami Zubaida, a British specialist on Islamic sociology, points out, 'It is conducted exclusively in traditional discussions with hardly any reference to western or western-inspired politico-ideological notions.'[19] There is no reference to nationalism, democracy or socialism.

It would be some years before Khomeini and his most important book were to have a devastating impact on the Pahlavi regime. In 1971, however, the Shah was busily undermining the influence of the traditional clergy by supplanting them with a new breed processed by the institutions of his regime. The Waqf Organization established the Department of Religious Corps and Religious Affairs. After initiating a programme of training groups of Religious Propagandists for posting to rural areas, this department undertook the formation of the Religious Corps in August 1971. The new corps was hailed as 'the mullahs of modernization'.

At the same time the Shah pursued the policy of dividing the ulama by using bribes to co-opt the fence-sitters and punishing those who refused to co-operate. In late 1973 he exiled forty prominent clerics to obscure parts of Iran for their sympathies with Khomeini. However, none of this had any impact on the traditional religiosity of the Iranian masses. If anything, the Shah's authoritarianism and repression of the ulama, and the rush of modernism, made ordinary Iranians more, not less, religious. The dramatic rise in the number of pilgrims to Imam Ali Reza's shrine in Mashhad was indicative of this. In 1964 Mashhad received 220,000 pilgrims; ten years later the figure was 3.2 million.[20] In a country of some 30 million people, or about 6 million families, this meant every other family sending a pilgrim to Mashhad once a year.

The Shah intensified his pressure on the ulama. Their publishing activities were banned when the government restricted religious publishing to the Waqf Organization. The agents of the Rastakhiz (i.e. Resurgence) Party, the sole ruling party formed in March 1975, began auditing the accounts of the religious endowments managed by the ulama. All this went hand in hand with the Rastakhiz government's attempts to project the Shah not only as the political leader but also as the spiritual leader. To make the point dramatically and universally, it introduced the royalist calendar, dating back to the pre-Islamic Achemenian dynasty, on the completion of half a century of Pahlavi rule on 24 April 1976. Since the calendar broke away from the Islamic heritage it was received with extreme hostility by the ulama. One of them, Hojatalislam Abol Hassan Shamsabadi of Isfahan, attacked it publicly. A few days later he was murdered.

During the autumn of 1976 James Carter, the Democratic candidate in the American Presidential election, named Iran as one of the major countries where the US ought to do more to protect civil and human liberties. Soon after assuming office in January 1977 Carter stressed human rights as an integral part of his foreign policy, hinting that the states violating human rights might be denied American weapons or aid, or both. Inadvertently, such statements set the scene for a revolutionary change in Iran.

Liberalization, which began in February 1977 with the release of 357 political prisoners, gathered momentum in the summer. Each concession by the Shah brought further demands from the opposition. Both the modern and traditional middle classes became active, but in different ways. Writers, academics, politicians, lawyers and even judges resorted to addressing open letters to the Pahlavi ruler, whereas bazaar merchants and theological students adopted militant methods: processions, demonstrations and clashes with the police. Being close to the urban poor, both politically and geographically, the traditional middle class provided leadership to the urban underclass which eventually adopted the revolutionary slogan 'Death to the Shah', and stuck to it. To be sure, popular demands were escalated in stages, and were orchestrated by Khomeini from abroad.

The revolutionary process went through several steadily rising stages over a two-year period from February 1977 to 11 February 1979.

Khomeini was by training and inclination a theological teacher, not a politician. He was certainly not a revolutionary, nor even a serious student of revolution. Despite his lack of knowledge of the dynamics of a revolution, he soon recognized the revolutionary potential of the protest which began in early 1977. He made astute use of Islamic history and Iranian nationalism to create and encourage anti-monarchical militancy. He relied heavily on Islam, and Islamic customs and festivals, to energize the revolutionary movement and destroy the Pahlavi dynasty. His spartan lifestyle won him a widespread following among people who were sick of corrupt and luxury-loving politicians. The fact that he was a man of God gave him the spiritual authority which secular leaders lacked. And he kept his message simple.

Of the various phases of the revolutionary movement the period from July to 8 September 1978 proved crucial. Working-class protest began mildly in June and caught on in September. It expressed itself in strikes as well as participation in demonstrations, swelling them to many times their previous sizes. On 22 July tens of thousands of workers joined a funeral procession for a Mashhad cleric killed in a car accident. In the police firing that followed at least forty people were killed. Most urban centres staged the seventh-day mourning processions for the Mashhad dead. This provided a prelude to the fasting month of Ramadan which started on 5 August. For the next twenty-nine days as the faithful prayed daily at a mosque and listened to the preacher's sermon – sometimes accompanied by Khomeini's taped speeches – before breaking the fast after sunset, anti-Shah sentiment rose sharply. 'Ramadan sermons provided a perfect and powerful vehicle for spreading a basically political message, urging men to rise and act against tyranny,' wrote the editors of *The Dawn of the Islamic Revolution, Volume I*. 'Preachers drew on the Shiite themes of struggle and martyrdom. The Pahlavis did not have to be directly mentioned. It was not difficult to draw a parallel between the hated figures of Yazid and Muawiya and the Shah, or between the Ummayad dynasty, with its bent for luxury and pomp, and the Pahlavi dynasty.'[21] On 31 August, the fortieth-day memorial of the Mashhad massacre, Ayatollah Abol Hassan Shirazi of Mashhad issued a fourteen-point manifesto which summed up the ulama's demands. With the co-operation of the opposition leader the government was able to secure peace on Eid al Fitr (i.e. Festival of the Breaking the Fast) on 4 September by promising to keep the army out of public view. Khomeini thanked the army for not firing on the huge Eid al Fitr marches in the country in which a total of 4 million people participated, and called on the troops to 'renew your bond with the beloved people and refuse to go on slaughtering your children and brothers for the sake of the whims of this [Pahlavi] family of bandits'. On 7 September half a million people marched from north Tehran to the Majlis in central Tehran, shouting 'Death to the Shah', 'Khomeini is our leader' and 'We want an Islamic government.' Khomeini referred to the marches of Eid al Fitr and 7 September as a referendum that the Shah's regime had no place in Iran. The next day, Friday, a massacre of demonstrators in Tehran's Jaleh Square by troops left more than 4,000 people dead.[22] This sealed the Shah's fate.

Ayatollah Khomeini had the sagacity and charisma to unite all the disparate forces behind the most radical demand: abolition of the monarchy. He kept the alliance together during a highly turbulent period by championing the cause of each of the groups in the anti-Shah coalition, and maintaining a studied silence on such controversial issues as democracy, agrarian reform, the ulama's role in the future Islamic republic and the status of women. He aroused hopes of deliverance and improvement in different strata of society. The traditional middle class saw in Khomeini an upholder of private property, a partisan of the bazaar, and a believer in Islamic values. The modern middle class regarded Khomeini as a radical nationalist wedded to the programme adopted earlier by Mussadiq: ending royal dictatorship and foreign influences in Iran. The urban working class backed Khomeini because of his repeated commitment to social justice which, it felt, could be achieved only by transferring power and wealth from the affluent to the needy. Finally, the rural poor saw the Ayatollah as their saviour: the one to provide them with arable land, irrigation facilities, roads, schools and electricity.

Actually Khomeini did more than merely hold the anti-Shah movement together. He helped to create an ever-increasing popular surge to push it forward in greater and higher tides. He did so by making consistent use of the fortieth day of mourning of those killed by the Shah's security forces, by using the month of Ramadan to charge the nation with Islamic revolutionary fervour, and by transforming the traditional Ashura processions into demonstrations for the revolution. With the aid of the re-enactment of the passion plays of the early days of Islam, he helped to create a revolutionary play of modern times.

The Ayatollah's other outstanding contribution was to devise and implement an original set of strategy and tactics to neutralize the Pahlavi's 440,000 strong military. Khomeini was aware of the strategy favoured by the Islamic Marxist Mujahedin-e Khalq (People's Combatants) and Marxist-Leninist Fedayin-e Khalq (People's Self-Sacrificers): guerrilla attacks on selected targets to lead to increased government repression which would arouse the masses to participate in an armed struggle against the regime. Khomeini disagreed with this, arguing that if people were to wage an armed struggle against the military this would create 'a chain of revenge'. Bloodshed would make the army close ranks and stand by the Pahlavis. He therefore chose the strategy of 'moral attack' on the army. 'We must fight the army from within,' he said. 'We must fight from within the soldiers' hearts. Face the soldier with a flower. Fight through martyrdom, because the martyr is the essence of history. Let the army kill as many as it wants, until the soldiers are shaken to their hearts by the massacres they have committed. Then the army will collapse, and thus you will have disarmed the army.'[23] Such advice appealed to the martyr complex that lies deeply embedded in the psyche of Shia Iranians. At the same time Khomeini tried to dissuade soldiers from firing by warning them that if they shot their brothers and sisters 'it is just as though you are firing at the Quran'.[24] Since these words came from a grand ayatollah, a marja-e taqlid, and since most of the troops were Shia, they were effective. In short, Khomeini devised revolutionary tactics which stemmed from the specific religio-cultural environment of Shia Iran, and therefore the Iranian people accepted and used these unhesitatingly and effectively.

The mosque played a crucial role in the revolution, both as an institution and as a place of prayer and congregation. Since it was impractical for the state regularly to suppress or disrupt activities in the mosque, it offered opportunities to the revolutionaries that no other place did or could. Khomeini knew this, and made maximum use of it. He urged the ulama to base local Revolutionary Komitehs (i.e. committees) in mosques. He thus spawned an institution which proved invaluable during the last, crucial months of the revolutionary movement. Of all the different revolutionary bodies that sprouted during the final stage of the anti-Shah movement, the Revolutionary Komitehs proved to be the most broad-based and most effective. They took over administrative and police powers once the Shah had departed on 16 January 1979, and consolidated their hold once Khomeini had overthrown the Shah's appointee, Prime Minister Shahpour Bakhtiar, on 11 February.

The Emergence of the Islamic State and Society

On his return to Iran from exile on 1 February 1979 Khomeini lost no time in dismantling the secular state he had inherited and installing an Islamic one. On 5 February when appointing Mahdi Bazargan – a widely respected pious layman who had suffered repeated imprisonment under the Shah – prime minister of the provisional Islamic government, Khomeini instructed him to 'change the political system of the country to an Islamic Republic'. Khomeini drew his own authority from the seventeen-point charter adopted by acclamation by the 2 million strong rally in Tehran on Ashura, 11 December 1978, which called for an end to monarchy, acceptance of Khomeini as leader, and the establishment of an Islamic government.

A referendum on the question 'Should Iran be an Islamic Republic?' was scheduled for 29 and 30 March. In order to include the Iranian youth, who had enthusiastically participated in the revolutionary movement, in the political process, the government lowered the voting age from eighteen to sixteen. Given the religious eminence of Khomeini there was a widespread feeling among Muslim masses that failure to vote for the Islamic Republic would mean being branded infidel.[25] Since the identity card of the person using his vote was to be stamped, a non-participant would have been easy to spot. No wonder, official sources announced the voter-turnout to be 89 per cent, an unprecedented figure, with 98.2 per cent of 20,251,000 voters saying 'Yes'. Khomeini declared 1 April to be 'the first day of the Government of God'.

The Bazargan administration functioned in parallel with the Islamic Revolutionary Council which Khomeini had appointed (in exile) on 13 January 1979, and which was charged with convening a constituent assembly to produce a constitution for the Islamic Republic, holding elections and transferring power to the elected representatives.

It was noteworthy that in Khomeini's view elections and representative government were at the core of an Islamic political system, a dramatic contrast to the stance of Saudi monarchs.

During the revolutionary upheaval Khomeini's aides had made a special effort to downgrade the importance of his book, *Hukumat-e Islami: Vilayat-e Faqih*. They thought that publicizing a definite outline of what Khomeini had in mind for post-Pahlavi Iran would destroy the unity of disparate anti-Shah forces which he had forged.

Indeed, the draft constitution leaked to the press by the Islamic Revolutionary Council in late April did not include the concept of the Vilayat-e Faqih, rule of the Just Jurist. Even then the document aroused much controversy. Some leading clerics opposed the idea of direct intervention by the ulama in the day-to-day running of the government as specified in the draft. The most prominent among them was Ayatollah Muhammad Kazim Shariatmadari, a senior cleric in Qom. There was also protest from the leaders of such ethnic minorities as Kurds, Arabs, Baluchs and Turkomans who wanted greater powers for non-Persian-speaking regions. The degree of controversy disappointed Khomeini, who had anticipated smooth sailing. The second draft, published officially on 18 June, failed to satisfy the critics. Radical Islamists and secular leftists wanted to revise it in a major way. Given this, and the unstable conditions existing in the country, leaders of the Islamic Republican Party (IRP), the leading Khomeinist force, decided to keep the doctrine of Vilayat-e Faqih out of the discussion on the constitution. But that did not mean they had abandoned the idea altogether.

IRP leaders found the results of the 3 August election to the seventy-three-member Assembly of Experts, charged with revising the draft constitution, very encouraging. Excluding the three representatives of religious minorities (Christians, Jews and Zoroastrians), and one disqualified member, the Assembly had sixty-nine Muslim members. Of these forty-five were clerics, with thirty-six of them either members of the IRP or allied to it. Of the twenty-four lay Muslim members, eleven belonged to the IRP or one of its allied groups. Most of the remaining Experts were independent. So the IRP and its allies had the two-thirds majority required to pass individual articles of the constitution.

By the time the Assembly met on 18 August a well-orchestrated campaign by provincial and middle-ranking ulama to incorporate the Vilayat-e Faqih doctrine into the constitution was in full swing. Both Ayatollah Hussein Ali Montazeri, chairman of the Assembly, and his deputy, Ayatollah Muhammad Husseini Beheshti, backed the idea. Beheshti, the general secretary of the IRP, emerged as the key actor in planning and revising the crucial clauses of the constitution.

The introduction of the Vilayat-e Faqih doctrine in the constitution led to controversy inside the Assembly and outside. Ayatollah Shariatmadari maintained that the concept was contentious – with some clerics interpreting it narrowly as guardianship of widows and minors and others (like Khomeini) doing so in broad political terms – and should not be incorporated into a constitution.[26] Inside the chamber Yadollah Sahabi, a lay member, argued that the faqih was expected to be knowledgeable not merely about the Sharia but also in politics, economics, administration and the day-to-day affairs of society. 'It may be possible to find a faqih with these characteristics and qualities, but [in general] the channels through which a faqih is trained are not designed to cultivate such knowledge and qualities,' he said.[27] Another lay member argued that whereas Khomeini was by virtue of his superior qualities and characteristics entitled to be the faqih for life there was no assurance that his successor would match him. This point was successfully addressed when the Assembly adopted an article which made a proviso for a Leadership Council of three or five when a single leader could not be 'so recognized by the majority of the people'.

But the large majority of the Experts who favoured the Vilayat-e Faqih doctrine saw it as the cornerstone of the Islamic polity, absolutely necessary to ensure the Islamic nature of the laws, and legitimize the actions of the president, prime minister and parliament. 'The government will not be Islamic unless the president, the prime minister and the chief justice are jurists or confirmed and supervised by the faqih,' stated Montazeri. The case for the Vilayat-e Faqih doctrine was summed up by Hojatalislam Hussein Taheri Khorramabadi thus: 'We entrusted the vice-regency to a Just Faqih so that our government is Islamic, so that Muslims regard themselves as responsible to the government and consider its commands to be God's commands and its dispositions to be legal and binding.'[28]

When the controversy persisted outside the portals of the Assembly, Khomeini intervened publicly. 'The Vilayat-e Faqih is not something created by the Assembly of Experts,' he said in a speech on 22 October. 'It is something God has ordained.'[29] This settled the matter finally and irrevocably.

The constitution, composed of twelve chapters and 175 articles, was completed on 15 November, and put to vote on 2 and 3 December. According to official sources, it won 99.5 per cent of the 15,785,956 votes cast.

Significantly, the constitution-makers conceded the demand of the predominantly Sunni Kurds, Baluchs and Arabs that non-Shia sects be officially recognized on a par with Twelver Shiaism. 'The official religion of Iran is Islam and the Twelver Jaafari school of thought, and this principle shall remain eternally immutable,' states Article 12. 'Other Islamic schools of thought, including the Hanafi, Shafii, Maliki, Hanbali and Zaidi schools, are to be accorded full respect, and their followers are free to act in accordance with their own jurisprudence in performing their religious devotions. These schools enjoy official status for the purpose of religious education and matters of personal status (marriage, divorce, inheritance and bequests), being accepted in the courts relating to such matters.'[30]

Article 5 states that due to the occultation of Hazrat Vali Asr (Lord of the Age, the missing Twelfth Imam), 'the governance and leadership of the nation devolve upon the just and pious faqih who is acquainted with the circumstances of his age; courageous, resourceful and possessed of administrative ability; and recognized and accepted as Leader by the majority of the people'. The duties and powers of the Leader, Rahbar, are listed in Article 110. As the commander-in-chief of the armed forces and the head of the Supreme National Defence Council, he has the authority to appoint or dismiss the chief of the general staff and the commanders of the military's three branches as well as the Islamic Revolutionary Guards Corps, and declare war or peace 'based on the recommendation of the Supreme National Defence Council'. He has the authority to approve presidential candidates as well as appoint the president on his election or dismiss him after the Supreme Court has convicted him of 'failure to fulfil his legal duties' or the National Consultative Assembly,[31] Majlis, has testified to 'his political incompetence'. He has the right to appoint 'the highest judicial authorities' and the Islamic jurists on the Council of Guardians, which vets all bills and regulations passed by the Majlis. In short, the Leader combines the roles of the head of state and the chief justice.

The procedure to find a successor, or successors, to Khomeini – who is specifically named in Article 1 as 'Grand Ayatollah Imam Khomeini' – is outlined in Article 107. 'Experts elected by the people' will investigate and evaluate all those qualified for leadership, it states. 'Whenever a candidate who has outstanding characteristics for leadership is found, he will be introduced to the people as the Leader. Otherwise, three or five candidates who fulfil the conditions for leadership will be appointed members of the Leadership Council and introduced to the people.'

On the question of sovereignty, a subject of much controversy in 1906, the Islamic constitution provides a compromise. 'Absolute sovereignty over the world and man belongs to God, and it is He who has placed man in charge of his social destiny,' reads Article 56. 'No one can deprive man of this God-given right nor subordinate it to the interests of a given individual or group.' How are the people to express their sovereignty? 'The affairs of the country must be administered on the basis of public opinion expressed by means of elections of the president of the republic, the representatives of the National Consultative Assembly and the members of councils, or by means of referendums in matters specified in the articles of the constitution,' states Article 6.

After stating that the powers arising out of the right of national sovereignty are 'legislative, executive and judicial', Article 57 adds, 'These powers are independent of each other, and communication between them will be ensured by the president of the republic.'

Next to the Leader, the president (who must be a male Shia Muslim) is the most powerful figure. 'His is the responsibility for implementing the constitution, ordering relations among the three powers, and heading the executive power except in matters pertaining directly to the Leadership,' reads Article 113. Elected directly for a four-year term by an absolute majority of the voters, the president is the chief executive who signs and executes the laws passed by the Majlis. He nominates a male Shia Muslim as a candidate for the position of prime minister; and once his nominee has won the endorsement of the Majlis, he administers the oath of office. He approves cabinet ministers proposed by the premier before they are presented to the Majlis for a vote of confidence.

To ensure that Majlis's decisions do not contradict 'the ordinances of Islam and the constitution', Article 91 specifies the establishment of a twelve-member Council of Guardians: '(a) six just Islamic jurists, conscious of current needs and the issues of the day, to be selected by the Leader or the Leadership Council; and (b) six lawyers, specializing in different areas of law, to be elected by the National Consultative Assembly from among the Muslim lawyers presented to it by the Supreme Judicial Council.' The tenure of the Council of Guardians is six years, and that of the Majlis four years. The Majlis must send all its laws and regulations to the Council, where its twelve members examine them for compatibility with the constitution's general principles, but only the six Islamic jurists do so for their compatibility with Islamic principles.

It is worth noting that in the case of the Islamic jurists of the Council of Guardians, a powerful and strategically placed body, and the Leader himself, the constitution specifically mentions that they must be fully conversant with 'the issues of the day . . . circumstances of his age'. That is, they must know how to apply and interpret basic Islamic precepts in the conditions prevalent in the late twentieth (Christian)/early fifteenth (Islamic) century.

One of the fourteen 'General Principles' listed in Chapter One outlines a multi-tiered system of government. 'In accordance with the command of the Quran contained in the verses "Their affairs are by consultation among them" (42:38) and "Consult them on affairs" (3:153),' states Article 7, 'councils and consultative bodies – such as the National Consultative Assembly, the Provincial Councils, the Municipal Councils, and the City, Neighbourhood, Division and Village Councils – belong to the decision-making and administrative organs of the country.'

In the judiciary the Supreme Judicial Council is the highest authority. It is on the basis of the standards and criteria laid down by the Supreme Judicial Council that the Supreme Court is to be established. The head of the Supreme Court and the Prosecutor General must be mujtahids, practitioners of ijtihad; and they are to be appointed by the Leader in consultation with the Supreme Court judges. The minister of justice, to be chosen by the prime minister from a list submitted by the Supreme Judicial Council, has the responsibility for 'all the problems concerning the relationship between the judiciary, the executive and the legislature'. One of the significant functions of the judiciary – described as 'an independent power' – listed in Article 156 is 'restoring public rights and promoting justice and legitimate freedoms'.

Chapter Three, consisting of twenty-three articles, concerns 'Rights of the Nation'. Article 21 guarantees the rights of women 'in all respects, in conformity with Islamic criteria'. Then follow the articles on private property, religious freedom and press freedom. 'Publications and the press are free to present all matters except those that are detrimental to the fundamentals of Islam or the rights of the public,' states Article 24. 'The formation of political and professional parties, associations and societies, as well as religious societies, whether they be Islamic or pertain to one of the recognized religious communities is freely permitted on the condition that they do not violate the principles of independence, freedom, national unity, the criteria of Islam or the basis of the Islamic Republic,' reads Article 26. 'No one may be prevented from participating in the above groups, or be compelled to participate in them.'

The right to property is qualified since it does not apply to illegitimately acquired wealth. 'The government has the responsibility of confiscating all wealth resulting from usury, usurpation, bribery, embezzlement, theft, gambling, misuse of endowments, misuse of government contracts and transactions, the sale of uncultivated lands and other categories of land inherently subject to public ownership, the operation of houses of ill-repute, and other illegal sources,' states Article 49. 'When appropriate, such wealth must be restored to its legitimate owner, and if no such owner can be identified it must be placed in the public treasury. The application of this principle must be accompanied by due investigation and verification in accordance with the law of Islam and carried out by the government.'

A citizen is guaranteed 'freedom of access' to courts of law. 'Both parties to a dispute have the right in all courts of law to select a lawyer,' reads Article 35. 'If they are unable to do so, arrangements must be made to provide them with legal counsel.' Article 38 forbids torture, and adds that punishment of those violating the ban 'will be determined by law'. Article 25 prohibits 'inspection of letters and the failure to deliver them, the recording and disclosure of telephone conversations, the disclosure of telegraphic and telex communications or the wilful failure to deliver them, wiretapping and all forms of covert investigation', except as provided by law.

In practice, many of the civil rights mentioned in the

constitution have not been granted to citizens. There have been persistent reports of the government torturing prisoners. The idea of freedom to from political parties within the principles of 'independence, freedom, national unity, the criteria of Islam and the basis of the Islamic Republic', enshrined in Article 26, has not been translated into reality. On the other hand, when it came to impeaching the Republic's first elected president, Abol Hassan Bani-Sadr, in June 1981, the constitutional procedures were followed meticulously.

There is, however, little doubt that Iran's 1979 constitution is a pioneering effort. While it draws its inspiration from Islamic precepts, it is designed to serve the needs of a community living in modern times, incorporating such concepts as the separation of legislative, executive and judicial powers, and basing the authority of the faqih and the president on popular will, expressed either directly, as in the president's case, or indirectly, through the Assembly of Experts to be convened to select the successor(s) to Khomeini.

Soon after the polling date for the presidential election was announced in mid-December 1979, Khomeini let it be known that he did not want the ulama to monopolize power. This ruled out Ayatollah Beheshti as a presidential candidate. The public endorsement of Abol Hassan Bani-Sadr – a layman member of the Islamic Revolutionary Council and minister of finance – by Khomeini's son, Ahmad, and son-in-law, Shahab al Din Eshraqi, made him the leading favourite. On the polling day, 25 January 1980, he received nearly 75 per cent of the popular vote. Elections to the 270-member Majlis were held between mid-March and early May. These polls helped the Islamic regime enormously in winning legitimacy.

The speed with which the Islamic leaders moved was remarkable. In little over a year they had conducted a referendum in favour of an Islamic Republic, framed and promulgated a constitution and held elections to the presidency and parliament on the basis of universal suffrage. They drew ordinary Iranians into the political system on a scale never witnessed before. The source of this success was the charismatic Khomeini, now seventy-seven years old, the undisputed leader of the Islamic revolution.

Khomeini argued that since both society and the regime were Islamic there was no place in them for those who were opposed to Islam or questioned the overriding importance of Islam in life. Such political parties as the Fedayin-e Khalq, which believed in and propagated Marxism, a materialist, atheistic ideology, were patently unIslamic. Then there were those who used Islam as a cover to hide their Marxist convictions and ideology, so ran Khomeini's argument. Such people were hypocrites, and ought to be exposed. To this category belonged the members of the Mujahedin-e Khalq. Finally came the deviants, those who accepted and acted on wrong interpretations of the Sharia. Khomeini considered himself to be the final arbiter of who or what was Islamic, and who or what was not. All non-Islamic elements had to be expelled from the government administration, military, judiciary, public and private enterprises, and educational institutions. This was to be achieved by a combination of government decisions and popular actions.

But identifying and neutralizing non-Islamic elements was only one function of the Islamic regime and its leaders. Their other major task was to purify society, which had been corrupted by alien influences over the past few centuries, and Islamize it. Corrupt behaviour and customs had to be ended. Alcohol and gambling were banned immediately, and so were nightclubs, pornographic films and mixed bathing. Society needed to be Islamized in a positive sense. Therefore Friday noon prayers and sermons were made the focal point of the week. The sermons were used to inform and educate the faithful. All Friday prayer leaders were appointed by Khomeini, and they were required to report to him.

Those who resisted the Islamic government were to be punished along the lines set out in the Sharia. Such crimes as raising arms against the Islamic state or spreading corruption in society were to be awarded capital punishment.

This was the ideological framework which Khomeini laid out, and within which he operated during the various phases that the revolution underwent.

With the takeover of the US embassy and diplomats in Tehran by militant students on 4 November 1979, the revolution entered a virulently anti-American phase. The focus now was on expelling the remaining vestiges of the influence of America, which had dominated Iran for the past quarter century, and sharpening the anti-imperialist image of the Islamic regime, thus lessening the attraction of the Mujahedin-e Khalq's mixture of Islam and Marxism to young Iranians.

Iraq's invasion of Iran on 22 September 1980 heralded another phase of revolution in which patriotism and Islam became inseparable. Traditional rivalry between Iraq and Iran worsened when, following the Islamic revolution, the Iranian clerical leadership began appealing to the faithful in Iraq to overthrow the secular Baathist regime of President Saddam Hussein. In return, the Iraqi president encouraged Iranian Arabs in the oil-rich province of Khuzistan to rebel against the Khomeini regime. Finally, encouraged by reports of low morale in the Iranian military and internecine fighting among Iranian leaders, Saddam Hussein attacked Iran. A side-effect of the Iran–Iraq war was to strain relations between President Bani-Sadr, who had been appointed the commander-in-chief of the military by Khomeini, and IRP leaders who exercised control over the Islamic Revolutionary Guard Corps, formed in June 1979 to safeguard the 'fruits of Islamic revolution'. Bani-Sadr took to lambasting 'the party [meaning the IRP] for being repressive, dictatorial and practising torture on political prisoners'.[32] Khomeini appointed a three-man commission to investigate the charges of torture.

When the American hostage crisis was resolved in January 1981 by the government of Prime Minister Muhammad Ali Rajai, a former student of Ayatollah Beheshti, without any reference to Bani-Sadr, the latter was incensed. In his paper, *Inqilab-e Islami* (Islamic Revolution), he attacked the government of Rajai for an agreement with the US 'which fell far short of what could have been achieved early in the crisis'.[33] Khomeini intervened in the controversy with calls for unity.

By early February a direct correlation could be discerned between the developments on the war front and those in domestic politics. An improvement on the battlefront encouraged dissent at home. By mid-February 1981 the Iranians were strong enough on the battlefield to block further Iraqi advances. The result was a stalemate. Not surprisingly conflict between Bani-Sadr and the IRP sharpened in early March. Khomeini tried to calm the situation by forbidding public speeches by both sides. There was peace for about two months. Then Bani-Sadr circumvented Khomeini's ban by addressing troops at their garrisons and giving interviews to foreign papers. In these he alleged that the IRP was leading Iran to a 'new despotism' and that the Rajai government had failed to revive the economy. The Majlis sided with Rajai, and increased his powers at the expense of Bani-Sadr. On 30 May 1981 Rajai attacked Bani-Sadr without naming him. 'Those who studied abroad when the revolution occurred had little contact with the people,' Rajai said in the Majlis. 'But after they returned [to Iran] they demanded a role in the revolution.'[34] From 1964 until 1 February 1979, when Bani-Sadr returned to Iran along with Khomeini, he had studied and taught in Paris.

From then on events moved fast. On 10 June Khomeini dismissed Bani-Sadr as the commander-in-chief of the military. Four days later the Majlis met to discuss Bani-Sadr's competence as president. On 20 June it was decided by 177 votes to 1 that Bani-Sadr was incompetent. Once Khomeini had received the Majlis decision by letter from the speaker, Hojatalislam Ali Akbar Hashimi-Rafsanjani, he removed Bani-Sadr from office. He then appointed a three-member Council of Presidency, consisting of the prime minister, the parliament's speaker and the chief justice.

The IRP described Bani-Sadr's ouster as 'the third revolution', the second revolution being the seizure of the US embassy. Bazargan's premiership until early November 1979 had reassured the modern middle classes and ethnic minorities that they would not have to live under an uncompromisingly Shia regime. Likewise, Bani-Sadr's election as president had made the less committed citizens feel that the Islamic fundamentalists were willing to share power with others. In reality, however, the comparatively moderate leaders were of temporary value to Khomeinists. They were used by the fundamentalists to buy time to build up their organizations and consolidate their hold over the state apparatus and the religious network.

From the beginning there had been tension between two kinds of leaders within the Islamic camp: those who had been educated in the West and had spent many years in exile before returning home after the revolution; and those who had stayed home, actively resisted the Pahlavis and suffered imprisonment and torture. The difference between them was epitomized by Premier Rajai and President Bani-Sadr. Rajai's somewhat scruffy appearance, modest demeanour, and refusal to speak English, a foreign language, in public contrasted with the haughty manner of the suave Bani-Sadr who revelled in his fluency in French.

There were deep differences between the two sides on the nature of the revolution and the direction it should take. Iranian revolutionaries faced a problem common to all revolutions: who should dominate the new order – the ideologue or the expert? Islamic militants put ideology first, Bani-Sadr professional skills.

With the outbreak of the war, this conflict was extended from running the civil service and the economy to fighting Iraq. The non-professional Islamic Revolutionary Guards Corps (IRGC) and the Basij-e Mustazafin (Mobilization of the Deprived) volunteers, possessing more enthusiasm than expertise, swarmed to the front to fight. They had accepted Khomeini's view that by invading Iran the Iraqi president, Saddam Hussein, had attacked not only Iranian soil but also the 'Government of God' and therefore Islam. Khomeini had constructed a connection between the duty to counter the aggression of Saddam Hussein, whom he described as 'a corrupt pagan', and the revolutionary struggle against the Shah. 'We will fight to the end . . . because we have to implement our religious duties,' Khomeini declared. 'We are religiously bound to protect and preserve Islam . . . This was the same logic we pursued in our fighting against the corrupt Pahlavi regime . . . Islamic teachings were going to be eradicated and Islamic principles erased, therefore we were bound by our religion to resist as much as we could.'[35] Military officers, who by and large were moved more by patriotism than religion, resented having to integrate non-professionals into their plans. In the dissension that developed, Bani-Sadr sided with the officer corps. This eroded his popularity among army troops who were being educated by the political–ideological department staffed by the ulama, and whose ranks were now swelled by fresh Islamic and leftist recruits.

The dramatic increase in the sizes of the IRGC and the Basij worked against the interests of Bani-Sadr, who had no control over these bodies. Since mosques were used as recruiting centres for these forces, their importance and standing rose. The ulama took to arms-training at a special camp near Qom, and parading in city strets, thus dramatically demonstrating their patriotism and Islamic fervour. Moreover, mosques became integral parts of the civilian administration when the Revolutionary Komitehs decided to use them to implement the rationing system introduced in the aftermath of the war. In general, revolutionary organizations showed themselves to be flexible and energetic in meeting the exigencies of the war. All this worked in favour of the IRP leaders, who controlled these bodies.

As a trained economist, Bani-Sadr was more aware of the poor shape of the Iranian economy, and the urgent need to repair it, than his rivals. He often urged ending the 'destructive phase' of the revolution and entering 'the period of reconstruction'. But his opponents felt differently. To them the political–religious aspect of the revolution was far more significant than the economic. They knew instinctively that the masses regarded the Shah's overthrow as such a stupendous political and spiritual victory that they would not mind bearing economic hardship in its wake. Believing that the revolution was incomplete, Islamic radicals wanted to complete it by keeping up a permanent political ferment among the faithful. Since the exodus of the rich and super-rich had reduced the extent of socio-economic inequalities and corruption, the fundamentalists wanted to build on this, and accelerate the pace of Islamization and redistribution of wealth.

The Islamic radicals' views on the economy were inspired by Ayatollah Taleqani's *Islam wa Malikiyat* (Islam and Property) and Ayatollah Muhammad Baqir Sadr's *Iqtisaduna* (Our Economics). Both works present Islam as having its own economic ideology as comprehensive as capitalism or socialism but superior to both. They argue furthermore that since Islam is wedded to the concepts of social justice, egalitarianism and the uplift of the underprivileged, it can be used as an instrument of social change.

Taleqani's premise is that God is bountiful; and given the vast natural resources he has bestowed upon humankind, there is enough for everybody. A major task of Islam is to guarantee equality of access to these resources to the members of the umma, Islamic community – a task it performs through moral appeals to the believers to behave fairly, and by prescribing general rules on economic exchange and activity, stressing its preference for social welfare over individual gain, and conferring on the Islamic authority the power to implement measures to ensure equity.

The assertion by Taleqani that ownership derives only from labour lands him in difficulties when dealing with Islamic laws on inheritance and contract. The very concept of inheritance runs counter to Taleqani's view on ownership. He tries to reconcile the contradiction by arguing that inheritance laws help to redistribute wealth, and that the motive behind accumulating wealth – to provide for the wife and children of the deceased – is worthy. He attempts to clothe in egalitarian garb the laws of contract in the

Sharia – rules on rent, sharing of crops, remuneration for employees either on the basis of output or fixed wages, or partnership – by stating that a Muslim worker has the choice of entering into partnership or settling for profit-sharing or accepting wages.

To the traditional Islamic taxes or khums and zakat Taleqani is prepared to add the proviso that an Islamic regime has the right to impose tax on agricultural land to any level it thinks fit for the general welfare of the peasantry.

The other major hurdle that Taleqani had to overcome to establish his unequivocally egalitarian view of Islam was to confront a body of interpretations, built over the centuries, which was decidedly capitalistic. He circumvents this by explaining that the past interpretations along capitalist lines had to do with the circumstances then existing, and not with the general ethos of Islam. The general tone of the Quran, he maintains, is egalitarian: it views wealth as a means to implement Allah's will and not an end in itself. It is this moral, ethical overview which must permeate the interpretations of the Sharia by present-day jurisprudents on private property, contracts, taxes and inheritance, he stresses. In any event an Islamic regime exists to create an egalitarian society and its leader, the faqih, is therefore entitled to oversee the acquiring and disposing of property in the name of upholding public welfare. From this stems the faqih's authority to limit a believer's right to exploit those resources which are the property of the umma. In case of conflict between the rights of an individual and those of society at large, the Islamic regime is entitled to 'limit individual ownership to a greater degree than the law may authorize'.[36]

According to Taleqani an Islamic government, being aware of 'the withering scourges and piercing swords that kings and slaveholders aim at the bodies of slaves and peasants', would refuse to back grasping landlords and capitalists.[37] The society that an Islamic regime would aim to create would parallel that which existed under Prophet Muhammad in Medina.

In this exemplary city, a portion of the private wealth of the ansars [Medinese helpers of Prophet Muhammad] was given to the muhajirin [émigrés from Mecca] and, except for a small portion of private fortunes, wealth was superintended by the state; apart from special allotments given to those participating in jihad, holy struggle, it was divided among all equally, to each according to his need. Individuals had no special distinctions, ruler and ruled were not set apart except in their capacities of governing and being governed. No noticeable differences existed in their houses and clothing.[38]

Sadr's *Our Economics* was of higher calibre than Taleqani's work. Instead of giving radical interpretations to traditional Sharia rules, as Taleqani had done, Sadr made a systematic attempt to present Islam as offering a self-contained economic system. In order to do this he defined such basic economic concepts as labour, added value, profit, rent, wages, structure and superstructure in Islamic terms. And in his arguments he relied exclusively on Islamic rulings and legal literature, quoting various rulings but choosing one, and stating his reasons for so doing. Thus he applied to economics the methodology used by senior ulama to other fields of life.

He gives radical interpretations to Islamic laws on economic transactions and activities by narrowing the definition of private property. According to him ownership means a 'special relationship between the individual and property which denies others the use of it', and no more.[39] To root his definition in Islam, Sadr refers to the way in which the conquered territories were incorporated into Dar al Islam during early Islamic history: the ownership of the lands rested with the umma, and an individual was given no more than the right to use land, a right which could be cancelled or withdrawn. But what about the instances during that period when the early converts to Islam were given the ownership of land? This right, Sadr argues, was not absolute: it was hedged with the condition that the owner would cultivate the land and thus contribute towards the welfare of the community. The same condition applied to the exploiting of other resources granted by Allah.

Sadr strengthens his argument by drawing on the Islamic prohibitions on excessive consumption, wastage and hoarding. Any of these, or even general misuse of wealth by its owner, is sufficient ground for the erstwhile owner to be deprived of his ownership rights. Sadr extends this concept to argue that an Islamic government is entitled to limit private property in order to guarantee a certain living standard to the community at large, and preserve social equilibrium.

A threat to social equilibrium would ensue, Sadr argues, if and when private capital acquires a domineering position in commerce and industry. In an Islamic state, he writes, 'Private economic activity will remain within reasonable limits . . . and will not create class differences. As a result, the creation of large industrial enterprises will fall within the sphere, authority and activity of the government.'[40]

In Sadr's scenario the Islamic government is to be headed by a jurist, called vali-ye amr, lord of the command, the equivalent of the faqih. He is to be the chief agent of socio-economic reconstruction of society and the one to resolve the thorny problems of doctrine. There is in Islam scope for flexibility in those areas of human actions which lie between the categories of 'obligatory' and 'prohibited' – recommended, allowed, unspecified, and undesirable – and which form the discretionary segment of the Sharia. It is here that the faqih/vali-ye amr has the right to issue secondary rulings. He can classify an 'unspecified' act as 'undesirable', 'prohibited', 'recommended' or even 'obligatory', depending on the circumstances. Since most of the Islamic laws on economic activities and transactions lie within the discretionary sphere, and the faqih has the authority to issue secondary rulings, there is in the Sharia an inbuilt flexibility. Thus the faqih is well-equipped to adjust relations between individuals, community and economic resources against the background of a continually changing social, cultural and technological environment.

Not surprisingly Sadr's book became the main inspiration of Iran's Islamic leaders not only in the economic and financial decisions they made in the early days of the revolution but also in the framing of the constitution. The chapter on the economy and financial affairs in the constitution is illustrative. Article 43 states that the economy of the Islamic Republic is to be based inter alia on 'granting interest-free loans [to citizens] or recourse to any other legitimate means that neither results in the concentration of wealth in the hands of a few individuals or its circulation among them, nor turns the government into a major or dominant employer', and 'the prohibition of extravagance and wastefulness in all matters related to the economy, including consumption, investment, production, distribution and services'. The next article describes the Islamic Republic's economic system as consisting of three sectors: state, co-operative and private. The state sector comprises 'all large-scale and major industries, foreign trade, major mineral resources, banking, insurance, energy, dams and large-scale irrigation networks, radio and television, postal, telegraphic and telephone system, aviation, shipping, roads, railroads and the like'. The co-operative sector includes 'co-operative companies and institutions concerned with production and distribution, established in both cities and the countryside, in accordance with Islamic criteria'. Finally, the private sector comprises 'those activities concerned with agriculture, animal husbandry, industry, trade and services that supplement the activities of the state and the co-operative sectors'.[41]

While Islamic leaders were deliberating these and other articles of the constitution in the summer of 1979, the country faced immense economic problems stemming from the tumultuous anti-Shah movement, which had consisted of long and bitter strikes by industrial and service workers as well as civil servants. With the flight of some 130,000 local and foreign industrial managers and technicians, hundreds of factories and workshops closed down or suffered steep falls in production. Shortages of raw materials bedevilled inexperienced managements. The cumulative effect of all this was the shrinkage of the pre-revolution labour force of 10.5 million by 2.5 million, and the reduction of the gross national product by 21 per cent.[42]

Premier Bazargan announced on 8 June that the government had acquired twenty-two privately owned banks.[43]
Two more nationalization decrees issued during the next
four weeks applied to fifteen insurance companies, including eight foreign-owned ones, and the factories assembling
aircraft and shipping vessel parts, and motor vehicles. All
this gave the government a tighter control over the economy
and was in tune with the regime's egalitarian tendencies.
In early July the Law for the Protection and Expansion of
Iranian Industry provided for the nationalization of heavy
industry, the factories of fifty individuals who had attained
their wealth through illegitimate means, and industrial
companies whose liabilities exceeded their assets. The next
month measures were taken to nationalize pharmaceutical
companies, cold storage plants, warehouses and trucking.

By now the Mustazafin Foundation, established in early
March under Khomeini's decree to consolidate the properties of sixty-three members of the Pahlavi royal family and
the assets accumulated by others through illegitimate
means, and to use the income derived from them for the
welfare of the mustazafin (needy or oppressed), had
emerged as the country's largest economic conglomerate.
Its immediate acquisition of the Pahlavi Foundation, which
owned 20 per cent of the assets of all privately owned
companies,[44] gave it a head start. Over the months it
acquired the assets of tens of thousands of affluent Iranians
who fled the country before and after the revolution, and of
all those who were executed. It was thus that the Mustazafin Foundation came to possess more than a hundred
companies engaged in such diverse activities as hotels,
construction, real estate, agriculture, household goods manufacture, tyres, paper manufacture, publishing and food
processing. The creation of the Mustazafin Foundation
combined with the nationalization measures gave the
regime powerful leverage in economic matters.

Among those who wholeheartedly supported the dominance of the state in the economy was Premier Rajai who,
following Bani-Sadr's impeachment in June 1981, became
the IRP's candidate for the presidency. The fact that he

was a pious layman with a humble background proved to be his strongest asset in the election campaign. According to the official returns, he secured 88 per cent of the popular vote. He was sworn in on 2 August, but his presidency proved short-lived. On 30 August the explosion of an incendiary bomb at a meeting of the National Security Council killed him as well as Premier Muhammad Javed Bahonar.

The responsibility for the bomb was claimed by the Mujahedin-e Khalq, whose leader, Masoud Rajavi, had declared guerrilla war against the regime following the ouster of Bani-Sadr. The organization now concentrated on thwarting plans for a presidential poll on 2 October. On 27 September hundreds of Mujahedin cadres clashed with revolutionary guards near the Tehran University campus in a central part of the city. The seven-hour-long battle left seventeen dead and forty injured. It was the most concentrated battle in the capital since the revolution. But Khomeini was unbowed. 'Disorder does not mean that the Islamic rule is weak,' he said. 'Islam is revived through this kind of bloodshed.'[45] The government met the Mujahedin challenge by unleashing its repressive machine. In the three months after Bani-Sadr's dismissal it executed more than a thousand people.

In the presidential election Hojatalislam Ali Hussein Khamanei won a little more than 16 million votes out of 16,847,00. He was helped by the fact that he was not only the general secretary of the IRP but was also Ayatollah Khomeini's personal representative on the Supreme Defence Council. In late October his nominee for prime minister, Mir Hussein Musavi, was accepted by the Majlis.

Since Musavi and Khamanei had been leaders of the IRP from the beginning, they were well suited to work in accord. With both the Majlis speaker Hashimi-Rafsanjani and the supreme court chief Ayatollah Abdul Karim Musavi-Ardebili belonging to the IRP, the party controlled the legislative, judicial and executive organs of the state. The daily administration was in the hands of second-rank ulama who were either IRP members or sympathizers.

Thus, in less than three years, Khomeini had brought the republic to the point where a fundamentalist party was firmly in power.

The Musavi government intensified the purging from all governmental and revolutionary institutions of those with 'insufficient Islamic convictions' (as the prime minister put it), and accelerated the pace of Islamization. The decision to dismiss all those Revolutionary Komiteh and IRGC officials whose sons had been found to be Mujahedin members was applied rigorously. The purge of the judiciary, which had so far affected thirty Islamic judges who had accepted bribes to commute capital punishment to life imprisonment, was extended. The recently passed law on Islamic dress for women in public was implemented strictly. Special judges were appointed under the overall direction of Hojatalislam Murtaza Hussein to combat 'impious acts'. These included 'adultery, homosexuality, gambling, hypocrisy, sympathy for atheists and hypocrites, and treason'.[46]

This chapter of the Islamic Republic's history was particularly bloody. Despite extreme security measures taken by the authorities, the Mujahedin-e Khalq claimed in early February 1982 that its members had assassinated over 1,200 religious and political leaders of the regime. In return the government had executed 4,000 guerrillas, most of them belonging to the Mujahedin-e Khalq. Masoud Rajavi, the party leader, put the number of executions at twice the official figure. Whatever the actual number, there was little doubt that the government action had been effective.

Why did the Islamic regime hit back as fiercely as it did? An explanation came from Hashimi-Rafsanjani in an interview with *Arabia*, a London-based magazine. 'It was imperative to take action immediately otherwise . . . Iran would have become [another] Lebanon,' he said. 'Islam commands determination.'[47] The reference was to the Lebanese civil war which broke out in April 1975 and was still in progress nine years later. During its most active phase, from April 1975 to October 1976, it had caused some 80,000 deaths in a country with a population of 3.5 million.

The consequences of a civil war in Iran – with a population of nearly 40 million and a long border with the Soviet Union – would have been much worse.

In the spring of 1982 the tide began to turn in Iran's favour in the Gulf War. In a major offensive in May the Iranians recaptured 5,380 square kilometres of their territory, including the port city of Khorramshahr, which they had lost to Iraq at the beginning of the conflict. In June Tehran rejected the Iraqi offer of an immediate ceasefire, and repeated its call for the overthrow of the Iraqi president Saddam Hussein, the 'corrupt infidel', whom it held responsible for aggression against the Islamic regime of Iran. Indeed, on 9 July the Iranian government threatened that if Saddam Hussein were not punished for invading Iran, and 100 billion dollars paid to it as war damages, then it would carry the war into Iraq. Four days later it did so with a view to capturing the Iraqi port city of Basra. It failed to achieve this objective. None the less, these events showed that the Gulf War had now entered a phase where the initiative lay with Tehran, a sign of strength of the Islamic revolution in Iran.

While the government was well on its way towards quashing the Mujahedin-e Khalq, it discovered an anti-regime plot in April 1982. It was hatched among others by Sadiq Qutbzadeh, who had been a member of the Islamic Revolutionary Council and foreign minister before falling into obscurity in September 1980, and Ahmad Abbasi, a son-in-law of Ayatollah Shariatmadari. The plan was to kill Khomeini by hitting his residence in Jamram, a Tehran suburb, with rockets, assassinate the members of the Supreme Defence Council, blame the outrage on the Tudeh Party, and seize power in order to avenge the killings.[48] The authorities arrested 170 people, including seventy military officers. The officers were tried secretly but Qutbzadeh's trial by a military tribunal was televised in mid-August. He was found guilty of conspiring to overthrow the Islamic government with arms, and executed on 15 September.

During his long political career, spent mainly abroad,

Qutbzadeh had actively pursued anti-Shah politics. In Paris, where he lived for many years, he was a leader of the Islamic Students Society. His execution marked a dramatic end to the co-option by the Islamic regime of lay Iranian intellectuals who had been active in the Islamic anti-Shah movement abroad. The process had begun in November 1979, and included Bani-Sadr. These leaders' many years in the West had cast them in a western mould; and this did not fit the Islamic state and society that were being forged in Iran under the active guidance of Khomeini.

Against the background of these dramatic events – the Mujahedin's guerrilla actions, anti-government plotting and conventional warfare against Iraq – the government kept up its programme of Islamization of society. On 30 May 1982 the cabinet approved comprehensive plans to bring the existing penal and legal codes, civil law, trade law and registration of documents and land in line with the Sharia. Adherence to Islamic dress for women was enforced strictly. In August the government declared all secular law null and void. The Majlis passed a law on moral offences on 21 September.

After protracted internal discussion the government finally decided to face the problem of Khomeini's succession. On 20 November it announced an election on 10 December for an eighty-two-member Assembly of Experts to deal with the question of the next Leader or Leadership Council. The Assembly of Experts was to be a permanent body, and only clerics were allowed to run for membership.

According to official sources, nearly 17,683,000 voters participated. Among the thirteen members elected from Tehran, Khamanei, Hashimi-Rafsanjani and Musavi-Ardebili were at the top of the list. This was a measure of their popularity and that of the regime they led.

Thus reassured, Khomeini launched what he described as 'a judicial revolution to protect the dignity and honour of individuals'. He issued an eight-point decree, entitled 'Islamization of Judiciary', on 15 December 1982. 'The laws regarding judicial matters . . . must be given priority over other measures,' read Point 1. The next point referred to the protection of 'the people's rights'. For this the criterion lay in 'the present deeds of individuals, overlooking certain mistakes they might have made during the former regime's rule'. Point 3 stressed that nobody was allowed to 'treat people in an unIslamic way'; and the next point specifically warned against 'arrest or summons by force'. Point 5 referred to the unlawfulness of usurping 'anybody's property or right except on a Sharia judge's orders'. Point 6 forbade unauthorized entry into somebody's house or business premises with a view to uncovering an offence or sin or to investigate people's secrets or spy on other people's sins. However, the next point stated that these restrictions did not apply to 'the cases relating to conspiracies and mini-groups opposed to Islam and the regime of the Islamic Republic'. The last point authorized the supreme court chief and the prime minister to implement the above instructions through 'trustworthy and reliable councils', to which the aggrieved persons could refer their complaints about 'violations and transgressions by enforcement officers against their rights and properties'.

The issuing of such an order by Khomeini was an admission that there had been transgressions of the Islamic law in the past and that these had caused much resentment. Expressing an official view, Premier Musavi called the decree 'a historic turning point' and 'a new phase in the revolution'. The leading papers in Tehran saw it as a confirmation of the strength and confidence of the Islamic state. 'The regime could rely on the sword only to a certain extent,' explained Musavi-Ardebili, the supreme court chief. 'In other cases reliance should be on justice, logic, faith and knowledge . . . Encouragement should be given to an individual's fear of justice rather than the sword.'[49]

Khomeini then turned his attention to methods being used by the vetting committees to determine the Islamic credentials of those employed by public agencies or applying for jobs with them. These committees had taken to giving tests to determine this. The tests contained many obscure theological questions which few lay persons, if any, could be expected to know. They also included questions which were unrelated to Islam. Parents of many job applicants had been subjected to extensive interrogation by intelligence agents about matters unconnected with the job. Khomeini found all this unnecessary. He instructed the Headquarters for the Implementation of the Imam's Decree to dismiss the vetting committees, whether they be in the armed forces, the civil service or educational institutions. He reiterated that present behaviour was the only criterion to be considered in choosing a candidate for a job with a governmental or revolutionary institution. Furthermore he instructed the headquarters to find means to identify and re-employ those who had been wrongfully dismissed in the past.[50]

In short, Khomeini took steps to rectify the excesses of the Islamic revolution which – following the example of earlier secular revolutions in various parts of the world – had occurred partly due to the revolutionaries' attempts to beat off the violent challenge to the regime by the counter-revolutionaries, and partly due to their over-enthusiasm in imposing values and laws stemming from their ideology.

A return to comparative normality, at the end of nearly four years of revolution, occurred in an environment where the revolutionary organizations, which had sprung up in the wake of the Shah's downfall, covered all spheres of life: political, military, security, judicial, economic, social, cultural and religious. Some of these bodies functioned independently, others in tandem with government ministries. Later, two of them were absorbed into existing ministries while a few others were transformed into new ministries. These organizations were so preponderant that one out of six Iranians above the age of fifteen belonged to one or more of them.[51]

With the Tudeh Party banned in May 1983, all pre-revolution parties, excepting Mahdi Bazargan's Liberation Movement, were eliminated. Political life thus became the near monopoly of the Islamic Republican Party and its smaller allies.

In the military a series of purges resulted in the dismissal or retirement of all but a thousand officers of the pre-revolution period. Moreover, the regime took steps to inculcate Islamic values and ideas among military personnel. A political–ideological department was instituted in the military. It was often manned by young ulama, who were fiercely loyal to the Islamic Republic. They educated officers and ranks in Islamic history and ideology. The information and guidance department performed the general task of creating and sustaining support for the actions and policies of the government, and the particular job of keeping an eye on potential dissidents or deviants. In addition there were the Islamic Associations among military personnel – voluntary bodies which concerned themselves with raising the Islamic consciousness of their members and guarding the security of their units.

One of the important motives behind the establishment of the Islamic Revolutionary Guards Corps was to create a counterforce to the army commanded by officers of dubious loyalty to the Islamic regime. As such, after the IRGC nucleus was formed out of small Islamic militias, which had sprung up during the anti-Shah movement, recruitment to the force was strictly controlled. A recruit had to pass tests in the Quran, *Nahaj al Balaghe* (Fountain of Eloquence) by Imam Ali, and *Hukumat-e Islami* by Khomeini.[52]

At first recruits underwent training for six months. But following the war the period was reduced to three months. Yet the standards of training–military, ideological and political – improved steadily, with the ulama playing a leading role in the ideological–political training. The IRGC was involved in the fighting at the front from the day the war erupted. As it expanded it acquired an air unit of its own. It became the force on which IRP leaders lavished their attention and resources. Following Bani-Sadr's dismissal, co-operation between the IRGC and the military improved dramatically. Revolutionary guards used unconventional tactics effectively on the front, and impressed military officers with their daring and flexibility. However, warfare was only one of the IRGC's functions, the others being maintaining internal security, and countering subversion and ethnic rebellions.

In November 1982 the Islamic Revolutionary Guards Corps ministry was created. Soon an élite division was formed within the IRGC with the specific purpose of protecting the capital against a possible military coup. In early 1983 the IRGC was 170,000 strong, and included both ground and air forces. It remains the Islamic regime's most reliable and most effective fighting force.

Following the US embassy takeover in November 1979 – which made an American invasion of Iran a serious possibility – Khomeini gave a call for the creation of 'an army of 20 million'. This led to arms-training for students at local mosques after school or college hours. In early 1980 the IRGC formally set up the Vahid-e Basij-e Mustazafin (Unit of the Mobilization of the Deprived). It drew volunteers from youths below the conscription age of eighteen, young women and middle-aged men, often from poor districts. Local mosques were used as recruiting and training centres. In March 1982 Basij volunteers were allowed for the first time to fight at the front. During the next year about a fifth of the total force of 2.4 million were posted at or near the battlefronts. Often young Basij members volunteered to act as vanguards in the human wave attacks that the Iranians mounted against the enemy, performing such highly dangerous tasks as removing mines. These teenagers had grown up in an environment of revolutionary turmoil, and were more dedicated to the cause of Islam than most adults.

The government has ensured that the families of those who die for Islam are properly looked after. This job has been assigned to the Martyrs Foundation which is funded generously by the government and affluent religious endowments. Since participation in the struggle against the Pahlavis was regarded by Khomeini to be an Islamic duty, Khomeini established the Martyrs Foundation initially to look after the welfare of the families of those 10,000 to 40,000 Iranians who had died in the revolutionary movement.[53] Following the Gulf War the size and budget of the Martyrs Foundation rose many times.

Unlike the institutions described so far, the Islamic Revolutionary Komitehs were not formally established by Khomeini's decree. They emerged in the heat of the revolutionary struggle. After the revolution they became the guardians of internal security. Later they were given the additional task of enforcing Islamic morality. They had their own armed militia. Following the war the Komitehs were authorized to administer the rationing system. With this, the Komitehs impinged on the life of every family. A local Komiteh works in collaboration with the IRGC unit, the mosques in its area, and the Islamic Associations which exist in all workplaces, schools, universities, hospitals, neighbourhoods and villages.

Following the Islamic revolution the judicial system and laws were changed radically. Islamic revolutionary courts were introduced in the civilian and military sectors. At first these courts dealt with counter-revolutionary activities and such serious offences as espionage and treason. Later, as Islamization got going, they were ordered to deal with moral offences as well as Islamic deviation, described as 'hypocrisy'.

However, once the regime had met the political challenge of the Mujahedin, Khomeini reversed the trend. Following his decree on civil liberties in December 1982, he transferred trials for moral offences from revolutionary courts to public courts, run by the justice ministry. A year later the Supreme Judicial Council decided to abolish the posts of the revolutionary chief justice and prosecutor-general, and placed revolutionary courts under the control of the state chief justice and the prosecutor-general of the justice ministry. The next step may well be to abolish revolutionary courts altogether. The normalization process is likely to be aided by the fact that by the end of 1982 all secular laws had been abrogated, and civil and trade laws as well as the penal code had been Islamized.

The Islamic revolution created a vast economic conglomerate in the form of the Mustazafin Foundation. In the spring of 1983 it owned, partially or wholly, 495 companies, with 200 being manufacturing firms, 250 trading, and forty-

five agro-industrial. With 85,000 employees, the Mustazafin Foundation became the largest employer after the civil
service, the military and the IRGC. Mindful of Khomeini's
directive to meet the needs of the mustazafin, deprived, the
Foundation decided in early 1983 to build 50,000 housing
units in 1984–5 for renting cheaply to the needy. It
dovetailed its plans with those of the housing ministry and
the Housing Foundation, formed after the revolution.

While the Housing Foundation had been given the
specific job of building houses, the task assigned to the
Reconstruction Crusade, formed in June 1979, was to
bridge the gap between town and village. Since half of all
Iranians lived in 65,000 villages,[54] this was a very important
assignment. In practice it meant helping economic development in the countryside, increasing literacy, propagating
Islamic culture and revolution among rural Iranians,
improving communication between villagers and educated
urban dwellers, and providing a constructive channel for
unemployed high school and university graduates. Not
surprisingly, the Crusade set up branches in high schools,
colleges and universities. Crusade members built civil
works – roads, bridges, irrigation works, public baths,
schools, health centres – distributed fertilizers, insecticides,
water pumps and tractors, and gave loans to small farmers.
In February 1984 the Reconstruction Crusade was transformed into a government ministry.

To help the needy in rural areas the regime set up Imam
Khomeini's Relief Committee in early 1979. During the
next five years the committee established 530 branches
covering 40,000 villages, and claimed to have provided
medical, educational and welfare aid to 1.1 million families.[55] Simultaneously, efforts were made to reduce illiteracy
in villages. For this purpose the Reconstruction Crusade
worked in co-ordination with the Special Movement for
Developing Education among the Deprived People, which
was launched in 1980.

All these measures stemmed from the view that an
Islamic regime is wedded to the concepts of social welfare
and uplift of the underprivileged.

In the wake of the cultural revolution initiated by
Khomeini in June 1980 came the University Crusade: it
was meant to rid universities of unIslamic ideologies as
well as staff and students. The 'committed Muslim students' were the Crusade's main force. Long before the
founding of this body they had proved their Islamic zeal by
engaging in pitched battles with their secular and leftist
colleagues.

Once all the 200 universities and colleges had been
closed down in June 1980, the authorities, acting on the
information collected by the University Crusade, dismissed
all those teachers thought to be imbued with eastern or
western ideologies: Marxism, capitalism, nationalism, liberalism, democracy. At the same time Iranian students
were not allowed the facilities of travel documents and
foreign exchange to join western universities.

Composed of seven clerics and scholarly laymen, the
Cultural Revolution Committee (CRC) concentrated on
countering cultural imperialism, whether of the eastern or
western variety, and imbuing universities with Islamic
values. It redesigned curricula; sponsored new textbooks,
or modified the existing ones in the light of Islamic teachings; helped the teaching staff gain a better understanding
of Islam; and replaced western concepts in education with
Islamic ones.

The ulama were active at different levels to help the
CRC. They were intimately involved in the running of the
Centre for Textbooks set up by the CRC. By the spring of
1983 this centre had produced 3,000 textbooks, either
original or in translation. Most of these were on pure
sciences, medicine and engineering: the disciplines where
conflict between published knowledge and Islamic tenets
was minimal. What proved daunting was the programme
of producing textbooks in social sciences which were
imbued with Islamic perspectives and values.

That is why the reopening of universities and colleges,
begun in mid-December 1982, was gradual. When all the
higher education institutions reopened fully in October
1983, they had far fewer students and teachers than before.

But within three years numbers were back to the pre-revolution level.

Schools underwent Islamization earlier and with far less upheaval. Within three years of the revolution, all coeducational schools had been transformed into single-sex schools, and about 40,000 teachers had been purged.[56] New Islamic teaching materials were made available to primary schools within six months of the revolution. Similar speed was shown in furnishing secondary schools with Islamic textbooks. Special stress was put on the teaching of Arabic, the language of the Quran. (Indeed, in an effort to popularize the language, lessons in Arabic were offered on television.) The resulting upsurge in Islamic devotion among teenage boys explained the enthusiasm with which they joined the Basij force and volunteered to fight at the front. In the aftermath of the revolution, Islamic Associations sprung up in all schools. They identified unIslamic teachers and watched suspected dissidents among older students, particularly after the Mujahedin-e Khalq had taken up arms against the state.

Efforts to Islamize such popular institutions as schools, colleges and the military went hand in hand with tackling specific moral ills like prostitution and drugs. The Office for Propagation of Virtue and Prevention of Sin, formed in the wake of the revolution, was in the forefront of stamping out moral degeneracy. In May 1980, at its behest, the red-light district of Tehran was pulled down, and about a thousand prostitutes rehabilitated.

A concerted campaign was conducted to eradicate the consumption of soft and hard drugs. Addiction to heroin was widespead during the Shah's days, with the number of addicts put at between 500,000 and 800,000.[57] Hojatalislam Sadiq Khalkhali, who was assigned the task of solving the drugs problem, resorted to awarding capital punishment to the dealers. Between 21 May and 18 July 1980, he ordered the execution of some 200 drugs traffickers.[58] This was effective. The consumption of drugs dropped dramatically. However, the problem did not disappear altogether.

All these actions by the regime were part of a two-pronged process of Islamization of society: purification and enlightenment. Purification was defined as cleansing the soul of all vice, and enlightenment as removing the ill-effects of all the sins committed so far by an individual. An overall objective of the Islamic government was to make the social environment such that it would offer less and less temptation to the believer to stray from pious living.

In a society where some women are veiled and others not (as was the case during the Pahlavi rule), unveiled women are seen as temptresses, agents of corruption of wholesome family life. So, say Islamists, all women must wear at least a hejab, loose-fitting clothing which hides the outlines of a female figure, and a headscarf. If some women go further and use a chador, shroud, of dark colour, so much the better.

Aware of the religious atmosphere prevalent during Ramadan (starting late June) in 1980, the government ordered on 5 July that all women in government and other public offices must wear a hejab. The order affected about 3 per cent of the urban female population above the age of twelve: the half a million urban women who had jobs formed 9 per cent of the total female population,[59] and a large majority of them worked in small, all-female work-shops or sections of factories. Due to this, and frequent reiteration by the media that prescribing a proper dress for women has the sanction of the Quran, resistance to the official fiat was minimal. Addressing the Friday prayer congregation in Tehran, Hojatalislam Ali Khamanei, the prayer leader, said: 'Hejab is an Islamic duty. Wearing of ornamental trinkets, elaborate hairstyles and make-up is unIslamic.'[60] A year later the Majlis passed the Islamic Dress Law: it applied to all women in Iran, whether Muslim or not. Violation of the law was punishable by a maximum jail sentence of a year.

Following the revolution, the Family Protection Law of 1967/1975, which restricted polygamy and gave women the right to initiate divorce proceedings, was first suspended and then abolished. However, in late 1983, a woman's right to divorce her husband was restored. Contraceptives, considered unIslamic, were banned. There were hundreds of instances of public flogging or execution for adultery. There were also capital and other punishments for homosexuality. These were in accordance with the Quranic verses which described allowable sexual relations, and punishments for transgressing them.

Relationships between men and women must conform to what the Quran has stated. 'Men are managers of the affairs of women: for that God has preferred in bounty one of them over another, and for that they have expended of their property,' reads verse 38 of Chapter IV, 'Women', of the Quran. 'Righteous women are therefore obedient . . . And those you fear may be rebellious, admonish, banish them to their couches, and beat them.'

Women's legal and financial positions are clearly defined by the Quran. 'God charges you, concerning your children: to the male the like of the portion of two females,' reads verse 11 of Chapter IV. 'And call in two witnesses, men; or if the two be not men, then one man and two women, such witnesses as you approve of, that if one of the two women errs the other will remind her,' reads verse 282 of Chapter II, 'The Cow'. Following another Quranic verse, the Islamic regime dismissed all women judges and barred women lawyers from practising.

Great stress is laid on women as mothers. This fits into the long-term goal of the regime to foster a new generation of pure Muslims by providing children with Islamic education at school and an Islamic environment at home, centred round the mother, who is modest in behaviour, faithful to her husband, and always demurely dressed in public.

Islamic principles are also being applied increasingly to the economic aspects of life. The Majlis passed the interest-free banking bill in June 1983. It provided a transition period of eighteen months during which depositors were required to divide up their sums into their bank's two sections: interest-free and term deposit. Once this was done the interest-free section of the bank began lending funds to needy customers without interest, and the term deposit section advanced funds to commercial companies according to Islamic contracts. The profits earned, or the losses incurred, by such loans to these firms were then shared by the depositors. In short, the idea of a fixed interest rate has been replaced by variable profit or loss margins by treating depositors as business partners.

However, some economic problems proved intractable. An example of this was land reform. The Musavi government's effort to implement radical land reform was thwarted by the Council of Guardians. In late 1981 the Majlis passed a bill which, among other things, imposed ceilings on landownership – from five to thirty hectares depending on the quality of land and other factors. But the ulama section of the Council declared the legislation to be unIslamic. It objected to the bill's provision which authorized the state to buy excess land above the ceiling. It argued that the blanket takeover of excess land meant that the state would buy up even the land acquired legitimately by an individual. This would undermine an individual's right to hold property – a right which, according to the Quran, is inviolable. The Guardians' verdict was final. It disappointed those who were committed to the concept of redistribution of wealth under the aegis of Islam. Naturally, it was welcomed by landlords, who owned and managed large holdings, as well as by those bazaar merchants who had bought agricultural land to improve their social standing, and who were absentee landlords. However, the Council of Guardians' decision did not affect the government's policy of reclaiming virgin lands belonging to the state and allotting it to landless peasants.

While these changes were going on apace, efforts were being made continually to create an Islamic ambience in the street, the media and the war front. One way to do this was by painting slogans on street walls. This was done on a vast scale in all Iranian cities and towns by the local Revolutionary Komitehs from a long, official list. Slogans were of three kinds: political, religious and the war effort. The political slogans denounced the regime's external and internal enemies: the USA, the USSR, Israel and the

Hypocrites (meaning Mujahedin). The religious slogans either paid homage to a divine figure or quoted the Quran or Khomeini to denounce or prescribe a certain behaviour. 'Imam Hussein, our third martyr, is the headlight of our rescue vessel,' is an example of the former.[61] Those pertaining to the Gulf War were full of confidence: 'War, war until victory'; or simply, 'Islam is victory.'

The mass media are helped in creating an Islamic ambience by the proliferation of Islamic events throughout the year, not to mention the daily prayers which are strictly observed on radio and television. Besides the whole month of Ramadan, there are ten days of Muharram, the six-day-long hajj pilgrimage, the birthdays of Prophet Muhammad and twelve Imams, and the two joyous eids, religious festivals. To this must be added the events of Iran's revolutionary Islam: ten days of celebration of the revolution, a week of commemoration of the Gulf War and the founding days of the Islamic Republic, the IRGC, the Basij, the Reconstruction Crusade and so on.

A believer had an opportunity to involve himself in the Islamic process by joining the Islamic Association at work or in the neighbourhood. These Associations performed many functions including identifying unIslamic elements in society, aiding the war effort, strengthening Islamic culture, and encouraging voter participation in elections and referendums.

In all these activities the ulama were in the forefront. They were now more numerous than ever before. Estimates of qualified clerics varied from 90,000 to 120,000.[62] In addition there was an unknown number of unqualified village preachers, prayer leaders, theological school teachers and procession organizers. To the important theological colleges in Qom, Mashhad, Tabriz, Isfahan, Shiraz and Yazd was added, in October 1983, the Imam Sadiq University in Tehran. The number of theology students trebled from the pre-revolution figure of 10,000.[63]

The number of mosques reached 22,000 in 1981, with urban mosques nearly doubling their pre-revolution total of 5,600. Some of these were newly built while others were created out of old property. Besides being the place for religious activities, larger mosques became centres for food and fuel rationing systems, consumer co-operative stores, recruitment for the IRGC and the Basij, collections for the war effort, teaching of Arabic, and offering interest-free loans to those in dire need. At the time of elections mosques were often used as polling stations.

Following the example of Prophet Muhammad, Khomeini set up his residence and administrative offices around a mosque in Jamran, a north Tehran suburb. As the marja-e mutlaq he stood at the apex of the religious network in which the local Friday prayer leader is a key figure. Every Friday this cleric delivers the main sermon which covers not only religious subjects but also political and social issues. In the main he supports official decisions, and galvanizes public opinion behind the Islamic government. Important excerpts from the Friday sermons in Tehran are broadcast on television nationally. Under Khomeini's overall guidance Friday sermons have become highly political. Khomeini, who has the authority to appoint or dismiss a Friday prayer leader, receives periodic reports from them on the mood prevalent in their cities or towns.

As the marja-e mutlaq Khomeini delivers periodic religious judgements on matters of import. He also looks after the religious welfare of the faithful. For instance, he instructed the Hajj Pilgrimage Committee in 1983 to provide funds to those poor Muslims who could not afford the journey to Mecca and Medina on their own. Since the revolution the number of hajj pilgrims has risen remarkably. In 1984 the figure was nearly 150,000 compared to 39,296 eight years earlier[64].

The Islamization process and the rise of revolutionary organizations have affected the lives of all Iranians. Most of them have either backed the change or gone along with it. A minority, consisting largely of upper-middle and upper classes, has grumbled about the onset of Islamic values and behaviour. Its strength is estimated to be about half a million families. They are almost invariably related to the 1.5 million Iranian exiles settled in the West. They stayed behind not because they sympathized with the Islamic revolution but because they wanted to safeguard their valuable properties. As long as there was a brother or sister, or a son or daughter, present in Iran, the properties of the whole family were safe from the threat of confiscation.

After the initial period of turmoil and revolutionary justice, the government decided not to continue pressuring the secular rich for a variety of reasons. They had been deprived of the political power they wielded during the Pahlavi era, and had more or less accepted their changed fortunes. Any pressure on them would negate the government's efforts to attract skilled Iranians living abroad, it was felt in official circles. Finally, the authorities felt confident that by Islamizing education they had sown the seeds of a process which would mature into conflict between children and their unIslamic parents. So the future was decidedly loaded against those unwilling to Islamize themselves.

For the present the secular upper-middle and upper classes found much for which to feel alienated from the regime: restrictions on women's dress in the street; the continued ban on music and dancing in public; the propagandistic output of radio, television and the press; the absence of good restaurants and places of public entertainment; and a constant fear of reprisals if they expressed their disenchantment too loudly or too often. At the same time they seemed to overlook a crucial fact: the Islamic regime upheld the right to property as inviolable. This meant that the wealthy were free to rent houses and flats, buy and sell properties, and receive dividends on investments and bank deposits.

The regime took steps to ensure a smooth transition after Khomeini's death. In November 1985 the Assembly of Experts resolved by a large majority that 'As the sole manifestation of the first part of Article 107 of the constitution, Ayatollah Hussein Ali Montazeri is acceptable to an overwhelming majority of the people for future Leadership.'[65] One of the factors that recommended Montazeri to high office was that he had actively opposed the Shah and suffered imprisonment and torture, something that could not be said of such senior clerics as Ayatollahs Marashi-Najafi and Golpaygani. Born in 1921, Montazeri was nineteen years younger than Khomeini, and had been his student in Qom. The campaign to popularize Montazeri had begun in the spring of 1982. Within a year his bespectacled face appeared as frequently on television screens as did Khomeini's, although less prominently. In all government offices Khomeini's portraits were accompanied by those of Montazeri. Iranian leaders wanted to settle the succession while Khomeini was still alive with a view to securing his endorsement, and thus aborting any damaging controversy which might erupt after his death. The November 1985 Experts Assembly decision was seen as an important step towards further stabilizing the Islamic regime. Since October 1981 the country had been ruled by the same leaders as president (Khamanei), prime minister (Musavi) and parliamentary speaker (Hashimi-Rafsanjani) – a fact which reinforced a sense of continuity and order among ordinary Iranians.

Not surprisingly, the Islamic regime began showing signs of normalizing relations with its Gulf neighbours, the only exception being Iraq.

Iran's Revolutionary Islamic Foreign Policy

Iran's foreign policy is guided by the principles outlined in three articles of the constitution, the first of which is pan-Islamic. 'In accordance with the [Quranic] verse "This your nation is a single nation, and I am your Lord, so worship Me," all Muslims form a single nation,' states Article 10. 'The government of the Islamic Republic of Iran has the duty of formulating its general policies with a view to the merging and union of all Muslim peoples, and it must constantly strive to bring about political, economic and cultural unity of the Islamic world.' Article 152 is more specific, and states that the Republic's foreign policy is based inter alia on 'the defence of the rights of all Muslims' and 'non-alignment with respect to the hegemonist superpowers'. Article 154 implicitly sanctifies the concept of export of revolution. 'The Islamic Republic of Iran considers the attainment of independence, freedom and just government to be the right of all peoples in the world,' states this article. '[It] therefore protects the just struggles of the oppressed and deprived in every corner of the globe.'

However, several months before the promulgation of the constitution, Khomeini's regime had declared it to be its 'Islamic duty' to support the national liberation movements of the 'deprived peoples' of the world. 'These liberation movements had stemmed from internal and natural conditions,' explained Ibrahim Yazdi, Iran's foreign minister, in July 1979. 'They only wanted to benefit from Iran's experience [of national liberation] and gain strength from Iran's support.'[66]

Later, as numerous attempts were made by internal and external forces to overthrow the Khomeini regime, Iranian leaders concluded that the arguments for exporting the revolution were not merely ideological but also pragmatic: an effective way to defend the revolution was by going on the offensive, by extending the influence of the revolution abroad. As President Khamanei put it in November 1983, 'If the revolution is kept within Iranian borders, it would become vulnerable.'[67]

There were obvious disadvantages in following this path. Iran's efforts to bolster a revolutionary organization in a foreign country vitiated relations between that state's government and Tehran, and further increased Iran's isolation in the international community. So this course of action proved unpopular with the officials of the foreign ministry headed by Ali Akbar Velayati, a comparative moderate, from November 1980 onwards.

The conflict was resolved by setting up a separate department in the foreign ministry to deal with national liberation movements. Later the functions of this department were taken over by an independent body, the World Organization of the Islamic Liberation Movements, led by Ayatollah Montazeri and based in Qom. Prominent among the affiliates to the World Organization were the Party of the Islamic Call, popularly known as Al Daawa, active in Iraq and Kuwait; the Islamic Liberation Front of Bahrain; the Islamic Revolutionary Organization of the Arabian Peninsula, based in Saudi Arabia; the Party of Allah, Hizbollah, and the Islamic Amal, in Lebanon; and the Army of the Guards, Sejah-e Pasdaran, and the Organization for Victory, Sazman-e Nasr, in Afghanistan.

The Islamic revolutionary parties based in the Gulf states found themselves in tune with the thoughts and actions of Khomeini. They accepted his interpretation of the Quran that hereditary power has no sanction in Islam.[68] They also endorsed his condemnation of the Gulf rulers as corrupt men who foster what Khomeini called 'American Islam' or 'Islam of gold'. He was scathing about their policy of depleting the valuable oil resources of their countries to satisfy the ever-growing demands of America, which he routinely described as the Great Satan, the prime source of corruption on earth. Khomeini denounced them for denying their subjects any role in the decision-making processes of the state. The creation of a representative system in Iran, with a popularly elected president and parliament, made his arguments for republicanism attractive to many in the Gulf kingdoms.

Khomeini's message proved particularly attractive to the Shia masses and ulama in the Gulf. This made Bahrain the most vulnerable to revolutionary upheaval. While 60 per cent of its 400,000 inhabitants were Shia, it had been ruled since 1783 by the Sunni Khalifa family. The current ruler, Shaikh Issa ibn Salman al Khalifa, had dissolved the elected national assembly and suspended the constitution in August 1975, and driven all opposition underground. The Iranian revolution in early 1979 buoyed the opposition. Aware of the popularity of Khomeini and the Islamic revolution among the Shia majority, the ruler banned all news on the subject. The security forces broke up a demonstration on Jerusalem Day (15 May) with 900 arrests. Undaunted, forty leading ulama issued a twelve-point charter demanding among other things an Islamic republic in Bahrain. The ruler responded by suppressing demonstrations by students and others in support of the charter, and expelling Sayyid Hadi al Modaresi, an eminent Shia leader.

With the seizure of American hostages in Tehran in November 1979, political tensions in the region sharpened. It was against this background that the information ministers of the Gulf states met in Riyadh and decided on guidelines for the state-controlled and state-guided media regarding the Iranian revolution. These guidelines stressed 'playing down the news from Tehran' and demoting 'the Iranian revolution from the status of an all-Muslim one to a purely Shia one, and then to downgrade it to a purely Iranian Shia one'.[69]

It was significant that Saudi Arabia was the main force behind calling this conference and shaping its outcome. It had just experienced pro-Khomeini demonstrations and riots by its Shia citizens in the oil-rich province of Hasa, not to mention the seizure of the Grand Mosque in Mecca by militant fundamentalists. This had made Saudi leaders extremely security-conscious and led them to seek internal security pacts with Kuwait, Bahrain, Qatar, the United Arab Emirates and Oman. The outbreak of the Gulf War in September 1980 gave urgency to this proposition. The Saudis were advised by Britain and France to create a supra-national body of the Gulf states which could call on the West for military assistance in case of serious internal or external threat to one or more of its members. It was thus that, in the wake of Iran's Islamic revolution and the Gulf War, the Gulf Co-operation Council (GCC) came into being in May 1981 with the objectives of co-ordinating internal security, procurement of arms and the national economies of the six member states: Saudi Arabia, Kuwait, Bahrain, Qatar, the UAE and Oman.

Anti-Tehran feeling reached a peak in the region in January 1982 when the Bahraini government arrested sixty people on charges of plotting a coup. It alleged that they had been trained by Sayyid Hadi al Moderasi, leader of the Islamic Liberation Front of Bahrain, who after his expulsion from Bahrain had based himself in Iran. The Bahraini prime minister stated, 'The Iranian regime is instigating the Shias in Bahrain and the Gulf under the slogans of the Islamic revolution . . . training them in the use of weapons and acts of sabotage and sending them to their countries [of origin] to foment chaos and destroy security.'[70] Prince Nayif, the Saudi interior minister, rushed to the Bahraini capital, Manama, and offered to send Saudi troops. 'The sabotage plot was engineered by the Iranian government and was directed against Saudi Arabia,' he said.[71] Clearly, in the face of subversion encouraged by Iran's revolutionary leadership, the Gulf monarchs were drawing closer together in order to retain their authoritarian status. They also felt that any sign of sharing sovereignty with their subjects would be seen as weakness, and so they clung to their monopoly of political power.

None the less, they had to take into account the balance of forces in the region: this was being settled by the developments in the Iran–Iraq War. As Iran began to score victories on the battlefield in the spring of 1982, GCC members paid close attention to what Tehran said or did. It was a prime objective of the Islamic Republic to wean the Gulf monarchs away from the American camp. Khomeini called on the Gulf states to abandon their 'obedience to the US and [other] international predators'. Addressing the people of the Gulf he stated, 'The people and government of Iran want to free you of the disgraceful load of being under the control of the superpowers. These powers want to force your black gold [i.e. oil] out of your throats.'[72]

Afraid of further gains in the war and their adverse impact on the stability of their regimes, GCC ministers, meeting in Riyadh on 2 June 1982, offered a peace plan: an immediate ceasefire, withdrawal of the parties to the 1975 treaty borders, negotiations to resolve the outstanding issues, and establishment of the Gulf Reconstruction Fund, to be financed by GCC members, to compensate Iran and Iraq for their war damages. But this effort was swept aside by the Israeli invasion of Lebanon a few days later.

Iran's advance into Iraq in July and its threat to block the Hormuz Straits the following month distressed GCC countries. In September the Arab League, composed of twenty-two members, adopted the earlier GCC peace plan. Tehran rejected it, and kept up its offensives against Iraq, which was being heftily aided, financially and logistically, by Saudi Arabia and Kuwait. Khomeini continued to appeal to the Gulf states in the name of the faith. 'Islamic Iran is ready to help the countries of the region in their liberation and salvation from the arrogant (alien) forces,' he said in an interview with the Tehran-based Voice of the Gulf Radio, in June 1983. 'We believe that the superpowers led by the US are trying to prevent the unity of Islamic countries, especially in this sensitive region of the world.'[73]

But the reasons for the split in Islamic ranks in the Gulf, and elsewhere, lay in Tehran's actions – so argued the Saudi government and media. 'Ever since the Iranian and Islamic peoples were afflicted by the Khomeini regime, this regime has failed to render any noteworthy service to Islam, and to Muslims,' said *Al Medina*, a Saudi daily, in July. 'This regime has tried to create schism among Muslims, not only in their politics but also in their mosques. The Khomeini regime sends its agents everywhere to foment discord.'[74]

Here were two fundamentalist states, deriving their inspiration from Islamic scriptures and basing their legitimacy on Islam, exchanging diatribes – the newer one, Iran, accusing the older of deviation from the faith, and the established, conservative polity condemning the revolutionary upstart for trying to create chaos in Muslim countries in the name of furthering the cause of Islam.

As the Gulf War entered its fourth year in late September 1983, Riyadh Radio announced that a joint military exercise by GCC forces would be conducted in the UAE desert in early October, a measure necessitated by 'the worrying and complex events as a result of the Iraq–Iran War and the situation in Lebanon'. It was reported elsewhere that the forces participating in the exercise would form the nucleus of the Rapid Deployment Force of the GCC. 'Who will the Rapid Deployment Force of the GCC confront?' asked Tehran Radio's Arabic service on 26 September

1983. 'Just as the formation of the GCC was intended to confront the Islamic tide, it is equally true that these exercises have the same purpose.'

One way Iran could retaliate against this was by intensifying its support for the Islamic liberation movements in GCC countries. In any case, there were periodic reports of Iranian agents landing secretly on the beaches of Bahrain and Kuwait, where 30 per cent of the 700,000 nationals were Shia. In the mind of the Sunni majority in Kuwait, Iran and Shia had become synonymous: both were considered dangerous and destabilizing. 'The Iranian revolution does not seem to accept the legitimacy of our system of government,' stated a Kuwaiti minister in early December. 'It exports Shiaism in the guise of pan-Islam.'[75] The government began to dismiss Shias from sensitive positions in the police and military.

On 12 December bombs exploded in the US and French embassies, in an American residential complex accommodating US missiles experts and at Kuwait airport. The government arrested eighteen Kuwaiti residents of Iraqi and Lebanese nationalities: they were reported to be members of Al Daawa of Iraq, known to have ties with the Qom-based World Organization of Islamic Liberation Movements. Alleging that these explosions were directed by the Iranian government, Iraq attacked five Iranian towns with ground-to-ground missiles. Such reprisals only steeled Tehran's resolve to continue the armed conflict.

With Iran showing no signs of stopping the war, the mood in the Gulf capitals became increasingly despondent. Iran's seizure of the oil-rich Majnoon Islands of Iraq in its offensive of February 1984 made GCC members realize that time was working against Iraq. GCC ministers, meeting in Riyadh in mid-March, made an attempt to mediate in the conflict. As before it was in vain.

All along, communication lines between Tehran and Riyadh remained open, mainly because Saudi Arabia was duty-bound to let in Iranian pilgrims for the hajj every year. Riyadh and Tehran disagreed on the right of pilgrims to shout slogans in favour of Islamic unity and against the enemies of Islam – America, the Soviet Union and Israel – with Riyadh insisting that using hajj for political purposes contravened Prophet Muhammad's injunctions to the believers to refrain from ill-temper, bad manners and violence during the holy pilgrimage. After protracted discussions, and violence between Iranian pilgrims and Saudi security forces, the matter was resolved in 1983, when Riyadh allowed Iranian pilgrims to raise slogans against the enemies of Islam at certain venues in Mecca and Medina. Having made this concession the Saudis thought it opportune to improve relations with Tehran. In mid-July the Saudi Hajj Office invited Hashimi-Rafsanjani to pilgrimage, due in September. Acknowledging the invitation the Iranian leader said, 'Such journeys could be useful.'

A few weeks later Khomeini publicly expressed disappointment at Iran's isolation. 'We have no more friends than can be counted on the fingers of one hand,' he said.[76] Two months later he declared that it was against 'reason and the Sharia' not to have relations with most countries.

Apparently Khomeini felt that Iran needed to channel all its energies to the overriding objective of toppling the Iraqi president Saddam Hussein by ending less significant disputes with the Gulf states. Still another factor to propel Khomeini and his lieutenants towards a pragmatic stance was the growing realization among them that there was much merit in balancing intransigence on the battlefield with flexibility in diplomatic and commercial links with Iran's neighbours.

Also there had been a natural cooling of the revolutionary fervour in Tehran while the confidence of the Gulf rulers in the durability of their dynasties, badly shaken in the early days of the Iranian revolution, had revived. Having weathered the squalls of Islamic republicanism in the wake of the Iranian revolution, the Gulf monarchs felt secure enough to normalize relations with Tehran. Also, much to their relief, the nightmarish scenario of the blocking of the Hormuz Straits had not materialized. What was more, they did not think it would. For they seemed to trust Iran when it said that it wanted to keep the waterway open.

This was the background against which the Saudi foreign minister, Prince Saud al Faisal, visited Tehran in May 1985 and met President Khamanei. Though the ceasefire in the Gulf War during the month of Ramadan he was seeking did not materialize, his initiative established dialogue at the highest level.

In December 1985 the Iranian foreign minister, Velayati, returned the Saudi visit. In Riyadh he met his counterpart a well as King Fahd. According to the Islamic Republic News Agency, King Fahd said that his country respected the Iranian nation and its leaders, and that the former regime (of the Shah) had been neglectful of Islam. Stressing the need for unity among Muslims, Fahd stated that both Iran and Saudi Arabia could play an important role in strengthening Muslim unity. In reply Velayati declared that 'peaceful co-existence with its neighbours' was an important principle of Iran's foreign policy.[77] The subsequent stoppage of hostile broadcasts by the two governments was a further sign of improvement in mutual relations. This well reflected the softened stance that Khomeini had adopted on the concept of 'export of our revolution', an idea to which he expressed his continued commitment. Addressing Iranian ambassadors on 2 November he said, 'The export of revolution is not one of military expedition. We want to convey to the world our views.'[78]

Iran improved ties with all the Gulf states except Kuwait. Indeed, Tehran's relations with Kuwait turned bitter in May 1985, when a group of Islamic fundamentalists of Lebanese and Iraqi origin made an unsuccessful attempt to assassinate the Kuwaiti ruler. Iran denied any involvement. Yet Iranian residents became the prime target for deportation by the Kuwaiti government.

The successful offensive by Iran in February 1986 in the Fao peninsula of Iraq in the extreme south made Kuwait particularly nervous. Kuwait condemned the Iranian assault, put its forces on alert and further strengthened its links with Iraq.

As Iranians prepared to celebrate the seventh anniversary of the founding of the Islamic Republic on 1 April 1986, Khomeini gave one of his strongest calls for the mobilization of all able-bodied men and the continuation of the war until the fall of Saddam Hussein. Describing the US as Iran's 'arch-enemy', Premier Musavi said, 'We will continue the struggle against America in Iran, in the Gulf region and throughout the world.'[79]

In the face of such determination Saudi Arabia considered it wise to continue its policy of mending its fences with Iran. This became apparent at the meeting of the Organization of Petroleum Exporting Countries (OPEC) in August. Saudi Arabia sided with Iran on a plan to lower quotas for its members, thus reversing its long-established policy of standing apart from Iran at OPEC conferences. On the eve of the October 1986 OPEC meeting the Iranian oil minister visited Riyadh and had 'brotherly talks' with King Fahd. As a result the Iranian-inspired ceiling on oil output was extended at the OPEC conference. More importantly, King Fahd sacked Shaikh Ahmad Zaki Yamani, the pro-American Saudi oil minister for twenty-four years, for his lack of enthusiasm for the Iranian strategy of raising the oil price by curtailing production.

Soon after, King Fahd made a symbolic, but highly significant, ideological concession to Tehran. As a gesture of goodwill to the republican Iran, King Fahd ordered that instead of 'His Majesty' he should henceforth be addressed as 'The Custodian of the Holy Shrines', the shrines being those in Mecca and Medina. This gesture was well received in Tehran.

Iran would have liked Riyadh to side with it in its demand that the venue of the forthcoming summit of the Islamic Conference Organization be shifted from Kuwait, a state closely aligned with its foe in the Gulf War. It was disappointed. The ICO meeting was held in Kuwait in late January 1987 under extremely tight security. The summit passed a resolution calling for a ceasefire in the Iran–Iraq War but, in a departure from its past practice, it did not send a delegation to the two warring capitals, thus sparing Tehran the odium of once again rejecting ICO advice.

However, given the crucial logistic and financial backing that Kuwait provided to Iraq, Iran made Kuwaiti ships the main target of its attacks in the Gulf. To secure protection for its oil tankers Kuwait approached the five permanent members of the UN Security Council: America, the Soviet Union, Britain, France and China. The Soviets agreed to lease three of their own tankers to Kuwait. The US followed with an arrangement whereby eleven Kuwaiti tankers were to be re-registered as American ships to qualify for protection by the US navy. An allegedly accidental missile attack on an American frigate by Iraq in late May 1987 was used by Washington to bolster the US military presence in the Gulf from four to fifteen warships, with plans to raise it further to forty. Tehran interpreted the American move as a ploy to intervene on behalf of Iraq in order to deprive it of its expected victory in the Gulf War. The dramatically increased American naval presence bolstered the confidence of the pro-Western Gulf monarchies, particularly Saudi Arabia. Iran condemned the American action vehemently, and reaffirmed its stance: security of the Gulf is the responsibility of the regional states, and all foreign powers must withdraw from the Gulf. Tension between Tehran and Washington escalated when, on 24 July, a reflagged American/Kuwaiti oil tanker, escorted by US warships, hit a mine (presumably laid by Iran) on its way to Kuwait.

It was against this background that 1.5 million foreign Muslims, including 155,000 from Iran, arrived in Mecca for the annual hajj – a six-day ritual – beginning on 31 July. A few days before the hajj Khomeini delivered a long speech in which he issued guidelines to the pilgrims. He combined the political message of 'Islamic unity against the superpowers' with the religious theme of 'disavowal of the infidels', one of the main pillars of monotheism, which the believer is enjoined to practise during the hajj. Khomeini urged the pilgrims to bear witness to 'the disavowal of the infidels headed by the criminal America' with as much ceremony as possible in the form of demonstrations and marches. His speech was broadcast several times daily at the vast compound accommodating the Iranian pilgrims in Mecca.

As in the past, the Saudi hajj minister and the leader of the Iranian pilgrims, Hojatalislam Mahdi Karoubi, worked out the details of the Iranian demonstration and procession as well as the contents of the slogans and banners. As before, there were to be three slogans against the satanical powers – America, the Soviet Union and Israel – and three for the oppressed Muslims: those in Afghanistan, Palestine and Lebanon. The demonstration was to be held in mid-afternoon for two hours at the Iranian hajj mission in Mecca, followed by a march of about half a mile to a square situated a mile from the Grand Mosque, with the dispersal of the marchers accomplished by sundown, around 7.15 P.M.

On 31 July, Friday, the demonstration occurred peacefully. But when the vanguard of the procession of some 100,000 Iranians, and 1,000 non-Iranians, led by women and invalid pilgrims in wheelchairs, was about 500 yards from the previously agreed termination point, it was blocked by Saudi police. Tempers flared and a riot broke out. When the marchers tried to retreat they found their exits blocked by the police. The riot lasted an hour, during which time the marchers were subjected to police clubs, tear gas and rubber bullets. Gunshots were heard too. As a result of the action by riot police and the stampede caused by it, hundreds of pilgrims and others died.[80]

According to Riyadh, the Iranians mounted a sacrilegious political demonstration and then stampeded, causing 402 people – 275 Iranian and 42 non-Iranian pilgrims, and 85 Saudi nationals – to die from suffocation and crushing in the ensuing panic. According to Tehran, however, armed Saudi police opened fire on pilgrims in an unprovoked assault which resulted in the deaths of 322 Iranians, many of them hit by bullets.

Voicing the official Iranian reaction to the Mecca tragedy, Hashimi-Rafsanjani said: 'We, as soldiers of God and executioners of divine principles, pledge ourselves to avenge the martyrs as soon as possible.' He declared that Iran would 'free the holy shrines from the mischievous and wicked Wahhabis'. Khomeini saw the hand of America behind the actions of 'those devious people, the ring-leaders of Saudi Arabia, the traitors of the holy shrines'. The Iranian leadership mounted a campaign against the Saudi rulers with the mourners chanting, 'Cut off King Fahd's hands.' The correspondents of Iran's Islamic Republic News Agency interviewed scores of non-Iranian pilgrims as they returned to their home countries about the events of the 'Bloody Friday' in Mecca with a view to proving that the Iranian pilgrims had behaved correctly and that it was the Saudi police which had mounted a pre-planned attack on them. The delegations despatched by Tehran to several Muslim countries made much use of these testimonials in order to convince their hosts that the fault lay solely with Saudi leaders for the Mecca tragedy.

On their part the Saudi authorities maintained that the deaths had been caused by a stampede and that the Iranian pilgrims were guilty of dual sacrilege: they had broken the Quranic injunction against violent or ill-tempered behaviour during the hajj, and they had tried to take pictures of Khomeini into the Grand Mosque, which had been free of statues and images since the day Prophet Muhammad had caused all idols around the Kaaba to be broken. There were further hints of an Iranian plot to take over the Grand Mosque and declare Khomeini the leader of all Muslims.

In reality the tragedy was probably caused by the convergence of two factors: the absence of the Iranian leaders at the front of the pilgrims' procession, a situation conducive to a violent flare-up; and the decision by the Saudi authorities, angered and exasperated by the recurrent Iranian demonstrations, to teach the disruptive Iranians a lesson.

Be that as it may, the Mecca killings ended the three-year-old rapprochement between Tehran and Riyadh. The two fundamentalist regimes were now firmly poised in vehement opposition, openly competing for the leadership of the faithful in the Muslim world.

Iran had undergone a similar vicissitude in the larger

context of the Islamic Conference Organisation. Before the Gulf War its regime enjoyed high standing in the ICO. The eleventh ICO foreign ministers' conference in Islamabad, Pakistan, in January 1980 supported the Islamic revolution in Iran and opposed 'the external pressures' being applied to it.[81] The situation changed with the Iraqi attack on Iran. Khomeini expected that the ICO would condemn Iraq for its aggression against another Muslim country. But nothing of the sort happened. On the contrary, the ruler of Saudi Arabia, which housed the ICO headquarters in Jidda, phoned Saddam Hussein to congratulate him on his actions.

At the December 1980 ICO foreign ministers conference in Rabat, Morocco, Iran argued that the item on the agenda for the forthcoming Islamic summit should read 'The Iraqi invasion and occupation of Iran' and not 'The Iraq–Iran War'. It was outvoted. Therefore it boycotted the third ICO summit held in Taif, Saudi Arabia, in January 1981. The conference appointed a nine-member delegation, headed by President Sekou Toure of Guinea, to bring about peace between the belligerents. Khomeini met the ICO delegates on 1 March 1981 but only to call on them to 'sit in judgment on Iraq' and fight whosoever had 'launched the aggression'.[82] Instead, the ICO team, following a visit to Baghdad, offered a peace plan: a ceasefire in a week followed by Iraqi withdrawal from Iran. Not surprisingly, the Supreme Defence Council of Iran rejected the ICO plan, and demanded the overthrow and trial of Saddam Hussein, the infidel aggressor.

The subsequent ICO attempts to mediate in the war were equally futile. Khomeini insisted that the aggressor must be punished to set an example for ICO members not to attack a fellow Muslim state in the future.

In June 1982, following the Israeli invasion of Lebanon, Iraq said that it was ready, in response to the ICO appeal to the belligerents in the Gulf War, to stop fighting and direct its arms against the common enemy of Iran and Iraq: Israel. Khomeini spurned the offer, arguing that Iraq was using the same tactic as Israel – first occupying alien territory and then seeking a ceasefire.

Due to stiff opposition from Tehran, the fourteenth ICO foreign ministers' conference in Dhaka, Bangladesh, in December 1983 failed to adopt a resolution on the Gulf War. Iran boycotted the fourth Islamic summit in Casablanca, Morocco, in January 1984 because the ICO did not send a delegation to Iran to inspect the results of Iraqi bombings of Iran's civilian areas.

When the ICO steering committee failed to shift the venue of the fifth summit from Kuwait, Iran once again boycotted the meeting, and called on others to do so. Those countries sympathetic to Iran responded by sending someone lower than the head of state to the conference.

Behind these moves of Iran's lay something more profound which informed Iranian policies towards other Muslim countries. Iranian leaders believed that it was only in their country that the will of Allah, as expressed through the Quran, was being implemented. A state such as Saudi Arabia was ruled by a monarchical system, which was unIslamic, and by a family most of whose adult members broke the Quranic injunctions on drink, extramarital sex, gambling, etc. In so far as its nationals were Muslim, Saudi Arabia was a Muslim state, but it was not an Islamic one. In Iran, on the other hand, the faithful had struggled in their millions to overthrow a corrupt, unIslamic regime and institute a government of God. Iran therefore provided a model for people in other Muslim countries to follow.

Such an assessment of their revolution and country made the Iranian leaders self-righteous. If this had isolated Iran in the community of Muslim countries, Iranians should not feel dejected by it, they argued. The faithful must look at the life of Imam Ali. He was a perfect Muslim. Yet he was ignored and made to suffer. But ultimately the umma realized his worth and elected him the successor to Prophet Muhammad. Like a true Muslim the Islamic Republic must stay firmly on a correctly interpreted Islamic path. Ultimately others will see the correctness of its policies and come round to its views and interpretations. It was a matter of faith, correct interpretation of the Quran, perseverance and time.

The Iranian leaders see their country as a pace-setter in re-creating a model Islamic society, and feel that their progress along this path is of general interest to Muslims everywhere, and of particular interest to the inhabitants of the forty-three other member-states of the ICO. They have shown that by carrying out an Islamic revolution they have ousted a corrupt ruling élite, freed their country from the domination of a superpower, and reclaimed its national independence. These achievements are highly valued in many Third World capitals, which find the choice of linking up with the Soviet or the American bloc incompatible with their newly acquired political independence. What Iran has shown to the Muslim states of the Third World is the Third Way of Islam, quite apart from the eastern or western path. In a world riven with superpower rivalries and tensions, it is an attractive proposition. When it is combined with the moral intransigence and radical anti-imperialism of a Khomeini, the mixture becomes irresistible, particularly to the young and educated in many Muslim states. Following Khomeini's line means not only rejecting the rise of capitalism, with its concomitant corruption, but also (atheistic) Marxism. This explains why it has followers everywhere in the Muslim world.

Islamic Iran tried to consolidate its support among Muslims abroad. The secretariat of Friday prayer leaders in Qom was used to maintain contacts with the ulama throughout the world. As it was, Qom had the distinction of seeing one of its local clerics, Imam Musa Sadr, become a leading religious–political figure abroad in the 1960s. He was sent to Lebanon in 1957 to offer religious guidance to Lebanese Shias who had been the poorest and most exploited group in Lebanon. As a result of his condemnation of the Shah's suppression of the June 1963 uprising in Iran, Sadr was deprived of his Iranian nationality. He became a Lebanese citizen. Four years later he formed the Higher Shia Communal Council under his leadership. He founded the Movement of the Deprived which attracted

Shias, dissatisfied as they were with their traditional, pro-establishment leaders. Being over 30 per cent of the Lebanese population of 3.6 million, Shias were the largest community, more numerous than the 900,000 Maronite Christians. Yet the National Pact, based on the 1932 census, gave Shias only nineteen parliamentary seats to the Maronites' thirty in a house of ninety-nine. In the 1930s Shias were concentrated in southern Lebanon, where they had arrived from adjoining areas several centuries ago to escape the persecution which followed the collapse of the Fatimid caliphate. Political convulsions in the Lebanon of the 1950s caused them to move north, to Sidon and Beirut, a trend which was strengthened by the 1967 Arab–Israeli war. Through strikes and demonstrations Musa Sadr made Shias aware of their political strength. But when a civil war between rightist Maronite Christians and an alliance of leftist Lebanese and Palestinians erupted in Lebanon in April 1975 the Shias found themselves in a weak position, because they lacked a militia of their own. With the assistance of Al Fatah, a Palestinian organization in Lebanon, Musa Sadr established a Shia militia called Al Amal, The Hope.

Throughout his stay in Lebanon, Sadr was in touch with Khomeini, who was his close friend. Not surprisingly, Lebanese Shias watched with growing interest the rise of the revolutionary movement in Iran under Khomeini. But Sadr did not live to see it succeed. During a trip to Libya and Italy in late August 1978 he 'disappeared'.

Following Sadr's death, leadership of the Higher Shia Communal Council passed to Shaikh Muhammad Mahdi Shams al Din. The Amal Congress of April 1980 elected a new Leadership Council, with Nabih Berri, a lawyer, as the general secretary. Under him the Amal expanded and became one of the most important fighting forces. In October 1981 an Amal delegation visited Tehran and had a meeting with President Khamanei.

However, Berri's policies were considered too constitutionalist by some of his colleagues, particularly Hussein Musavi, a young teacher. Musavi left the Amal to form the

Islamic Amal with its headquarters in Baalbek in the Syrian-controlled Bekaa valley. Baalbek was also the centre of the Hizbollahis of Lebanon, led by Shaikh Muhammad Hassan Fadlollah and Shaikh Ragheb Harb. Later it was in Baalbek that Iranian revolutionary guards were to set up their offices in order to repulse the June 1982 Israeli invasion of Lebanon.

Baalbek was reported to be the centre of the Islamic Jihad, a shadowy organization which claimed responsibility for the bombing of American and French barracks in Beirut in late October 1983, and a similar attack on the Israeli headquarters in Tyre on 4 November. In retaliation Israeli and French warplanes raided Baalbek on 20 November. Of the forty-four people killed, fourteen were Iranian revolutionary guards.

This set off a fresh cycle of violence and counter-violence, leading to an intensification of hit-and-run attacks on Israeli forces in south Lebanon, where 60 per cent of the 1 million inhabitants were Shia. On 3 and 4 January sixteen Israeli warplanes bombed Baalbek and two adjoining villages, killing nearly 100 people and injuring 400, most of them civilians. Two days later Hussein Shaikholislami, an Iranian deputy foreign minister, visited Baalbek. In his statements he was reported to have praised suicide bomb attacks on American, French and Israeli troops. This was taken to be an affirmation of the earlier allegations by the US, French, Israeli and Lebanese intelligence officials that Iran was masterminding suicide assaults in conjunction with Syria.

Tehran denied these charges, and replied that the western powers and Israel were looking for excuses for the failure of their policies in Lebanon: a Muslim majority country ruled by a Maronite Christian minority allied to the West and Israel. Ayatollah Hadi Khosrowshahi, the Iranian ambassador to the Vatican, explained the religio-political context of suicide attacks. Arguing that the Muslim peoples of Iran, Afghanistan, Palestine and Lebanon had the right to defend their 'freedom, faith, honour and independence from the aggressor' by 'whatever means they see fit', he said: 'This honourable defence is a right for every free human being, and dying in this noble cause in our view is martyrdom in the way of God.'[83]

Soon Lebanese Shias showed themselves to be well-versed in conventional means of fighting as well. When President Amin Gemayal's order to the Lebanese army to flatten the Shia suburbs in south Beirut was carried out on 3 February 1984, Berri ordered the Amal militia to attack the army. Aided by the militia of the Druze Progressive Socialist Party, operating mainly from the adjoining Shouf mountains, the Amal captured West Beirut, and dealt Gemayal's army and administration a body-blow. The Lebanese army disintegrated and the government collapsed. The success of the Muslim forces, supported by Syria, over the Gemayal administration, backed by the US and Israel, pleased Tehran as much as it did Damascus.

Tehran saw the victory of Lebanese Muslims in the Beirut area as a step towards the expulsion of the Israelis from south Lebanon. The escalating attacks on Israeli forces in southern Lebanon by the members of the Amal, Islamic Amal and Hizbollah, among others, led to the withdrawal of Israel from Lebanon in June 1985. Encouraged by this, Iran and its Lebanese allies resolved to carry on the struggle to achieve their final goal of liberating Jerusalem, the city of the Holy Rock, the site to which Prophet Muhammad miraculously flew by night and was escorted up a staircase of light by the archangel Gabriel to receive divine instructions for his followers, the event heralding his prophethood.

The liberation of Jerusalem from its Zionist usurpers is a goal that is universally shared and reaffirmed by the delegates of more than forty countries who attend the annual World Congress of Friday Prayer Leaders in Iran. During their visit to the Islamic Republic these delegates are exposed to the Islamic and other achievements of the revolutionary regime. It is significant that while the Saudi-sponsored ICO stays in touch with Muslim countries at state level, Iran has opted for contacts outside official circles. Through the World Congress Iranian leaders attempt to create and sustain goodwill towards their Islamic revolution in the religious quarters of Muslim societies abroad.

The perseverance and energy with which Iran has pursued its war with Iraq's Saddam Hussein has given succour to pro-Iranian elements among Muslims everywhere. For its part the Iranian regime constantly reiterates the Islamic nature of the struggle. It always refers to its forces as 'combatants of Islam'. The new corps it has raised in the course of the war are named after Prophet Muhammad, Mahdi and Khomeini. Almost always it names its war offensives after Islamic personalities, places or rituals: Ashura, Karbala, Muslim ibn Aqil, Ramadan al Mubarak (the Blessed Ramadan), Bait al Muqaddas (The Sacred House, i.e. Jerusalem) and Tariq al Quds (The Road to Jerusalem).

The references to Jerusalem reinforce Tehran's assertion that the struggle to overthrow the unIslamic regime in Baghdad is a step towards the liberation of Jerusalem and Palestine from their Zionist occupiers. By so doing Iran pressures the (Muslim) Arab states to sharpen and heighten their endeavours to bring about the overthrow of Zionism in Palestine. It also helps Iran to place the Palestinian issue in a global context of Islam rather than merely in an Arab framework.

There is no doubt that, were Tehran to succeed in causing the overthrow of Saddam Hussein, pressures on Arab states, aided by a victorious Iran, would mount to confront Israel militarily.

While addressing foreign policy problems along its western border and beyond, Iran has not neglected its eastern frontier. There it has been assisting Afghan Islamic guerrillas fighting the Marxist regime in Kabul since early 1980.

7

AFGHANISTAN: CHANGING FORTUNES
OF FUNDAMENTALISM

Special geographical and historical circumstances shaped Afghanistan into a landlocked society which clung to medieval Islam and tenaciously resisted modernization well into the last quarter of the twentieth century. The present state of Afghanistan, the Land of Afghans, was created out of numerous tribal fiefdoms in the mid-nineteenth century as a buffer between Russia, British India and Iran by imperial Britain and Tsarist Russia.

As for historic Afghanistan, it became part of Dar al Islam with the rise of the Abbasid caliphate in 750. The weakening of the caliphate, which followed a century later, led to the emergence of semi-independent dynasties which ruled Iran, Afghanistan and parts of central Asia. The most prominent of these was the Ghori dynasty (1000–1215), which ruled present-day Pakistan, much of Afghanistan and eastern Iran. In the first quarter of the sixteenth century Zahir al Din Muhammad Babar, a descendant of Jenghiz Khan and Timur Lang, seized a territory in Afghanistan and governed it from Kabul. In 1525 he ventured out to India and established the Mogul dynasty. From then on the Mogul and Safavid empires competed for the control of Afghanistan. In 1729 Nadir Shah Afshar, having expelled the Afghan tribes from Iran, went on to subdue Qandhar in southern Afghanistan. He was assassinated in 1747 by Abdali Afghans, centred around Qandhar, who chose Ahmad Shah Abdali as their leader. On assuming power he took the title of Durr-e Durran, Pearl of the Age, which became transformed into Durrani. He seized parts of the decadent Safavid and Mogul empires, and added to them bits of Tajik territory in the north. In 1776 the capital was moved from Qandhar to Kabul. The new political entity was shaken by a civil war which lasted from 1818 to 1826.

Later, rivalry between Britain and Tsarist Russia led to two wars between Afghanistan and British India: in 1839–42 and 1878–80. The occupation of eastern Afghanistan, which followed the First Anglo-Afghan War, was resisted by the Afghans. In the wake of the second war the British left, but kept control of Afghanistan's foreign relations. The overall result of these conflicts was to engender a sense of Afghan identity as well as to isolate Afghanistan politically and diplomatically. Furthermore, the bloody experience made the traditional tribal and Islamic leaders view all reform and modernization as western innovations which had to be resisted.

It was against this background that Abdur Rahman assumed power in 1880. Starting with firm control of Kabul and its environs, he staged several campaigns to subdue the Pushtun tribes in the south and south-east, and then the Uzbek and Turkoman tribes in the north. In 1888 when Shia Hazaras, who over the centuries had been pushed into the inhospitable Hazarajat mountains, rebelled, Abdur Rahman rallied Pushtun, Uzbek and Turkoman tribes under the banner of Sunni Islam, and subdued the Hazaras in 1891. Four years later he seized Kafiristan, Land of the Infidel, to the east of Kabul, dotted with Christian missions, and converted its pagan inhabitants to Sunni Islam, renaming the area Nuristan, Land of Light. This made Afghanistan 99 per cent Muslim: 80 per cent Sunni of the Hanafi school, and the rest Shia of the Jaafari school.

Islam in Afghanistan was a mixture of orthodoxy and Sufism. In cities and towns there were properly trained ulama. But in most of the 26,000 villages, where 85 per cent of Afghans lived, the locally appointed mullahs were often semi-trained, having been educated by an alim at a local madrasa, a religious high school. There were very few Islamic seminaries of repute in Afghanistan. For proper training in Sunni Islam an aspiring alim had either to go to

Al Azhar in Cairo or the seminary in Deoband, sixty miles north of Delhi, India, a seat of orthodoxy which, while opposing the cult of saints, was tolerant of such orthodox sufi orders as Naqshbandi.[1] For the Shia, advanced theological education came either in Mashhad in eastern Iran or Najaf in Iraq.

A typical village mullah was an integral part of the rural élite by either marriage or birth, often himself being a substantial landlord. Besides performing religious rites he imparted elementary religious and other education to village children, and was also a folk healer.

While Afghan tribes had embraced Islam they had not totally discarded their (pre-Islamic) traditional law and values. An example among Pushtun tribes, who formed half of the Afghan population, was Pushtunwali, or Nang-e Pushtun, the Way of Pushtun. Pushtunwali is both an ideology and a corpus of common law with its own institutions and sanctions. Some of the major features of the Pushtanwali are: 'To avenge blood; to fight to death for a person who has taken refuge with me no matter what his lineage; to defend to the last any property entrusted to me; to be hospitable and provide for the safety of the person and property of guests; to pardon an offence (other than murder) on the intercession of a woman of the offender's lineage, a sayyid or a mullah; to punish all adulterers with death; to refrain from killing a man who has entered a mosque or the shrine of a holy man.'[2] There are many instances where the provisions of the Pushtunwali and the Sharia are at odds. The Sharia requires four witnesses to adultery; in the Pushtunwali mere hearsay is enough. Divorce is easy in the Sharia, particularly for the husband, but almost impossible in the Pushtunwali. Women are entitled to inheritance in the Sharia but not in the Pushtunwali. Retribution is total in the Sharia but limited in the Pushtunwali. On the one hand the Pushtunwali has perpetuated feuding among tribes, on the other it has proved adequate in providing a semblance of law and order among warrior tribes.

The dominant Sufi orders are Qadiriya and Naqshbandi.

Qadiriya had reached Pushtun tribes in eastern Afghanistan from India where it had become established in the
sixteenth century. After the First World War Naqib Gailani
arrived in the Pushtun area from Baghdad, the original
source of the Qadiriya, to gain greater control over the
brotherhoods. In contrast, the Naqshbandi order had permeated Afghanistan in the course of its expansion from
Bukhara, the city of its founder, and encompassed both
Pushtun and non-Pushtun tribes. In the late 1800s descendants of Shaikh Ahmad Sirhindi, an eminent Naqshbandi
leader, called the Mujaddid Alf-e Thani, arrived from India
to settle in Kabul's Shor Bazaar district. In due course the
patriarch of the Mujaddidi family came to be called the
Hazrat of Shor Bazaar, the first one being Qayum Jahan.
These two sufi orders had the whole gamut of supreme
guides (pirs), aspirants (murids) and lay members, a string
of lodges and holy shrines, coupled with the practice of
pilgrimage to these shrines where the faithful called for the
intercession of the saint. The fact that orthodox ulama
considered such practices heretical had no impact on their
continued popularity.

It was in this milieu that Abdur Rahman exercised
power which, according to traditional Afghan thinking, he
derived from the tribal jirga, assembly. While not disputing
this view he insisted that only 'divine guidance' could
assure that the people would choose a true and legitimate
ruler. The throne, he argued, was the property of Allah
who appointed kings as shepherds to guard his flock. Thus
kings were vice-regents of Allah who derived their duties
and responsibilities from the will of Allah. Among the
duties and responsibilities he saw himself performing were
championing the cause of Islam and freeing Afghan soil
from the domination of infidel and foreign forces. It was in
the name of Islam that he subdued ethnically heterogeneous tribes and founded a centralized state, a strategy
which Abdul Aziz ibn Saud was to use later in Najd. Abdur
Rahman set up an Executive Council and a Loya Jirga,
National General Assembly, consisting of aristocrats from
the royal family or clan, village notables and landlords, and

ulama. Since he had no intention of sharing power these bodies were purely advisory.

Among the ministerial departments he established were those of justice and education, which had so far been the monopolies of the ulama. He thus came into direct conflict with the religious establishment. He resolved this by assuming the dual role of the Leader of the Islamic community and the sole interpreter of the Sharia, something Emperor Akbar had done in Mogul India in the late sixteenth century. He attacked the ulama for disseminating strange doctrines which were never part of the teachings of Prophet Muhammad. He deprived them of the right to declare jihad which, he asserted, could be waged only under the orders of a ruler. As a self-proclaimed mujtahid, interpreter of the Sharia, he published various pamphlets on the foundations of Islam, jihad and religious advice. To underline his status as the leader of the umma, Islamic community, he took over the religious endowments, thus destroying the economic self-sufficiency of the ulama. He reduced the clergy to the status of government bureaucrats. He ordered that they should undergo formal examination to prove their suitability as state officials. By depriving the ulama of their right to interpret the Sharia, turning them into state employees dependent on his treasury, and controlling their numbers by introducing a formal examination, Abdur Rahman severely undermined their position. He rationalized the legal system by dividing it into the Sharia, qanun (administrative and civil law), and tribal law. He assigned the judgment of business disputes to boards of commerce. He appointed himself the supreme judge.

Such concentration of power was bound to elicit countervailing demands. These arose during the reign of his successor, Habibullah (1901–19). However, the calls for the constitutional monarchy came not from the clergy but from liberal secularists who were inspired by the Constitutional Revolution in Iran. They got short shrift from the ruler: he executed some of their leaders and jailed many more.

Habibullah pursued the idea of the Triple Alliance of the Ottoman empire, Iran and Afghanistan as a barrier to

Russian expansion in the Middle East that had been conceived by his predecessor. From 1911 onwards Afghanistan experienced a surge of pan-Islamism which was actively encouraged by Habibullah. He found in it a useful concept to unite his ethnically divided subjects and consolidate national independence. Pan-Islamism appealed to both traditionalists and modernists. The latter saw in it an opportunity to rationalize reform and innovation as a means of reinforcing monarchy and defending Afghanistan and Islam. Yet Habibullah failed to side with Ottoman Turkey during the First World War, a failure which led to his asassination in 1919.

His successor, Amanullah (1919–29), set out as a fervent pan-Islamist. He waged a jihad against the British along the border with India to recover the Pushtun land Britain had annexed and retrieve the right to conduct his country's external relations, thereby strengthening Islamic bonds between him and the border tribes. His campaign was a military failure but a political success: he gained the right to conduct Afghanistan's foreign affairs. In March 1921 he concluded a treaty with Turkey whereby Afghanistan recognized Turkey as the guide of Islam and custodian of the caliphate. Three months later he signed a treaty with Iran, thus moving towards Islamic solidarity along the lines first mooted by Afghani some decades earlier. Amanullah's actions united the ulama and modernists behind him.

However, he was aware that his landlocked country, lacking financial resources of its own, needed to normalize relations with its powerful non-Muslim neighbours: British India and Bolshevik Russia. He signed a treaty with Britain in November 1921, having concluded a comprehensive treaty with Soviet Russia nine months earlier.

At home he could not sustain the simultaneous support of modernists and the ulama. When he opened government schools to train future administrators and professionals, and liberalized women's position by banning child marriage and transferring the regulation of family affairs from the clergy to the state, he ran into stiff opposition from the religious establishment. The first sign of disaffection came with a tribal rebellion in the east in March 1924. Amanullah successfully crushed it, but his hiring of German and Russian pilots for the aircraft used in the campaign incensed the traditionalists: they found the intrusion of infidels into the internal feuds of Muslims intolerable. Amanullah capped his victory with a ban on contacts between the armed forces and mullahs, and the enrolment of military personnel in sufi brotherhoods. He thus enlarged his power at the expense of the ulama.

He formalized the situation by offering the nation a written constitution in 1923 along the lines of the Iranian constitution of 1906–7. In it he declared Islam to be the official religion of Afghanistan, where the name of the ruler had to be mentioned in religious sermons.

Having thus consolidated his position Amanullah undertook a nine-month-long tour (from October 1927 to July 1928) of India, the Middle East and Europe, a sojourn which laid the seeds of his deposition. At receptions in Europe his wife, Soraya, appeared unveiled, and photographs of such appearances began circulating in Kabul. He returned home via Turkey, then in the midst of militant secularism, and Iran, then undergoing rapid modernization under Reza Pahlavi Shah.

The special Loya Jirga that Amanullah convened on his return went along with his proposal for a representative government based on votes for all, and military conscription for men. But it opposed modern education for girls and age limits for marriage. When he tried to implement legal and financial reform the ulama responded with the argument that the Sharia, having been derived from Allah, was enough, and needed no elaboration.

But Amanullah was not to be stopped. He issued decrees outlawing polygamy among civil servants, permitting women to discard the veil, and requiring all Afghans residing in or visiting Kabul to wear western dress complete with a European hat from March 1929 onwards. Clerics regarded the dress order as blasphemous, particularly the insistence on the European hat.[3] The king forbade theological students from enrolling at Deoband seminary and banned foreign-trained ulama from teaching. To crown it all, in October 1928 a hundred women led by Queen Soraya appeared unveiled at an official function in Kabul. For the religious and traditional establishments this was the limit. The ulama's attitude was summed up by a cleric's quip: 'When reforms come in, Islam goes out.'

When Fazl Muhammad Mujaddidi, the Hazrat of Shor Bazaar, began collecting signatures against the reforms, King Amanullah arrested him. Violent rioting broke out in Kabul. In November Shinwaris in the east joined other Pushtun tribes in a revolt against the king. Amanullah despatched royal forces, but they defected to the other side. Disaffection within monarchist forces stemmed from the ruler's secular reformist actions as well as his employment of European military advisers.

In early January 1929 forces led by Bacha-e Saqqao (literally, Son of a Water-Carrier), a Tajik highwayman based in the Shamali plain north of Kabul, a stronghold of fundamentalism, laid siege to the capital. He had the active support of the ulama, who in turn had popular opinion on their side. Under pressure from Bacha-e Saqqao, Amanullah agreed to close girls' schools, withdraw permission for women to discard the veil, cancel the western dress order, allow religious students to join Deoband seminary, and rescind the requirement of a teaching certificate for a cleric imposed by Abdur Rahman. He promised to appoint muhtasibs, religious supervisors, in provinces to ensure that Islamic precepts were being observed. Most importantly, he agreed to abide by the Sharia as interpreted by orthodox ulama, and rule in consultation with a council of fifty religious and tribal leaders.

But all this proved inadequate to save Amanullah his throne. On 14 January, aided by defectors from the royal troops, Bacha-e Saqqao captured Kabul and promised to establish the rule of the Sharia. On assuming power he confirmed all the cancellations of Amanullah, and went on to dissolve the education and justice ministries and hand over the task of running courts and schools to clerics.

While Bacha-e Saqqao performed the job of deposing

Amanullah, the inspiration for his actions, and the crucial popular backing they received, stemmed from the ulama. In short, clerics were the main agents who brought about the downfall of the monarch in Afghanistan, a Sunni country – an achievement they were to repeat fifty years later in Shia Iran. The event was all the more remarkable because most of the clergy were state employees. Only sufi leaders and their followers formed an independent Islamic force. It was not accidental that it was the Mujaddidi family in Kabul who took the lead in expressing and mobilizing Islamic sentiment against the monarch. Unlike Reza Pahlavi Shah in Iran, who rose to power as a military leader and built up a strong army before challenging the clergy, Amanullah lacked a strong, secular force in the form of a properly trained, disciplined and, above all, loyal army. It was not until 1953 that the army came into its own in Afghanistan when, under the leadership of Muhammad Daoud Khan, it seized effective power.

Bacha-e Saqqao failed to consolidate his position. Political anarchy and severe economic crisis overwhelmed him. In October 1929 he was overthrown by Muhammad Nadir Khan – a third cousin of Amanullah and a brother of King Habibullah's second wife – with the aid of Fazl Umar Mujaddidi in Kabul and Sher Agha Naguib, a religious leader in the eastern city of Jalalabad.

The brief reign of King Nadir Shah marked the zenith of Islamic fundamentalism in Afghanistan. Obligated to religious luminaries for his position, he set out to found a fully-fledged Islamic state. He established the Jamaat-e Ulama, Society of the Ulama, and authorized it to interpret the Sharia and vet all government laws and regulations in its light. One of the Jamaat's interpretations held that women were not entitled to vote. The ministry of justice, placed under Fazl Umar Mujaddidi, was given the task of enforcing the Sharia. Nadir Shah ordered that all civil and criminal laws should be based entirely on the Sharia. He set up the department of ihtisab, religious observance, to supervise adherence to Islam with instructions to enforce strictly the Islamic dietary restrictions, particularly on alcohol. He consulted the ulama on all important social, educational and political issues. So beholden was he to the clergy that when they opposed his plan of establishing a central bank on the ground that it would amount to creating an instrument of usury, he dropped the idea. Never before in modern times had the ulama enjoyed such power and prestige, with the Hazrat of Shor Bazaar acting as a close adviser to the monarch. Islam and tradition were the two pillars which firmly supported Nadir Shah's regime.

In the constitution of 1931 Nadir Shah formalized the role of religion and religious leaders. The first four articles described Islam of the Hanafi school as the official religion, required that the king be a Hanafi Muslim and that his name be mentioned in Friday sermons, and barred non-Muslims from becoming government ministers. Other articles institutionalized the powers that Nadir Shah had conferred on the ulama and Sharia courts, and recognized the supremacy and orthodoxy of the Hanafi school. Still another provision authorized Afghan citizens the right to impart 'Islamic scholastic or moral sciences' either in private or public. This confirmed the right of the clergy to educate Muslim children. With this primary-school teaching reverted to the mullahs, and religious instruction became the central preoccupation of the system.

The constitution incorporated the Quranic injunctions on popular consultation – 'Consult them of affairs' (3:153) and 'Their affairs are by consultation among them' (42:38) – by prescribing a consultative assembly based on votes for all male Afghans.

The first parliament assembled in 1931, but Nadir Shah did not live to see the second parliament three years later: he was assassinated in November 1933. The throne went to his son Muhammad Zahir Shah, a youth of nineteen. Power was exercised in his name by his three uncles, one of whom, Muhammad Hashim Khan, became prime minister, and held the position until 1946.

During these years much intellectual energy was spent in diagnosing the reasons for the backwardness of Afghanistan and the poor condition of Muslims at large. The pious traditionalist thinkers blamed the present sorry state on Muslim leaders' deviation from the true path of Islam and the Sharia. But nationalist modernists disagreed. They said that there was no inherent contradiction between Islam and progress. In fact Islam enjoined upon the believers to seek knowledge. Social welfare and national defence demanded knowledge and science. They argued furthermore that the Sharia offered guidance towards public well-being, progress and justice, and that such principles could be learned by reason which could be cultivated only through education and learning. In other words they called for ijtihad, creative interpretation, dormant in the Sunni world for many centuries.

Every so often even *Al Falah* (The Good Path), the journal of the Jamaat-e Ulama, would publish an article in this vein. One author argued that the ethical precepts of Islam and the Quran were sources of inspiration for social reform. Another, Abdul Razak Khan Tulimsher, argued that in modern times Muslims could preserve their societies and spiritual legacy through military power which could be achieved only through knowledge. The sword was essential, he wrote, but Islam also needed knowledge and progress to defend itself.[4]

However, these were the views of a tiny minority among the clergy, the vast majority holding modernization to be antithetical to Islamic and traditional values. Tribal chiefs shared this belief. With these two important centres of power – the ulama and tribal leaders – wedded to the status quo, the monarchical regime became static.

The Second World War, in which Afghanistan remained neutral, underlined the importance of science and technology. It made the ruling dynasty realize the pressing need for rapid reform and modernization in order to preserve itself and Afghan independence as well as tackle the rising socio-economic problems.

Modern education grew, but at a very slow pace. Kabul University, founded in 1932, with a Faculty of Medicine affiliated to Lyons University in France, acquired Faculties of Science, and Law and Political Science, during the next decade.

Religious education continued to have priority. Curricula in primary and secondary schools, designed in the main by the ulama, laid heavy emphasis on Islam, Islamic history, moral lessons, Islamic precepts and law, and Persian classics. In 1944 the government established a School for Instruction in the Sharia, and upgraded it six years later to Faculty of Theology at Kabul University in conjunction with Al Azhar in Cairo. Thus the monarchical regime established a state-run system through which an Afghan could become an alim without leaving the country: a breeding ground for a new type of religious scholar.

Overall, the nationalist modernists seemed to be gaining ground at the expense of traditional and religious leaders. One symptom of it was the emergence in 1947 of the Awakened Youth movement of intellectuals who demanded constitutional reform. Prime Minister Shah Mahmud allowed comparative freedom to voters in parliamentary elections whose results in the past had been predetermined by the royal family. Of the 120 members of the Seventh Parliament (1949–52), between forty and forty-five were considered liberal. They were instrumental in allowing a degree of freedom to the press. With this the differences between the traditional–religious and nationalist–reformist camps sharpened. The liberals' demands for further extension of freedom of speech and the press, and the formation of political parties, was rebuffed by the palace. This made them virulent. Students at Kabul University, a stronghold of nationalist–reformists, formed a union and began discussing such blasphemous subjects as communism and atheism. The three opposition magazines became strident and attacked religious luminaries, including the Hazrat of Shor Bazaar, for their fanaticism and conservatism. An example of their conservative interpretation of Islam was their opposition until 1949 to smoking tobacco, which they regarded as a narcotic. Radical students staged plays which ridiculed the royal family and Islamic figures. Premier Mahmud found these developments intolerable. He banned the Students' Union in 1951, and then the Awakened Youth. He arrested top opposition leaders before the 1952 parliamentary poll.

Clearly the royal family, the ultimate arbiter of power, found Islamic and tribal leaders unrealistically conservative and a continued barrier to modernization. At the same time they saw in the rival group of constitutional modernizers a threat to their unchallenged supremacy in the political arena. Fortunately for the royalists, the mounting hostility between the competing forces of religious tradition and secular modernization had left them both weak. Thus the time was ripe for the palace to inject into the political drama its own active player: the military.

In September 1953 Muhammad Daoud Khan, commander of the Central Forces in Kabul, and a cousin of King Zahir Shah, mounted a coup against Premier Mahmud with the active consent of the palace, and became the prime minister. His first priority was to modernize and strengthen the military. For this he relied heavily on the Soviet Union – a neighbour with which Kabul had built up a special relationship after the Bolshevik Revolution – for historical and contemporary reasons. By concluding a treaty with Soviet Russia in early February 1921 Afghanistan under Amanullah became the first country to recognize the Russian revolutionary regime. Following two serious border incidents in 1925, the two countries signed a Treaty of Neutrality and Non-aggression which was reiterated and strengthened five years later. Good relations between the two neighbours were undisturbed by the Second World War due to the neutrality that the Afghans maintained in the conflict. Oddly, the creation of Pakistan, a Muslim state, in August 1947 was badly received by Kabul. Britain's departure from the Indian sub-continent led to the revival of Afghan irredentist claims on the Pushtun lands in Pakistan, which had been kept in abeyance since 1893 when Abdur Rahman had signed an agreement with British India to delimit the border which caused a division of the various Pushtun tribes in the region. Now Afghanistan sponsored a movement for an independent Pushtunistan consisting of Pushtun tribes living east of its pre-1947 border with British India. Pakistan vehemently opposed the Pushtunistan movement. Relations between Afghanistan and Pakistan worsened. As Pakistan drifted towards the western camp, formalizing its links with the US with a Mutual Security Pact in 1954, Kabul tilted towards Moscow. In order not to upset its ally, Pakistan, America refused to sell arms to Afghanistan. Unsurprisingly, Daoud Khan began attaching Soviet advisers to the Afghan military academies and despatching military officers to the Soviet Union for further training. At the same time, anxious to develop Afghanistan economically, he successfully solicited funds and experts from America and other western nations for economic projects.

An autocratic personality, Daoud Khan wanted to centralize state authority through the military, and implement socio-economic progress through executive decrees rather than democratic debate and consensus. He was intolerant of such independent power centres as the Jamaat-e Ulama and deprived it of the powers vested in it by Nadir Shah. He began supplanting orthodox clergy by fresh graduates of Kabul University's Faculty of Theology in the justice and education ministries. Also he tried, quietly, to effect women's emancipation. In 1957 Kabul Radio introduced female singers and announcers. Mild protest followed but did not linger. The following year the government sent a woman delegate to the United Nations in New York, an unprecedented step. The state-owned Ariana Afghan Airlines employed female receptionists and hostesses, and they went about their job without a veil. Also unveiled women were employed as telephone operators. It was against this background that at the independence day celebrations, on 25 August 1959, wives and daughters of senior government officials appeared unveiled on the review stand: an act which reminded senior traditionalists of what had occurred under Amanullah thirty-one years earlier. As before, the ulama protested vehemently. Daoud Khan replied that if they could find indisputable evidence for the veil in the Sharia he would impose it. Although the ulama failed to do so they refused to accept the discarding of the veil. Soon they began to preach against the regime, arguing that Daoud Khan was an anti-Islamic leader who among other things was letting atheistic communists and western Christians undermine the Islamic way of life. They were particularly upset about the presence of Russian advisers, military and civilian, in Afghanistan, apprehensive that the Russians would steer Afghans away from Islam, something they had done to the Muslim inhabitants of the central Asian republics of the Soviet Union. The government arrested fifty clerical leaders on charges of treason and heresy. The severity of the charges dampened the spirits of the ulama, who were well aware of the iron fist with which Daoud Khan ruled the country. The chastened clergy were released after a week, and the protest against the unveiling of women died down. This was in marked contrast to what had happened under Amanullah. The major difference between then and now was that Daoud Khan controlled a loyal, well-disciplined and modern army, which was not the case with Amanullah.

Daoud Khan's continued passion for setting up the independent state of Pushtunistan brought him into open conflict with Pakistan in September 1961. The two states broke off diplomatic links. Pakistan closed its frontier with the landlocked Afghanistan, causing high inflation and an acute fuel shortage there. On King Zahir Shah's advice Daoud Khan resigned in March 1963. Two months later Pakistan reopened its border with Afghanistan.

The exit of Daoud Khan from the premiership did not alter the fact that the military was the single most important centre of power and that it was ultimately loyal to the monarch. This reassured King Zahir Shah, who had so far been overshadowed first by his uncles and then by his cousin Daoud Khan. Now he decided to come to the fore. Realizing the need for political reform he promulgated in October 1964 a liberal constitution, which inaugurated constitutional monarchy, better known in Afghanistan as 'New Democracy', and which proved to be the last chapter in the long history of monarchy in the country. This period witnessed an important change in the composition of Islamic forces.

As before, the new constitution assigned Islam a prime place in society. Article 1 stated that Islam was the sacred religion of Afghanistan and that the king had to be a Hanafi Muslim. Article 64 ruled out any law 'repugnant to the basic principles of the sacred religion of Islam'. Another article stated that where no law existed the provisions of the Hanafi school of the Sharia would apply. (As in the past the National Centre of Legislation at the ministry of justice was to continue to examine whether the existing laws were unconstitutional or unIslamic.)

The 1964 constitution provided for a parliament composed of a fully elected Wolesi Jirga, House of the People, and a partly elected Meshrano Jirga, House of Nobles. The first Wolesi Jirga which met in October 1965 consisted of four main groups: clerics led by the Mujaddidi family; nationalist centrists who looked to the monarch to implement progressive policies; democrats who wanted to adopt western-style democracy; and Marxists.

For the clergy, parliament provided a national platform, an improvement on the past when they had functioned on a regional basis. But they were now losing power since they were being supplanted by the graduates of Kabul University's Faculty of Theology who had been appointed to important administrative and religious posts during Daoud Khan's premiership. Also, like the freshly established parliament, Kabul University had been fostering inter-tribal and inter-regional contacts since half of Kabul University's 3,000 students (in 1962) were from the provinces.

The twelve-year-old Faculty of Theology was headed by Professor Gholam Muhammad Niyazi, who during his education at Al Azhar had come under the influence of the Muslim Brotherhood. At certain times two Egyptian professors, and one Indian, a follower of the Islamic thinker Sayyid Abul Ala Maududi (1903–79), taught at the faculty. Through them and a local cultural group, led by Sibghatullah Mujaddidi, Persian translations of the works of Sayyid Qutb and Maududi became available to theological students and others. These books presented Islam as a modern ideology – not an obscurantist faith associated with traditional ulama and village mullahs. *Majale-ye Shariat* (Review of the Sharia), published by the Faculty of Theology, proved to be a fruitful channel for discussion to the new breed of Islamic fundamentalists.

By 1965 the expanding body of Islamist students felt confident enough to mount a demonstration and distribute a pamphlet entitled *A Tract of the Holy War*. The Organization of Young Muslims was the public face of Islamic fundamentalists who functioned secretly under the guidance of a council headed by Professor Niyazi. In 1970 the council decided to branch out of the university campus and establish cells in the army. Two years later they shifted their focus from spiritual revival of the community to acquiring political power. Following the adoption of a constitution, the fundamentalists elected Professor Borhan al Din Rabbani, a Tajik, as president and Professor Abdul Rasul Sayyaf as his deputy.

Gahiz (Morning), a pro-Islamic, anti-Marxist publication established in October 1968, provided a popular platform for Young Muslims and other fundamentalists. This was a consequence of the press legislation passed by parliament in 1965 and endorsed by King Zahir Shah. However, when parliament passed a bill on political parties the monarch refused his assent. He did the same to the legislation on provincial and local councils. So the much flaunted 'New Democracy' was stillborn.

By the late 1960s secondary education had expanded so rapidly that only a minority of applicants to Kabul University were able to gain entry. Student protest at teaching and other facilities often took a political turn, and the university became a hotbed of Marxists and Islamic fundamentalists. The latter were as much opposed to the autocracy and corruption of the royal family as they were to the rising tide of Marxism. In secondary schools, teacher-training colleges and technical institutes too dissent grew, with a large body of students and rising numbers of unemployed graduates blaming the corrupt monarchy for their problems and backing the radical solutions offered by Marxists or Islamic fundamentalists.

The palace found Marxists particularly threatening since leftist students had taken to allying with industrial workers and their strikes. It ensured the defeat of all Marxist candidates in the 1969 parliamentary poll. In April 1970 the publication in the *Parcham* (Flag), a Marxist magazine, of a poem entitled *Dorud Bar Lenin*, a benediction normally reserved for Prophet Muhammad, on Lenin's birthday provided the government with an opportunity to apply popular pressure against the Marxists. It encouraged the ulama and their followers to demonstrate against the leftist magazine, which they did. But they did not stop there. They went on to attack the regime's steady drift towards secularization and the growing presence of female students in secondary and higher educational institutions. They argued that injecting large doses of non-traditional education into the system was fast eroding the morals of the youth and undermining traditional social values. What reinforced, for them, a sense of general moral decadence was the presence of thousands of young western men and women and their licentious behaviour in Kabul, which was then on the trail that western hippies followed from Europe to India.[5] In 1972 the Kabul-based press reported famine in the provinces due to the failure of rains for two consecutive years, which claimed about 100,000 lives. Islamists staged demonstrations against foodgrain hoarders and called for limits on personal wealth. All in all, therefore, in the early 1970s there was a general sense of drift, decadence and turmoil in the country; and Islamists held the royal family responsible for it.

On 17 July 1973, while King Zahir Shah was in Italy for medical treatment, Muhammad Daoud Khan seized power. This time he abolished the monarchy and set up a republic. He declared that he had assumed power in order to return Afghanistan to Islamic principles. But instead of ordering the immediate and total application of the Sharia he announced land ceilings of twenty and forty hectares for irrigated and unirrigated land. Through this measure he expected to win popularity in rural Afghanistan. To enlarge his popular base, particularly in urban areas, he secured the co-operation of the Parchami group which had split with its radical rival Khalqi faction in 1966, a year after the formal founding of the (Marxist) People's Democratic Party of Afghanistan in January 1965. Parchamis regarded Daoud's republic as an improvement over the corrupt, autocratic monarchy whereas Khalqis did not.

As before Daoud Khan tried to monopolize authority. With Parchami Marxists supporting his regime, the only party which hindered his path to total power was that of the Islamic fundamentalists, who had established themselves at Kabul University as the dominant force. In 1972 Young Muslims, led by Gulb al Din Hikmatyar, an engineering student, had secured the majority of seats on the Students' Council. Young Muslims drew most of their support from rural high school graduates, who felt frustrated at every step: university admission, jobs and career advancement. By and large they were more pious than their Kabul counterparts. As for the parent body of Young Muslims, now popularly called the Ikhwan, (Muslim) Brothers, it was winning recruits among military officers.

While senior fundamentalist leaders kept in touch with traditional ulama, Young Muslims were dismissive of them, regarding them as conservative compromisers. Consequently, no united front of old and new fundamentalists emerged. This helped Daoud Khan as he increased pressure on the Islamists. In one swoop in June 1974 his government arrested 200 Islamic fundamentalists in Kabul as they gathered to discuss a blueprint of an Islamic republic where the Sharia would be applied in its totality. Hikmatyar fled to Pakistan. But Niyazi and Rabbani made one more attempt to persuade Daoud Khan to break with Parchamis. They failed. Rabbani escaped to Pakistan, but Niyazi was subsequently imprisoned.

In exile Rabbani, leader of the Ikhwan, proposed a long-term strategy of infiltrating the military and seizing power through a coup in Kabul. By contrast, Hikmatyar was for immediate armed struggle. This suited Pakistan's Prime

Minister Zulfikar Ali Bhutto. He wanted to strike at Daoud Khan, who had once again revived the contentious issue of Pushtunistan. Bhutto readily agreed to aid Hikmatyar and his followers with arms and training. July 1975 was chosen as the date for a national uprising. But very little happened except in the north-east. Daoud Khan used the trouble caused by the armed fundamentalists to tighten his grip on the state and society. He banned all privately owned publications. He set up his own political party called the National Revolutionary Party. Much to the chagrin of the ulama he secularized commercial and civil laws, thus undoing the work of King Nadir Shah and proving the hollowness of his earlier claim that he had seized power to revive Islam.

Following the failure of their uprising the Islamists took refuge in Peshawar, Pakistan. Here the split between Rabbani and Hikmatyar became final in 1976; and that marked the final demise of the Ikhwan and Young Muslims. Both leaders were now free to form their own parties. They did. Since he lacked a classical religious education, Hikmatyar failed to win the respect or support of the vast majority of the ulama. On the other hand he was a charismatic figure and an outstanding organizer who had spent many years in student politics at Kabul University. He formed Hizb-e Islami, the Islamic Party, which believed inter alia that the piety of a believer should be judged primarily on the basis of his political actions and only secondarily on his religious behaviour. Rabbani, a graduate of Al Azhar and a literary critic, was much respected by orthodox ulama as well as leaders of the sufi orders. Rabbani named his party Jamaat-e Islami (Islamic Society) of Afghanistan, taking a lead from the Jamaat-e Islami that Maududi had established in India in 1941, followed by the Jamaat-e Islami in Pakistan six years later. Maududi and his party were well known in Kabul's Islamic circles, and through *Gahiz* magazine efforts had been made in the early 1970s by Afghan Islamists to establish formal links with the Pakistani party. By then Maududi had emerged as the most important non-Arab Islamic theorist and propagandist in the Sunni world: his books in Urdu had been translated into Arabic, Persian and English.

Born in Jabalpur, India, in 1903 in a religious family, Abul Ala Maududi started his working life as the editor of a religious journal. He believed that the character of a social order flowed from the top to the bottom, and therefore to change society one had first to change the theoretical thinking of its leaders. He founded the Jamaat-e Islami to produce a cadre of sincere and disciplined Muslims capable of bringing about the victory of Islam in India. When India was partitioned in August 1947 he moved to Pakistan.

The author of sixty books, Maududi developed Islam, through ijtihad and literal exposition, into a modern ideology with answers for all individual and social problems. Unlike traditional ulama who spent their energies in tackling arcane and largely irrelevant matters, Maududi faced modern life armed with the Sharia. Like Abdul Wahhab he attacked orthodox ulama for confusing the fundamentals of Islam with the details of its application, and diluting Islam by attaching their own rules to the injunctions of the Sharia. He advocated ijtihad but only in accordance with the spirit of the Sharia's commandments.

What made Maududi particularly attractive to young urban pious Afghans – caught in the web of western cultural influences and Soviet military and commercial links – was his argument that Islam was self-sufficient and quite separate from, and indeed opposed to, both western and socialist ways of life. Describing the West as morally decadent and corrupt, he stated 'Islam and Western civilization are poles apart in their objectives as well as in their principles of social organization.'[6] He wanted Muslims to acquire scientific knowledge – which he seemed to regard as finite – for the benefit of Islam.

While regarding the government under Prophet Muhammad and the First Four (Rightly Guided) Caliphs as the model, Maududi gave it a democratic interpretation. He prescribed that the Leader of an Islamic state today – heading the legislative, judiciary and executive organs –

must be elected by the faithful; so must the Consultative Council. Its members should be able to judge whether or not the Leader was following Islamic policies. Maududi had no objection to candidates contesting elections on party tickets, but ruled that once they had been elected they must give up party labels and owe allegiance only to the Islamic state, and vote on issues according to their individual judgement.

Maududi's innovation, however, failed when it came to tackling social and family issues. Here he followed an ultra-orthodox line. He was for sexual segregation and the veil for women. He insisted that a woman must cover her face when she leaves home. Arguing that since the objective of the Sharia is to curb indecency and obscenity, 'nothing can be more unreasonable than to close all the minor ways to indecency but to fling the main gate [i.e. face] wide open'.[7]

But the merit of Maududi's blueprint was that rejection of some of its elements left the whole edifice still intact and self-sufficient. More specifically, Maududi's thesis provided a modern interpretation of Islam as an alternative to the secular and atheistic ideologies that were being disseminated in Afghanistan.

Though Rabbani called his organization Jamaat-e Islami, he did not share Maududi's élitist views about his party. Indeed, Rabbani wanted it to be a mass organization. Aware that the structure of a modern political party was unsuited to the social conditions prevailing in the tribal regions of his country, he wanted to adapt the Jamaat-e Islami to tribal institutions.

In a different context President Daoud Khan proved himself to be equally flexible. Having crushed the rebellion in the north-east, he put the Pushtunistan issue on a back-burner. When the Shah of Iran offered his services to improve Afghan–Pakistan relations, Daoud Khan responded positively. He had a meeting with Bhutto, an unprecedented event in the history of the two neighbour states. In 1976 the Shah promised to underwrite nearly half of Afghanistan's 2,392 million dollar seven-year plan. This was indeed a generous offer, and Daoud Khan responded by tilting Kabul's foreign policy towards the West.

At home too Daoud Khan's policies took a right turn. He purged the Parchamis from his administration. Then he resorted to persecuting them as well as the Khalqis. Under this pressure the Parchami and Khalqi groups merged in July 1977 to re-establish the People's Democratic Party. Daoud Khan continued his earlier policies of enhancing his powers, and persecuting the fundamentalists. The new constitution that he promulgated in January 1977 provided for a strong president and a weak legislature. It gave equal rights to men and women, and allocated only a passive role to Islam. In December, following the confession of the assassin of the planning minister, Ahmad Ali Khorram, the government arrested fifty-four fundamentalists on charges of plotting to assassinate President Daoud Khan and his cabinet. Meanwhile, the persecution of the Marxists had taken the form of murders of their leaders by government agents. This aroused much disquiet in leftist ranks who did not know how to react to this tactic.

However, the assassination of Mir Akbar Khyber, a respected trade union leader and a former editor of *Parcham*, on 17 April 1978 changed the situation. The PDP leadership organized massive anti-government demonstrations in Kabul. Daoud Khan ordered the imprisonment of all PDP leaders. But Nur Muhammad Taraki, the party chief, escaped arrest. He activated the leftist network in the military that had been built up over the years. The result was a coup by leftist military officers on 27 April 1978, an event officially described as the Saur (April) Revolution. Daoud Khan was killed in the fighting at the presidential palace, and his official positions of president and prime minister went to Taraki. The coup was the culmination of the Marxists' efforts to recruit military officers over the past many years, and the policy of the Kabul government (initiated by Daoud Khan in the mid-1950s) of sending its officers for further training to the Soviet Union. Since they received this training at military academies in the central Asian republics of the Soviet Union, they felt racially and culturally at home, and could not avoid comparing the economic, social and educational progress of the (Muslim) inhabitants of these regions with the backwardness of Afghans. These experiences made them pro-Soviet and a suitable quarry for recruitment into the military network of Afghan Marxists.

Marxist Revolution and After

Once in power, the differences between the PDP's two components came to the surface. The Khalqi faction led by Taraki and Hafizullah Amin wanted rapid changes; the Parchami wing, led by Babrak Karmal, advocated a gradualist approach. As it was, Taraki described his regime not as socialist but 'national democratic', based on an alliance of workers, peasants and national bourgeoisie in conflict with feudal lords and comprador bourgeoisie subservient to foreign capital. Aware of national history and popular culture, the revolutionary leaders reiterated their faith in Islam and began all their public utterances with 'Bismillah', 'In the name of Allah'. So too did all official statements, and radio and television broadcasts. Taraki and other PDP leaders offered Friday prayers in different mosques in the capital. They repeatedly assured the public that all reforms would be in line with the Sharia.

The reform package they offered the nation from May to November 1978 affected the lives of most Afghans directly or indirectly. The motive behind it was promotion of the social and economic welfare of the vast majority of the people, which seemed quite in line with Islam. There was opposition to reforms from various quarters, all of whom rationalized their stance in Islamic terms.

In May the government declared a 'jihad' against illiteracy, and prescribed compulsory primary education for both sexes. The extent of female education had been exceedingly low. Only 5 per cent of girls were then attending school versus 30 per cent of boys.[8] The campaign went well in urban areas, but not in rural. Here opposition to the mixing of the sexes, particularly in adult education, was very strong. What made the situation even more tense was the fact that due to the paucity of female teachers the task of teaching women fell on male teachers who had arrived from towns and cities, considered by rural folk as hotbeds of licentiousness. The textbooks portrayed the urban lifestyle favourably, and were tinged with Marxism. Furthermore, the literacy campaign completed the process of expelling mullahs from the local educational system, and swelled the ranks of anti-government clerics. The result was periodic murders of secular, revolutionary teachers by fundamentalists. The literacy campaign in villages reached a peak in early 1979 and then declined rapidly.

The next major step, taken in early July, was meant to benefit the peasants burdened with mortgages and heavy interest charges levied by landlords and moneylenders. Decree 6 abolished all pre-1973 mortgages and debts, and drastically reduced the excessive interest (often 100 per cent a year) on later loans. The government estimated that this reform would benefit four out of five peasant families. In practice, however, in the absence of a socially committed bureaucracy, the decree created unprecedented problems for the new regime, and dulled its beneficial impact on rural life. More often than not village mullahs, having blood ties with landlord-moneylenders, ruled that cancellation of debts amounted to stealing, and was therefore unIslamic. (On the other hand the pro-regime minority among clerics cited the Quranic verse against riba, usury.) Many rural mullahs began preaching against the government in an environment where armed resistance against the regime took the form of murdering Marxist teachers and civil servants. The authorities responded by dismissing or arresting rebellious mullahs. Indeed, in September 1978, encouraged by the ruling issued by a group of pro-regime ulama in Kabul and elsewhere, the government mounted a jihad against the Ikhwan, the generic term used for militant fundamentalists.

By then the conflict within the ruling party had been resolved in favour of the Khalqis. So the pace of reform and secularization quickened. In mid-October the government replaced the national tricolour – black, red and green – with a red flag, flagrantly similar to the standards of the Soviet Central Asian republics. The disappearance of the Islamic green from the national flag aroused popular suspicion that the state had taken the path of atheism. This view was reinforced when the practice of invoking Allah, 'In the name of Allah, the Merciful', at the beginning of broadcasting programmes or governmental statements was dropped by the official media as well as political leaders. These two steps effectively undid all that had been achieved by months of state propaganda that the new regime believed in Islam and wanted to uphold it. They provided evidence to a rising number of clergy that the state was unIslamic: a sufficient basis for them to call on the faithful to resist it.

These steps virtually neutralized the immediate impact of Decree 7 concerning marriage and family relations which was issued at about the same time. Women were granted equal rights, forced marriage was banned, and the minimum age for marriage fixed: sixteen for females and eighteen for males. The decree fixed the bride price at 7 dollars, its going rate then being 1,000 dollars. This provision was meant to help poor prospective bridegrooms; but it was extremely hard to enforce in villages. However, the decree did not interfere with mahr, the provision of guarantees for the welfare of the wife, sanctified by the Sharia.

Finally, in late November 1978, came the most important reform. It concerned landownership, land being the primary source of income in a predominantly agrarian Afghanistan. Forty per cent of the peasants were landless, and another 40 per cent possessed only 1.5 to 6 acres each. In contrast, the top 2.2 per cent of elandowners, holding 30 acres or more each, owned 42 per cent of the total of 25 to 29 million acres.[9] Decree 8 divided land into three categories, and fixed ceilings of 30 acres for first-class, perennially irrigated land to 300 acres of dry land. The government expected to secure 2.5 to 3 million acres of excess land for distribution to landless peasants. To implement the reform it set up land committees composed mainly of urban-based

PDP members. Beginning in January 1979 these committees, backed by radicalized, well-paid police, began visiting villages to hand over the title deeds to the landless. This was a major means by which the revolutionary regime planned to break the socio-economic power of the traditional–religious élite which had effectively ruled rural society for many centuries. Rich landlords protested while their religious allies, local mullahs, issued verdicts that taking somebody's land was tantamount to robbery, a crime, and that those receiving such property would be transgressing the Sharia.[10] This, and the fear of violent reprisals from the landlords, discouraged many landless villagers from accepting title deeds offered to them by the visiting land committees. None the less, by March 1979, the government claimed to have distributed 512,000 acres to 104,000 families.[11]

Abroad, the Marxist government strengthened its ties with the Soviet Union by signing a Treaty of Friendship and Co-operation with it in December 1978. The treaty, modelled on the ones Moscow had earlier concluded with Ethiopia, Angola and Vietnam, specified close military, political and economic links between the two neighbours. Article 4 of the Treaty stated that the signatories 'shall consult with each other and take, by agreement, appropriate measures to ensure the security, independence and territorial integrity of the two countries'.[12] It was this provision which was later to be invoked by Kabul to invite Soviet troops.

The aggregate effect of these developments was to polarize society, with opposition becoming more vociferous and gaining more supporters. Such Islamic luminaries as Muhammad Ibrahim Mujaddidi, the Hazrat of Shor Bazaar, condemned the reforms as unIslamic and preached against the government. After a period of hesitation the authorities moved against the religious opposition in January 1979. They seized the offices of the Hazrat of Shor Bazaar, arresting all adult male members of the Mujaddidi family. They executed some religious figures, but did not make this public. Their actions caused alarm in religious circles. Many Islamic and sufi leaders fled the country, and joined the resistance groups based in Peshawar. The Afghan–Pakistani border became an active centre of resistance and subversion.

Resistance against the Marxist regime hardened during the winter of 1978–9, with the (seasonally) inaccessible Nuristan slipping out of the control of the central government and falling into the hands of the (Islamic) Nuristan Front. A similar situation prevailed in the Hazarajat highlands, now ruled by the Revolutionary Council of the Islamic Union of Afghanistan. Thus the regions which had been the last to be integrated into the central Afghani system were the first to be lost to the leftist regime.

But the event which caused much worry in Kabul and a shift in the balance of forces within the PDP was the uprising in Herat, situated sixty-five miles from the Iranian border, in mid-March 1979. Several dozen Afghan fundamentalists returned to Herat from Iran in the wake of the Islamic revolution there in early February. Some of them established contacts with pro-Islamic officers in the local garrison while others mobilized the faithful in the surrounding villages on the issue of compulsory education for women being imparted by male teachers. On 16 March, Friday, the demonstrating villagers murdered government teachers, and then converged on Herat in a series of armed marches. Here their ranks were bolstered by disaffected townsmen and defectors from the local garrison. Together they went on a rampage, killing PDP cadres and military officers, and Soviet advisers and their families. The insurgents took over Herat. A few days later when they found a column of armoured cars approaching from the direction of Qandhar, waving a green flag and a copy of the Quran, they thought that they were being joined by another contingent of rebels, and let the column pass. These were in fact government troops. Once they had entered Herat, and received air cover, they attacked the insurgents and recaptured the city. The five-day-long insurrection caused some 5,000 casualties, including several hundred loyalist troops and PDP functionaries. Kabul blamed Islamic Tehran for the insurgency. To meet the rising danger of counter-revolution a government of 'national deliverance' was formed on 1 April, with Amin as the prime minister.

Amin was an uncompromising hardliner whose policy of purging the administration of Parchamis fell foul of President Taraki. In the ensuing power struggle Premier Amin gained ground and took over the defence ministry, and thus counter-insurgency operations. In mid-September there was a shoot-out between the aides of Amin and Taraki. On 6 October the official media announced that President Taraki had died after a 'serious illness'.

Soviet leaders, who had provided refuge in Moscow to such leading Parchamis as Karmal, advised Amin to take conciliatory steps to allay public hostility towards the regime. Aware of Kabul's dependence on Soviet aid, economic and military, Amin accepted the advice. He released several thousand political prisoners. He reintroduced the invocation of Allah in official statements and broadcasts, and ordered the repairing of mosques at state expense. While reiterating 'complete freedom of religion, and profound respect for and widescale support to Islam', he vowed to combat 'religious fanaticism'.[13] He tried to woo sufi leaders, and instructed the committee on drafting the new constitution to 'pay special attention to Islam'. Proclaiming an amnesty to a quarter of a million refugees, he invited them to return. This was a futile gesture. Anti-government sentiment among the refugees had risen to the point where members of the Hizb-e Islami had initiated a programme of assassinating PDP leaders in the capital.

The Hizb-e Islami's terroristic actions in Kabul were symptomatic of the upsurge in anti-government activities along the Afghan–Pakistani border. The eastern province of Paktiya became a hotbed of insurgents. Amin was obliged to call on the Soviets to help him fight the rebels. Together, they defeated the insurgents in Paktiya. Following this, Marshal Ivan Pavlovsky, head of the Soviet ground forces, toured Afghanistan to prepare overall plans for countering insurgency. This was the beginning of a process which culminated in the arrival of tens of thousands of Soviet troops.

From late October 1979 onwards Soviet Central Asian contingents began taking over guard duties from Afghan troops in order to relieve the latter to fight the rebels. In mid-December two Soviet battalions arrived at Bagram air base near Kabul, which came increasingly under Soviet control. Following an attack on Assadullah Amin, head of the secret police, at the downtown headquarters of President Amin, the Afghan leader moved to Darulaman Palace on the outskirts of the capital. By 24 December there were some 8,000 Soviet troops and 4,000 military advisers in Afghanistan. Three days later Soviet forces seized military installations in Kabul, and attacked Darulaman Palace: Amin was killed. Babrak Karmal, who had been in exile in Moscow for over a year, arrived to lead the new regime. Soon there were 50,000 Soviet troops in Afghanistan. The strength of the Afghan military was then put at 80,000. The arrival of Soviet troops in such large numbers to bolster the Afghan state was an admission that the local Marxist regime had alienated large sections of society, and that its rulers had failed to assess the mood of their people correctly and calibrate the pace and nature of reform accordingly. Since then, in various ways the moderate PDP leadership has been trying to undo the damage done to the regime's popular standing due to the excesses committed by the over-zealous Khalqi faction, led by Amin, which exercised effective power from August 1978 to December 1979.

On assuming power Karmal proclaimed the release of all political prisoners, abolition of 'all anti-democratic, anti-human regulations, and all arrests, arbitrary persecutions, house searches and inquisitions', respect for 'the sacred principles of Islam', protection of family life, and observance of 'legal and lawful private ownership'.[14] It was obvious that after the excesses of the Amin regime Karmal wanted to take palliative action, and not only in the religious field. In this he had the wholehearted backing of the Kremlin whose despatching of Soviet troops to Afghanistan, stemming from Article 4 of the year-old Afghan–

Soviet Friendship Treaty, was described by Karmal as ushering in the 'second phase' of the Saur Revolution.

Moscow's military intervention also marked the second phase of the Afghan resistance. The arrival of Soviet troops was a severe blow to Afghan national pride, and resulted in thousands of nationalist-minded professional men leaving their homes either to join the resistance active in the countryside or enrol with the resistance parties based in Pakistan or Iran. The organizations operating from Pakistan continued to exist as independent entities after the failure of an attempt to include them in a 110-member council proposed by a provisional Loya Jirga, Grand National Assembly, held in May 1979 in Peshawar. Describing the Loya Jirga as unrepresentative and illegal, the leaders of these parties rejected the constitution for an Islamic republic drafted by it.

By the spring of 1979 there were six Pakistan-based (Sunni) Islamic parties of Afghans, and they had a vested interest in maintaining themselves as independent bodies: the Pakistan government had decided to channel Islamic charity to Afghan refugees through them rather than its own bureaucracy. Three of these parties were fundamentalist: the Hizb-e Islami (led by Hikmatyar), the Jamaat-e Islami (led by Rabbani) and the breakaway Hizb-e Islami (led by Maulavi Yunus Khalis). The rest were traditional religious parties: the National Islamic Front of Afghanistan (led by Sayyid Ahmad Gailani), the National Liberation Front of Afghanistan (led by Sibghatullah Mujaddidi), and the Islamic Revolutionary Movement (led by Maulavi Muhammad Nabi Muhammadi). The latter parties wanted to return Afghanistan to the pre-1973 set-up with King Zahir Shah as the constitutional monarch; and they drew their support from village mullahs, tribal chiefs, landlords and sufi leaders.

In 1981 the active cadres of the six parties numbered 73,000 with the fundamentalists accounting for two-thirds of the total, the contingent of Hikmatyar's Hizb-e Islami being by far the largest. In contrast the three traditional religious parties were even in strength.[15]

Not surprisingly the Karmal regime directed its fire, military and ideological, at the fundamentalist parties, with Hikmatyar's Hizb-e Islami being the prime target. Both the Hizb-e Islami and its predecessor, the Ikhwan, drew their inspiration from the ideology of the Muslim Brotherhood of Egypt. Hikmatyar was unimpressed by the calibre of traditional Afghan mullahs who, he stated, had failed either to offer intellectual stimulation to the faithful or constitute themselves into a strong independent force ready to confront an unIslamic ruler. That the fault lay partly in the absence of seminaries in Afghanistan with a tradition of offering excellent religious training or producing outstanding Islamic personalities did not alter the validity of Hikmatyar's argument. He was equally scathing about sufi leaders whom he often described as 'decadent, superstition-ridden self-seekers' who had corrupted Islam. According to Hikmatyar, returning Afghanistan to the true path of Islam meant having to reform the religious establishment, eradicate sufism and sufi orders, and implement the Sharia in its totality. The last requirement could only be achieved by abrogating such traditional laws as the Pushtunwali. Also it would mean imposing the veil on women in rural Afghanistan where it was not the norm. 'The moral and religious reformation' of Afghan society, stated a publication of the Hizb-e Islami, included 'revival of the role of the mosque, revival of Islamic learning, centres for training scholars to impart religious education, character building in the light of Islam . . . elevating the status of the mullah through state assistance.'[16]

Given Hikmatyar's critical attitude towards traditional ulama, it was not long before he fell out with one of his colleagues in the party leadership: Maulavi Yunus Khalis, a Deoband-trained cleric who was also a tribal leader. The specific reason for the split was Khalis's insistence on engaging in the armed struggle immediately and his involvement with the uprising in Paktiya in the spring of 1979, something Hikmatyar opposed. He wanted to build up an extensive network in Afghanistan before striking at the regime. Khalis lacked the organizational genius and charisma of Hikmatyar, and his breakaway faction was only a fraction of the parent body.

Hikmatyar, who ran a very tightly knit party, was unwilling to adjust its structure in order to accommodate the peculiarly Afghan social reality of tribes, sufi brotherhoods and traditional rural élite. In contrast, Rabbani, the leader of the Jamaat-e Islami, swiftly abandoned the élitist nature of his party to integrate supporters who were not fully committed to the party ideology, which was inspired by the works of Maududi and Qutb. Rabbani's flexible attitude extended to Shias: alone among Sunni leaders he conceded the Shia demand that the Jaafari school of law be applied to them. During his years as a theology professor in Kabul he had concentrated more on ridding Afghan society of non-Islamic influences and less on attacking Islamic traditionalists. Now he was able to draw on the existing networks of clerics, sufi orders and the newly emerging Islamists – leaving out only the tribal network – to strengthen his party. His weakness was that he was a Tajik, and not a Pushtun like Hikmatyar. Tajiks, forming only a quarter of the total Afghan population of 19 million, are only half as numerous as Pushtuns.

While both Rabbani and Hikmatyar were committed to full implementation of the Sharia in a future Islamic state, Rabbani envisaged a multi-party system, as expounded by Maududi, which was not the case with Hikmatyar. An authoritarian figure, he was for a single-party Islamic state. He vehemently attacked his rivals, describing them variously as monarchists, religiously corrupt or deviant, or pro-western. His party, he stressed, was a contrast to theirs: it was republican, religiously pure and committed to the 'Neither East nor West' policy. Whereas the aim of other parties was to bring about the withdrawal of the Soviet troops from Afghanistan and restore Afghan independence, the Hizb-e Islami talked of carrying the guerrilla raids beyond the Oxus river into Soviet Central Asia and rolling back communism by freeing the Muslim lands of Bukhara, Tashkent and Dushabe.

Both Hikmatyar and Rabbani labelled the Kabul regime

as infidel and exhorted the believers to wage a holy war against it and die as martyrs if necessary. Hikmatyar's dogmatic ambition and exceptional organizational ability made the Hizb-e Islami by far the strongest party with a command structure stretching as far as Herat, with a network of recruitment centres, training camps, medical facilities, warehouses and offices. His party claimed to have set up parallel government in the areas it controlled inside Afghanistan. In the case of Rabbani, his ally Ahmad Shah Masoud in Panjshir valley near Kabul had proved to be one of the ablest guerrilla commanders. While successfully resisting central control he had established a parallel political–administrative infrastructure in the valley. This bolstered the prestige and credibility of the Jamaat-e Islami.

Within Afghanistan, besides the areas controlled by the Peshawar-based parties there were territories in the central Hazarajat highlands ruled by Shia organizations which maintained offices in Iranian cities as well as Quetta, Pakistan. The Revolutionary Council of the Islamic Union of Afghanistan, which set up its administration in the Hazarajat region in September 1979, consisted of moderate and radical Shia Islamists. In the spring of 1984 the coalition of the pro-Iranian Sazman-e Nasr and the Sejah-e Pasdaran, Army of the Guards, overthrew the Revolutionary Council and assumed control of the region, thus strengthening Iran's role in the ultimate solution of the Afghanistan crisis.

Fundamentalist parties derived their recruits mainly from young college-educated men with rural or small-town backgrounds from the families of civil servants, teachers or traders. They were often radical, dogmatic and intolerant, mirror images of the young cadres of the People's Democratic Party.

The traditional Islamic camp stemmed from the religious establishment of Afghanistan which had been close to King Zahir Shah. The leader of the National Liberation Front of Afghanistan (NFLA), Sibghatullah Mujaddidi, a graduate of Al Azhar and an Islamic teacher, was a nephew of the

Hazrat of Shor Bazaar. Due to the cosy relations between the Mujaddidi family and the king, the NFLA attracted many monarchists. Indeed the NFLA used the emblem of monarchy as a nationalist and Islamic symbol. Ahmad Gailani, the leader of the National Islamic Front of Afghanistan and the head of the Qadiriya (sufi) order, had been a close adviser to King Zahir Shah. He was the least religious of the Pakistan-based Afghan leaders, and a realist, who recognized that the Soviet Union had a permanent interest in Afghanistan and advised co-existence. Nabi Muhammadi, the leader of the Islamic Revolutionary Party, was a cleric who had run an Islamic college in Logar, south of Kabul, and a leading figure in the Qadiriya order. His party contained both traditional mullahs and young men with modern education. He was at ease with both religious and secular figures, modernistic or traditional, and was in a sense a bridge between the traditionalist camp and the fundamentalist camp.

The common denominator of these parties was that they were pan-Islamic and anti-Marxist, and used Islam as the exclusive, or at least a major, rallying cry to mobilize popular resistance against the leftist regime. To put it differently, Islam played a crucial role in providing a sense of purpose to these organizations. Yet this proved insufficient to bring them under one umbrella and one leader.

After the failure of the provisional Loya Jirga in May 1979, attempts were made at the Islamic Conference Organization foreign ministers' meetings in January and May 1980 to forge a united front of the exile parties. These failed. What did happen, though, was that such leaders as Hikmatyar and Rabbani were successful in soliciting funds from the oil-rich states of the Gulf. Strengthened by this financial aid Hikmatyar's Hizb-e Islami tried to expand its turf into the regions where other parties and tribes were dominant. This worsened inter-party relations, and brought some 300 mullahs from Afghan provinces to Peshawar in April 1981 to foster unity. Under this pressure Gailani, Mujaddidi and Nabi Muhammadi set up a joint council. The three fundamentalist parties formed an umbrella organization called the Islamic Alliance of Afghanistan under the chairmanship of Professor Abdul Rasul Sayyaf. Educated at Al Azhar and Medina University, Sayyaf was fluent in Arabic, an asset which won him a warm reception in the Gulf capitals. The establishment of these coalitions helped to co-ordinate the distribution of arms from America, Saudi Arabia and Egypt which in the summer of 1981 were arriving at the rate of two planeloads a week. Sayyaf used his exalted position to win over many floating Afghan groups with supplies of weapons, and transformed the Islamic Alliance of Afghanistan into a party of his own, a development which revived inter-party discord.

However, this did not discourage Saudi Arabia from keeping up its pressure on the Islamic parties to unite. In early 1983, fearing that they would be excluded from the negotiations in progress under the United Nations aegis between Kabul, Moscow, Islamabad and Tehran to solve the Afghanistan problem, the Islamic parties tried hard to create an umbrella organization. The result was the seven-party Islamic Alliance of Afghan Mujahedin in May 1983 under the chairmanship of Sayyaf with Mujaddidi as his deputy.

The Kabul regime ignored the traditional Islamic groups and concentrated its attacks on the fundamentalist ones, particularly the Hizb-e Islami (both factions) and the Jamaat-e Islami. It coupled this with a policy of projecting itself as a guardian of Islam. President Karmal took a lead in this. Having relegated the red flag to the People's Democratic Party in January 1980, he restored the national tricolour on the eve of the second anniversary of the Saur Revolution in April. 'The tricolour has taken deep root in our society and is permanently interlinked with the ups and downs of the struggles of our people,' he said.[17] Karmal prayed in public regularly, and began his statements with an invocation to Allah. His audience responded to his public speeches with intermittent cries of 'Allahu Akbar' (God is Great). He instituted the Office of Islamic Teachings under his direct control, and radio and television reintroduced recitations of the Quran. In a speech in mid-June, he restressed that respect for Islam was part of official policy. Various steps were taken to illustrate this. A higher profile was given to the Ministry of Religious Affairs and Waqfs whose activities were widely reported in the media. Among other things this ministry awarded hefty salary increases to the ulama and gave them enhanced importance. In return the clergy became more willing to explain official policies and reforms to their congregations. The ministry initiated a well-advertised project of building new mosques and religious schools. It also introduced a programme of exchange of Islamic delegations with the Soviet Central Asian republics. The purpose was to reassure Afghan Muslims that Islam and Islamic institutions continued to exist in these constituents of the Soviet Union. Radio broadcasts from these republics in Persian, Azeri, Tajik, Uzbek and Turkoman languages stressed that Islam was safe in the Soviet system and that danger to it came from America, Britain, China and Israel.

As for Islamists, the government tried to challenge the monopoly over Islam they claimed, and took measures to block the movement of the guerrillas to and from Pakistan. With the assistance of such prominent clerics as Sayyid Baha al Din Jan Aqa, it mounted a campaign portraying the resistance as unIslamic. It tried to win over the tribes along the Pakistan border with bribes and promises of regional autonomy. Given that the relations between the fundamentalist parties, led mainly by personalities who lacked traditional status, and the border tribes had been tenuous, the government met with some success. Those tribals who switched their loyalty to Kabul – following the receipt of cash and weapons, the traditional means of bribery in the tribal world – began harassing the resistance fighters as they tried to cross into the Afghan interior or out of it.

The Karmal administration intensified its efforts to expand its popular base. In early 1981 it organized the founding of the National Fatherland Front with due consideration to the composition, characteristics and qualities of various nationalities, tribes and clans that constituted the Afghan nation. Among the Front's components were the Jamaat-e Ulama and numerous tribal jirgas, assemblies. The Front's major task was to publicize and explain official policies to the masses. By March 1981 the Front claimed to have 100,000 members affiliated to 400 local councils. The number of full and candidate members of the People's Democratic Party was officially put at 90,000.[18] But the activities of both organizations were limited mainly to urban centres since large parts of the countryside had slipped out of the control of the central authority.

How extensive the resistance's actions had been could be judged by the official statements in early 1983 that the counter-revolutionaries had destroyed or damaged nearly half of the schools and hospitals (1,814 and thirty-one respectively), 111 basic health centres, three-quarters of communications lines, 800 heavy transport vehicles and 906 peasant co-operatives.[19]

Human casualties were mounting too. By early 1984 the number of dead or injured Afghan troops was put at 17,000 and among guerrillas 30,000. The estimates of Soviet casualties varied between 13,500 and 30,000.[20]

By now firm lines were drawn between the two sides. The Kabul regime, heavily dependent on 115,000 Soviet troops and generous military aid from Moscow, was committed to subduing the continuing resistance in rural Afghanistan. On the other side the Pakistan-based Afghan parties, receiving arms and cash from the US, Saudi Arabia, Egypt and China to an approximate value of 500 million dollars a year – twice the Afghan budget, including foreign aid, in 1980 – were equally determined to maintain the jihad against the Marxist government until the expulsion of the Soviet forces and the collapse of the infidel regime.

It was against this background that UN-sponsored talks between the various parties proceeded, the points in dispute being the timetable for Soviet withdrawal, the cessation of foreign arms aid to the Afghan groups, and the return of the refugees to their homes. The rate of Soviet withdrawal became the most intractable point. The Kabul–Moscow side offered a period of four years after the stopping of foreign military assistance to the Afghan resistance. The Islamabad–Washington axis specified three to four months. The Afghan parties wanted an immediate and unconditional Soviet withdrawal.

After Mikhail Gorbachev had become secretary-general of the Communist Party of the Soviet Union in March 1985, the Kremlin began to show flexibility on Afghanistan. Gorbachev described the conflict in Afghanistan as 'a bleeding wound' and expressed his wish to scale down Soviet commitment to Kabul. The Kremlin's serious intent was illustrated by the offer by the Kabul–Moscow axis to shorten the period of Soviet withdrawal from forty-eight months to eighteen. Moscow was keen to see the anti-Marxist forces negotiate with the Karmal government to bring about national reconciliation. When it realized that resistance leaders inside and outside the country were unwilling to deal with Karmal, it worked behind the scenes to ease him out, in May 1986, in favour of Dr Muhammad Najibullah. By announcing shortly afterwards that it would withdraw 6,000 Soviet troops in October, Moscow underlined its wish to settle the Afghanistan crisis.

These moves by the Kremlin were likely to be seen by the Islamist parties and the US as signs of weakness. In order to disabuse its adversaries of such an interpretation, Moscow increased its counter-insurgency activities in Afghanistan. It began using crack units instead of regular troops to shut off rebel supply lines from Pakistan. In a joint operation in November 1986 Afghan and Soviet forces seized Kama Dakka, a vital staging post for western and Chinese weapons from Pakistan. They also continued their campaign of exhorting and bribing the border tribes to impede the passage of arms and guerrillas into Afghanistan along its 1,500-mile border with Pakistan.

The Islamists and the Americans were not idle either. Having forced the Kabul–Moscow axis to adopt an openly compromising stance, they tried to raise the Soviet cost of continued presence in Afghanistan. They knew that whatever the strength of Islam's appeal to Afghans, the balance of forces could only be settled on the battlefield. Here the extensive deployment of helicopter gunships by Afghan and Soviet troops gave them an overwhelming advantage over their Islamist adversaries. In order to neutralize Kabul's air superiority Washington decided to arm the guerrillas with British-manufactured Blowpipe and US-made shoulder-held Stinger anti-aircraft missiles. About 150 Stingers were shipped to the area in the late spring of 1986 followed by 300 Blowpipes several months later. They were put to extensive use in the autumn, and proved more effective than the Soviet-made SAM-7s that had been in use before. Afghan sources in Peshawar claimed to have shot down sixty government helicopters in the last three months of 1986.[21]

Given this, resistance leaders had good reason to believe that the unilateral ceasefire that Najibullah declared on 15 January for six months stemmed from the growing weakness of his side in the face of the Islamists' intransigence and perseverance. As for Najibullah, he visualized his move as a prelude to total Soviet withdrawal and the formation of a government of national reconciliation to include among others some guerrilla leaders.

The seven-party Islamic Alliance of Afghan Mujahedin rejected the ceasefire offer, and decided to form an interim government to take over from the Najibullah administration.

Najibullah was undeterred. In a move reminiscent of Karmal's National Fatherland Front six years previously, Najibullah established the Commission for National Reconciliation which in turn set up hundreds of branches in the country to encourage the opposition to give up their armed resistance and participate in normal political life. The media stopped calling guerrillas 'bandits' or 'counter-revolutionaries', and instead referred to them as 'misguided brothers' with whom the government was prepared to share power. Concerted efforts were made to downplay the radicalism of the Saur Revolution. 'We call it revolution, but actually it is a type of evolution,' explained Abdur

Rahim Hatef, head of the Commission for National Reconciliation.[22] The key words in the political and administrative officials' vocabulary were 'gradual' and 'voluntary'.

The Islamic resistance retaliated by assassinating provincial leaders of the Commission for National Reconciliation. By late March the ceasefire had virtually collapsed. Whatever gains the government made were modest. It claimed that 44,000 refugees had returned and that 21,000 guerrillas had given up their violent activities. Given that, by official accounts, there were 2 million refugees and a quarter of a million (intermittently active) guerrillas,[23] the results of the unilateral ceasefire were unimpressive.

With the consensus on the Soviet withdrawal informally settling around the period of eleven months, the main point to be tackled, outside the UN framework, was the composition of the government in Kabul that would be acceptable to the Islamic opposition and its backers. In June Najibullah declared himself ready to negotiate with the supporters of King Muhammad Zahir Shah, in exile in Rome, to form a coalition government. In a way this was an invitation to the traditional Islamic parties in the Islamic Alliance of Afghan Mujahedin to negotiate their entry into the Afghan administration, a step bound to break up the Alliance, and help secure the Kabul government universal legitimacy. But Zahir Shah refused to share power with Najibullah. At the same time he continued to spurn plans to form a government in exile around him. What Zahir Shah wanted was the restoration of tradition in Afghanistan which the PDP was very unlikely to concede. As for the fundamentalist parties and Marxist PDP, the differences were too basic to be fudged. While upholding Islam the PDP believed firmly in separating religious Islam from political Islam. This was anathema to the fundamentalists for whom Islamic ideology permeated all aspects of life: religious, political, social and economic.

Neither Kabul nor Moscow was prepared to cede the dominant position that the People's Democratic Party visualized for itself in any future coalition government. During its nine years of rule it had engendered its own constituencies: the peasants who had secured land; the emancipated women who dreaded the prospect of being returned to the four walls of home and the veil; and all those who had benefited, materially and otherwise, from the literacy campaign.

On the opposite side the traditional Islamic parties had merely managed to maintain the networks their leaders had headed before the Saur Revolution. It was the four fundamentalist parties which, like the PDP, had created new constituencies both inside and outside Afghanistan. Being the main beneficiaries of the aid by foreign powers – running in 1987 at 640 million dollars from the US, matched by an equal amount from Saudi Arabia[24] – they had the means to sustain the vastly enlarged networks to promote the fundamentalist cause in political and military terms. In other words, the Marxist revolution, and the resources and facilities provided by Pakistan, Iran, the Gulf states, Egypt and America had been the main reasons for the upsurge in Islamic fundamentalism among Afghans.

Yet no observer seriously believed that the fundamentalist parties, singly or jointly, would or could assume power in Afghanistan. Firstly, there were differences among them on such vital issues as the right of women to vote, and whether the future Islamic Republic of Afghanistan would be a single- or multi-party state. Secondly, these organizations clashed with the traditional Islamic ones on such basic questions of doctrine as monarchy. The traditionalists were monarchists whereas the fundamentalists regarded hereditary power as unIslamic. Finally, on the subject of co-existence with Moscow, such traditionalists as Gailani were prepared to accept the exceptional interests that the Soviet Union had in their country. In contrast, for the fundamentalist Hikmatyar the future Islamic Republic of Afghanistan was to become a springboard for exporting Islamic revolution to the southern states of the USSR. That this was not mere rhetoric became apparent when a Hizb-e Islami group tried in April 1987 to capture a frontier guard post near Pianj in Soviet Tajikistan.[25]

All in all Afghanistan provides a complex picture of

Islam and Islamic forces. Afghan society has none of the homogeneity that Egyptian Muslim society has. It is extremely heterogeneous, and economically underdeveloped. Until the Saur Revolution the state had made minimal inroads into the individual or social life of Afghans. In a way the resistance offered by rural Afghans to the central government is as much a rebellion against rapid socio-economic reform as it is against the state itself.

Traditional Islamists had their heyday in the 1930s and 1940s. The growth of Islamic fundamentalism was patchy until the turmoil of the April 1978–December 1979 period. It has now become a substantially important part of the political–military scene in the country. What is more, quite uniquely, it has been sucked into the balance of power equation of the superpowers. Since it is part of the American side its future depends primarily on the policy Washington assumes towards it, and secondarily on the stance Islamabad adopts. Unlike in Iran, therefore, fundamentalism in Afghanistan does not have a strong, secure and united base at home, which is self-sufficient with a dynamic of its own. Unlike Iran, again, Afghan fundamentalists are not in practice following the 'Neither East nor West' policy which they, in theory, profess.

In short, there is no single model for Islamic fundamentalism, whether in power or opposition.

CONCLUSION

Two conclusions are self-evident in this study. Revival and reform have been recurring phenomena in Islamic history. And they manifest themselves differently in different circumstances.

Closely related to Islamic revival is the movement to return to the fundamental scriptures of the faith: the Quran and the practices of Prophet Muhammad as recorded in the Hadiths, which together form the Sharia, Divine Law. When it comes to applying the Sharia to the everyday life of Muslims, the choice is between taqlid – that is, dependence on or imitation of the opinions and interpretations of the ulama of the past – and ijtihad, independent interpretation. By and large Islamic reformers have reiterated the believer's right to practise ijtihad. This applies more to Sunnis than Shias: unlike Sunnism, Shiaism almost always kept the gates of ijtihad open. But irrespective of their sectarian persuasion, fundamentalist reformers have been unanimous that what the Quran offers is final, unique and most authentic, and that in Islam there is no room whatsoever for synthesizing the Quranic message with any non-Islamic doctrine or practice.

Thus fundamentalist reform means returning to the Sharia, creative interpretation of the Divine Law in the context of changing circumstances, and rejection of non-Islamic accretions to Islam.

The dynamic of fundamentalism derives from the conflict that exists between the egalitarian message of the Quran and the exploitation and iniquity of the real world, between the demands of virtuous existence made on the believer by the Sharia and the actuality of life surrounded by temptation and vice.

It was their commitment to the Quran and pious living that drove the Shiat Ali, followers of Imam Ali, to struggle against his enemies. In that sense Shias were the first fundamentalists. Later, the rise of the pragmatic, yet despotic, Ummayads was seen by true believers to be an affront to the teachings of Islam, and to bring about their downfall became the prime objective of the fundamentalists. They succeeded.

In subsequent centuries the Islamic community became vast and complex due to the spread of the faith throughout much of Asia, Africa and Europe, the firming up of the Sunni–Shia divide, the codification of the Sharia into four Sunni and one Shia schools, and the emergence of sufism as a prime agent of popularizing Islam. Sufism included the heterodoxy of Hallaj as well as the orthodoxy of Ghazali, who attempted to fit the mystical experience within the limits of the Sharia – a stance which has been consistently maintained by such sufi orders as Naqshbandi.

There was creative tension between popular Islam, as represented by sufi brotherhoods, and establishment Islam, as represented by the ulama. Sufism itself had an uneasy existence between pure and syncretic versions of Islam. When the Mogul emperor Akbar, who was close to the Chisti sufi order, launched Din Illahi in the late sixteenth century, it was an example of someone offering the world syncretic Islam, a development which elicited a frontal attack from Baqibullah, a Naqshbandi leader: a position vehemently maintained by his disciple Sirhindi. He reaffirmed the sufi orthodoxy that a true believer's mystical experiences had to adapt themselves to the Sharia. It was left to another Naqshbandi personality, Waliullah, to combine an assault on syncretic Islam with one on establishment Islam by calling for perpetual ijtihad to cope with contemporary problems.

However, the credit for mounting simultaneous attacks on popular Islam, syncretic Islam and establishment Islam went to Abdul Wahhab in the mid-eighteenth century. He condemned sufism as well as pre-Islamic practices and beliefs of the tribes in Najd, and upheld the believer's right to ijtihad. His uncompromising stance was moulded by the social and geographical conditions of Najd. He functioned in a tribal society in an underpopulated central Arabian desert where Islam did not have to compete against any other well-developed religious creed – an environment vastly different from the populous Indian subcontinent with a long-established pantheistic Hindu civilization.

Abdul Wahhab and the Islamic reformers in India were grappling with doctrinal and other problems of the faith in an environment where Islam was either the only organized religion (as in Najd) or the dominant political–administrative force (as in India). But beginning in the mid-eighteenth century, as the Muslim world became increasingly subservient to the West, and exposed to western secular ideas, practices and political models, the situation changed substantially. Now fundamentalist reform acquired the twin task of releasing Islam from the legal–scholastic tradition of fossilized jurisprudents and purging it of the secular concepts which had penetrated Islam under the cloak of modernism.

The credit for conceiving Islam's global predicament and offering solutions must rest with Afghani, the father of the modern Islamic reformist movement. Having lived in all the important countries of the Muslim world – as well as Britain, France and Russia – he acquired an unrivalled breadth of understanding. He propagated pan-Islamic ideas and called for a jihad against Britain and Russia, the leading European imperialists of the age. He advocated opening up the long-shut doors of ijtihad, and went on to pronounce the parliamentary system as being in line with basic Islamic tenets. He urged Muslims to study science and scientific method. Since he preached his gospel during a period of irreversible decline of the Ottoman empire, the seat of the caliphate, his message fell on receptive ears. In 1876 the Ottoman emperor became the first Muslim ruler in Islamic history to adopt a written constitution, albeit under political pressure from a powerful group called the Young Ottomans.

Abdu, one of Afghani's disciples, interpreted the Islamic concept of shura (consultation) as parliamentary democracy, ijma (consensus) as public opinion and maslah (choosing that interpretation of the Sharia which causes maximum good) as utilitarianism. Finally Rashid Rida, a disciple of Abdu, offered a blueprint of the modern Islamic state. Only a mujtahid, chosen by representatives of all Islamic sects, was qualified to rule this state. He needed the assistance of popular representatives to legislate, where the Sharia had to be supplemented by civil and administrative law, qanun, which was in tune with the spirit of broad Islamic teachings. The believers must obey the ruler so long as his actions were in line with Islamic precepts and served the common weal. When his decisions seemed to contravene Islamic principles or the public interest, the popular representatives must exercise their religious right to challenge him. Here was an outline of Islamic democracy well suited to the temper of the times.

Once Islamic reformers had offered political and other interpretations of the Sharia which took into account contemporary circumstances, it was only a matter of time before the tools of propagation and implementation of ideas employed by them too followed suit.

Hassan al Banna, for instance, went beyond pamphleteering and soliciting the support of the élites in Muslim countries, the techniques used by Afghani and Abdu. In tune with the times of mass participation in political movements, he engaged the attention and energies of ordinary Muslims and created in the late 1920s the Muslim Brotherhood, a popular party with a slogan which included the Quran, Prophet Muhammad, God, constitutional government and martyrdom.[1] The timing was right too. The Muslim masses were feeling disheartened and bewildered at the disappearance of the thirteen-century-old caliphate, and the message disseminated by the Muslim Brotherhood gave them succour and hope. It also provided a countervailing force to the tide of secularism sweeping Egypt not only from the West but also from the post-caliphate Turkey of Kemal Ataturk.

But Banna did more than found a mass party. By insisting that every branch of the Brotherhood should have its own mosque, centre, school and club or home industry, he gave flesh to the idea that Islam is all pervasive. By so doing, he also offered an institution which helped its predominantly poor and lower-middle-class membership to overcome the spiritual and social alienation it felt in an environment dominated by secular, westernized classes.

Since then as economic development has accelerated in Islamic countries in the wake of political independence, and latterly a dramatic rise in the price of oil – a mineral found in many Muslim states – cities have attracted vast numbers of migrants from villages. They feel lost and rootless in their new environment. This reservoir of alienated masses packed into the poor quarters of urban centres provides a ready audience and recruiting ground for radical and revolutionary groups, secular and religious.

Muslim fundamentalists try to rally the alienated and underprivileged on the basis of Islam. They present it as a religion of justice and equity and decry the current ruling élite as unjust, unIslamic and corrupt which deserves to be overthrown, or at the very least replaced non-violently, by true believers. The tactics used to achieve this objective vary: from setting up secret cells to addressing large congregations inside a mosque or outside, from bloody confrontations with the security forces to peaceful participation in elections, from carrying out terroristic actions to holding non-violent demonstrations, from subverting official institutions through infiltration to total withdrawal from society, from waging open warfare against an infidel state to conducting intelligent debate with secular adversaries.

As a rule large organizations tend to function openly and small ones clandestinely. One could argue that because certain bodies are not allowed to operate openly they remain small. On the other hand, a popular party such as the Muslim Brotherhood in Egypt had an underground apparatus even when it was permitted to function legally.

But whatever the size and structure of a fundamentalist organization, or the intensity of its commitment to the cause, its ultimate goal remains to install a truly Islamic regime in the country.

One way to accomplish this is by transforming social protest into a revolutionary movement, in stages, using Islamic symbols, language, customs and festivals. This is what happened in Iran, except that there was no Islamic party like the Muslim Brotherhood functioning there – but, more significantly, a general body of Shia ulama with its own independent economic base and widespread network. Another path to the goal of installing an Islamic regime is for a fundamentalist group to assassinate the ruler (like Sadat in Egypt) or capture an important urban centre (such as Hama in Syria) or holy shrine (like the Grand Mosque in Mecca), hoping that the incident will trigger an uprising against the state, enabling the fundamentalist forces to seize power.

But whatever method is used the key element is the loyalty or otherwise of the military. The regimes in Egypt, Syria and Saudi Arabia survived the severe blows struck by radical fundamentalists because they continued to retain the loyalty of the military. Only in Iran was Khomeini able to undermine the morale of the army, gradually, to the extent of making it an ineffective tool for restoring law and order. This happened for the following reasons. The army was used as a police force to quell civil disturbances for such a long time that it ceased to terrify, or even awe, the people. Secondly, the army had a high proportion of conscripts, and they found it hard to ignore continued exhortations by a religious leader of such a high calibre as Khomeini to abandon the Pahlavis. The deeply rooted martyr complex of Shias, which led thousands of Iranians to bare their chests to the bullets of the army, was an important factor in demoralizing the ranks. The onset of the emotional and highly charged Ashura festival at the height of the anti-Shah movement finally turned the scales against the secular, westernized Pahlavi dynasty.

Among the case studies presented in this survey, Syria, Iran and Afghanistan fall in the category of a sustained struggle by the fundamentalists to overthrow a secular regime, and Egypt and Saudi Arabia in the category of 'one-off' attempts.

There are several reasons for the Afghan fundamentalists' failure to assume power. Fundamentalism did not flower as a movement of protest against the repressive autocracy and corruption of the nominally Muslim regimes of King Zahir Shah and President Daoud Khan, but grew as a reaction to an attempt by leftist military officers and intellectuals to transform the April 1978 military coup into a fully-fledged Marxist revolution. Just as the leftist regime in Kabul has found its powerful northern neighbour, the Soviet Union, indispensable to its survival so have the fundamentalist and traditional Islamic groups become deeply dependent on the Muslim neighbours of their country – Pakistan and Iran – for their sustenance and growth. In short, the Islamist leaders are not full masters of their movement.

Having created propitious conditions for the growth of Islamic fundamentalism by its extreme actions during the first twenty months of the revolution, the leftist regime has been on the retreat on socio-economic reform and secularization of society. At the very least this has helped to stop the inflow of fresh recruits into the Islamist camp.

The policies of the leftist government have activated previously dormant sections of society – urban illiterates, women and landless peasants – and this has strengthened its hands. At the same time it has done much to end the alienation that the ulama felt during the early months of the revolution. Being the paymaster of the ulama has given an advantage to the government, which it has tried to use in winning at least tacit approval for its much-moderated policies. By taking an initiative to bring the civil war to an end it has been able to present itself as a genuine peace-seeker to an increasingly war-weary people, and thus win the backing of many fence-sitters inside the country. It has done this without much slackening in its counter-insurgency activities, including the bribing of border tribes along the Afghan–Pakistani frontier.

In the final analysis, as the party exercising power in Afghanistan's urban centres, the PDP retains the initiative in the conflict. In any compromise that may be reached between the PDP and the Islamic resistance, the Marxist party is unlikely to agree to a programme of moulding the state and society according to the doctrines of fundamental Islam, or to give up such vital ministries as defence, foreign affairs, police and intelligence.

A similar mixture of internal and external factors explains the failure of Syrian fundamentalists to overthrow the Assad regime. By the time the Syrian Brotherhood declared a jihad against the Assad administration in 1976, secular pan-Arab Baathism, which reveres Islam as an inherent, cultural component of Arabism, had been in power for more than a decade, and engendered its own constituencies. These consisted of sectarian and religious minorities like Alawis and Christians, as well as large social classes like peasants and workers, who had benefited from the decrees on land reform and nationalization of industry and wholesale trade. During the earlier, less serious confrontations between the fundamentalists and the authorities these segments of society had rallied around the Baathist flag and beaten back the Islamist threat. Assad had thus inherited government and party machines with an experience of repelling Islamic fundamentalist assaults through official and popular actions.

When in early 1980 the Muslim Brotherhood, drawing on the experience of Iran, forged an alliance with secular opposition forces before staging a determined attack on the regime with massive demonstrations and strikes, Assad clearly saw the contours of an Islamic revolutionary movement along Iranian lines. But, unlike the Shah, he did not have to grapple with a towering and astute Islamic personality of the stature of Khomeini. And he had a greater area of manoeuvre than the Shah. He made specific political, economic and administrative concessions to meet the general charge of corruption and specific grievances of merchants – the major financiers of the fundamentalists – and professionals, demanding relaxation of import quotas and long-suspended civil liberties. Side by side went military operations to quash the armed fundamentalists and their active sympathizers. During the crisis the state-controlled media conducted a virulent campaign against the fundamentalists, taking care to make a clear distinction between the moderate and extremist sections of the movement, and highlighting state decisions to increase the number of mosques and raise the salaries and status of the ulama. Under the mounting pressure of the fundamentalist-led agitation, Alawis and Christians actively sided with the government, afraid that a future Islamic regime would annihilate them. In contrast, merchants, apprehensive of the anarchy that would follow the overthrow of the Assad regime, began to distance themselves from the insurrectionary aspirations of the Islamists. What clinched the outcome in the government's favour was the fundamentalists' failed attempt to assassinate Assad.

All along, external factors were very much part of the struggle waged by the fundamentalists. They had sanctuaries in Iraq and Jordan, and received aid from Riyadh. The other important external element was Israel. Indeed, what finally settled the issue in Assad's favour was the Israeli invasion of Lebanon in June 1982, which led to the closing of Syrian ranks.

In the case of Iran the mosque–state divide – stemming from the independent economic resources which the Shia ulama possessed and which gave them a degree of freedom of action not witnessed anywhere in the Sunni world – was a significant factor in causing the Shah's downfall. Since clerics in Iran were not civil servants, the Shah's control over them was minimal. Secondly, unlike Assad, the Shah did not have an alternative ideology like Baathism, comprehensive and self-contained, and a well-oiled party apparatus to underwrite the legitimacy of his regime. Thirdly, unlike the Syrian leader, the Shah did not enjoy the deep, unflinching loyalty of a substantial minority like the Alawis or Christians – scattered throughout society, the party and the state's civilian and military machines – on which he could rely absolutely. Fourthly, unlike Assad again, the Shah found himself pitted against a charismatic religious personality, Khomeini. His predicament was compounded by the fact that Khomeini directed the protest movement from abroad and was therefore beyond his writ. Fifthly, while Assad remained crystal clear and determined about his objective and the means to achieve it during the long crisis, the Shah wavered at crucial moments of the popular protest partly because of his failing health[2] and partly because of the indecisiveness prevalent in Washington, the ultimate underwriter of his power. Finally, there was no external threat, actual or potential, that the Shah could credibly present to his subjects to divert their energies into confronting a foreign foe.

Having galvanized millions of his countrymen in the cause of upholding Islam, which was threatened by the Pahlavis, Khomeini channelled their energy and attention into Islamizing society – that is, deepening their knowledge of and commitment to Islam. He has also channelled part of their energy and commitment into prosecuting the war against the Iraq of Saddam Hussein who invaded the Islamic Republic of Iran.

Before the revolution Iran was ruled by a secular, westernized élite. This is at present the case with most Muslim countries: subjugated in the nineteenth century by Europeans, they recovered their political independence in the third quarter of the twentieth century, with the local élite, moulded in the image of the departing European imperialists, taking over the reins of power. In that sense the manner in which the revolutionary regime has transformed a secular system into an Islamic one in Iran is relevant to a large majority of the members of the Islamic Conference Organization which includes the former French colony of Mauritania facing the Pacific Ocean in the extreme west and the former Dutch colony of Indonesia in the extreme east.

In contrast, Saudi Arabia is a case unto itself with very little, if any, relevance even to its immediate neighbours along the western coast of the Gulf.

The Saudi ruling élite, untouched by western imperial rule, has several strong factors working for it. With the country possessing the world's largest oil reserves, the Saudi royal family has enough material resources to co-opt whatever opposition arises, whether among technocrats or dissident tribal leaders at home, or even Saudi opposition leaders in exile. Being the custodians of the holy shrines in Mecca and Medina gives it unique status among Muslims throughout the globe. This also aids it in securing and maintaining the absolute loyalty of the ulama who enjoy higher rank and material well-being in the kingdom than anywhere else in the Sunni world. Since the shock of the 1979 Mecca insurrection by the revived Ikhwan, now preaching the (republican) salafiya doctrine, the state has sharpened and deepened its instruments of intelligence and coercion.

None the less, major weaknesses remain. The House of Saud has an enormous territory to protect whereas the number of its nationals is puny: no more than 6 million. There is among its princes a propensity towards venality and deviation from pious living; and this tarnishes their public image and erodes their legitimacy. At heart the royal family remains deeply insecure, a fact highlighted by its continued opposition to promulgating a written constitution and sharing power with an elected consultative council. It has tried to secure its future by tightening its military, economic and intelligence links with the US. But American assistance cannot help it to counter subversive Islamists at home.

So far Saudi royals have been able to blunt the republican message from revolutionary Tehran by stressing the fact that those who rule Iran are Shia, a sect held in low esteem by most Saudi Sunnis.

However, the future of Saudi Arabia as well as other Gulf monarchies and Iraq hinges on the outcome of the Iran–Iraq War.

Ever since its outbreak in September 1980, Khomeini has presented the war in Islamic terms. By invading Iran, President Saddam Hussein attacked not just Iranian soil but the government of God, and thus Islam. While his troops have since then been expelled from Iranian territory, the infidel aggressor has yet to be punished for his misdeed. Therefore, to fight until the overthrow of Saddam Hussein is a religious duty of all true Muslims, Khomeini argues, so those who perish in this conflict die for Islam. Their fate is described in the Quran thus: 'Count not those who are slain in God's way as dead, but rather living with their lord, by Him provided, rejoicing in the bounty that God has given them.'[3] On the eve of its seventh anniversary in September 1987 the Gulf War had claimed the lives of nearly a quarter of a million Iranian fighters and about half as many Iraqis. Yet with 422,000 male Iranians reaching the conscription age of eighteen every year, there is no dearth of recruits. Also, war is consuming only 8.6 per cent of the Iranian gross domestic product whereas the figure for Iraq is a staggering 57.1 per cent.[4]

Tehran's victory in the conflict would result in a pro-Iranian regime in Baghdad, with the country's Shia majority ascendant in the portals of power for the first time in Iraq's history. Iran would exert pressure, overt and covert, on Gulf monarchies to fall in line with the basic Islamic tenet about consulting the community in the running of the country, and installing a representative government at home. Gulf rulers would find it hard to defy Iran on this point for political and religious reasons.

Islamic Iran will also argue that God has been bountiful to the Muslims of the area by bestowing the Gulf region with 55 per cent of the known world oil reserves, and that it is the duty of Gulf governments to co-ordinate their plans to exploit this precious resource in order to maximize the benefits to the Muslim masses and use the surplus earned to transform the region into a hub of industry and advanced technology. In other words, Iran would offer plans to its neighbours of an Islamic Common Market along the lines of the European Economic Community. This would be presented as the first stage of a wide plan to draw all Muslim countries into a single economic network and thus transform Islam into a global economic system on a par with capitalism and socialism.

This would strengthen further the hands of Islamists who have always taken for granted the moral and spiritual superiority of Islam over other social systems. One important element that provides evidence for such a notion is that the moral challenge which fundamentalist leaders like Khomeini and Qutb throw at a secular, corrupt or repressive regime flows not from the socio-economic interest of certain segments of society with which they identify but from an unshakeable belief that they are acting out the will of Allah. Such behaviour defies analysis from a liberal or Marxist perspective, the two powerful analytical tools of the West.

The other conflict which impinges directly on the Islamic world is the Arab–Israeli dispute concerning Palestinian rights. Were the Israelis to return the West Bank and Gaza, and let it be constituted as a Palestinian state – a highly unlikely scenario – the radical leftist and Islamic forces would then press for a struggle to recover the rest of pre-1948 Palestine from the Israelis. Either because of this, or due to the continued refusal of the Israelis to vacate the occupied Palestinian territories, a war between Israel and Arabs could erupt. Defeat by Israel of one or more Arab states would heighten opposition to America and such pro-American regimes as the ones in Saudi Arabia and Egypt.

What happens in Egypt is crucial to the shape of things to come in the heartland of Islam. The overt signs of a rise of fundamentalism are unmistakable: a growing number of women wearing the veil and men growing beards, and a dramatic rise in the number of religious publications. But much depends on the military officer corps. One of the damaging consequences of Sadat's unilateral peace treaty with Israel in September 1978 was that almost overnight the officer corps, which had been reared on a steady diet of secular Arab nationalism for a quarter century, found itself stripped of ideology. A vague notion of becoming part of western defence plans in the Middle East was a poor substitute for what Nasser had offered them and what was also genuinely indigenous. Since then Islamic fundamentalists have intensified their efforts to fill the ideological vacuum in the military and gain recruits. Given this, and the persistence of Nasserist tendencies among some senior military officers and their junior assistants, the possibility of an alliance between Islamist and Nasserist colonels cannot be ruled out. Two contingencies can make this possibility real. One is the continued disturbances by ordinary citizens or even aggrieved policemen which the army is repeatedly called on to quell, as was the case in the Shah's Iran. The other is defeat of one or more Arab countries by Israel in an all-out war.

In the civilian sphere moderate fundamentalists have been slowly but surely infiltrating professional syndicates and administrative organs of the state, thus preparing the ground for the day when Islamist leaders, civil and military, would occupy top official posts, possibly as a result of a peaceful election or probably through a military coup. But the major weakness of fundamentalists in a Sunni country like Egypt is that the ulama, being state employees, have no independent economic base of their own, and that the right of ijtihad is seldom exercised by anyone lower than the rector of Al Azhar, who is always in league with the current ruler. Still, contemporary Egypt has thrown up such popular, independent-minded ulama as Hafiz Salaama, Abdul Hamid Kishk, Yusuf Badri and Abdullah Samawi, who keep on speaking out fervently for an immediate and total application of the Sharia and the abrogation of the peace treaty with Israel. Also, the rise of affluent Islamic investment companies, functioning on the fringe of the national economy and providing funds to fundamentalist organizations, is an unprecedented phenomenon, signalling the emergence of an independent, self-sustaining economic base for the Islamist forces of Egypt.

However, it seems such external factors as the developments in the Gulf War and/or the Arab–Israeli conflict will determine the course of events in Egypt more than internal developments.

One thing is certain. The emergence of a revolutionary fundamentalist Egypt, a strategically situated Sunni country, will shake the Muslim and non-Muslim worlds even more than did the 1979 Iranian revolution.

EPILOGUE*

Following a good performance by the Muslim Brotherhood-dominated Alliance in the April 1987 elections in Egypt, there was an upsurge in Islamist activity. In the main this was conducted by some 40-plus radical groups, known generically as Jamaat al Islamiya. They challenged the government's right to appoint prayer leaders by clashing with the security forces outside mosques, confronted the university police over the unIslamic environment of the campuses – mixed classes and women students without hijab – and intimidated Christians by attacking their churches.

The radical Islamists were particularly active in Upper Egypt, where one-third of the national population lives. In such cities as Asyut and Minia they closed down discotheques and restricted the sale of alcoholic drinks to a few luxury hotels. They then tried to enforce the Islamic code of behaviour in certain suburbs of Cairo, particularly Ein Shams, and set up Islamic courts. In this tense atmosphere a policeman was murdered in Ein Shams in late September 1988. The government responded by saturating the suburb with troops and security police and, using emergency powers, arrested 2,000 Islamic militants nationally.

But there was growing evidence that state repression of the radical groups was proving increasingly counter-productive. Research by Dr Saad Ibrahim, a sociologist, revealed that a typical Islamist prisoner found his inspiration in Prophet Muhammad's edict: 'Any of you who sees evil must change it by his hand' – and perceived his

* Notes are at the end of the chapter.

militant actions as part of his religious duty to function as a 'good Muslim', and was indifferent to the consequences of his acts.[1]

As it was, the government repression, including torture, of Islamic militants came under increasing attack by Muslim Brotherhood journalists and parliamentarians. In the National Assembly the Brotherhood deputies had improved their standing by transforming their simplistic slogan, 'Islam is the solution', into demands for an end to the emergency and release of detainees, more houses and better health services, Islamic banking, and the introduction of zakat as a means of providing social welfare. Three of the five opposition magazines, manned chiefly by fundamentalist journalists, had emerged as important tools in forging pro-Islamist public opinion. The continuing economic crisis provided the Islamic forces with a favourable environment in which to enlarge their popular base.

Indeed, some of the official policies inadvertently helped the fundamentalist camp. By maintaining its ban on the Nasserites, and sticking to its rule of a minimum of eight per cent of the popular vote for a party to enter the National Assembly (thus disenfranchising the secular leftists), the government left the discontented public little choice but to back the Brotherhood and its radical allies.

What was more, in early 1989 signs of division within the religious establishment began to appear. Referring to the mosques controlled by militant Islamists, the Grand Shaikh of Al Azhar university stated: 'Poisonous mosques in our age are those which seek to stir up the people, where they hide weapons and other instruments of violence.' In contrast, alluding to the government's attacks on the mosques controlled by independent and outspoken clerics, the Grand Mufti of Egypt stated that such an action was a 'big crime' except when it was taken for security reasons.[2]

As for external events, the fundamentalists were buoyed by the Palestinian agitation against the Israeli forces which originated in Gaza, where in October 1987 the security forces killed seven members of the Islamic Jihad. Two months later a Palestinian uprising emerged in the occupied territories, with the Islamists actively cooperating with the secular Palestine Liberation Organization. On the other hand, Iran's acceptance of a ceasefire in its conflict with Iraq had a depressing effect on the Egyptian fundamentalists.

Iran

As the Gulf War entered its seventh year on 22 September 1987, Iran found itself facing the combined strength of the Iraqi air force, now possessing 400 combat aircraft, and the US naval force of some 40 warships.

Diplomatically, too, Iran was in a weak position. On 20 July the UN Security Council unanimously passed a comprehensive, ten-clause Resolution 598 on a ceasefire in the Gulf conflict, including a provision for an international commission to establish who started the war. While Baghdad accepted the resolution immediately, Tehran prevaricated.

During the winter of 1987–88, Iran was unable to mount a major offensive in the southern sector due to shortages of manpower and military hardware. The ceaseless Iraqi bombing of bridges, factories and power plants had begun to affect Iran's war effort seriously. Moreover, by staging an all-out assault against Iraq, Iran was bound to alienate the UN Security Council, thus inviting an international arms embargo.

Aware of Iran's predicament, Baghdad initiated the War of the Cities on 27 February 1988, introducing a surface-to-surface missile, with a range of 380 miles, called Al Hussein. This brought Tehran into Iraq's firing range. By the time the War of the Cities ended on 20 April, Iraq had fired 200 Al Hussein missiles at Iranian cities, principally Tehran. Iran's score was 77 surface-to-surface missiles, most of them directed at Baghdad.

In mid-March, Iran and its Iraqi Kurdish allies captured Halabja, a town of 70,000 people, situated 15 miles inside Iraq. The Iraqi air force attacked the town with chemical weapons and killed at least 4,000 persons, mainly civilians.

Among other things, this provided Iran with an effective propaganda opportunity. The pictures of men, women, children and animals frozen to instant death shocked the world. But by giving wide publicity to Iraq's chemical bombing of Halabja, Iran engendered a heightened fear among its citizens that Baghdad would equip its surface-to-surface missiles with poison gas payloads. This had an adverse effect on public morale, already low due to frequent Iraqi missile attacks.

It was against this background that Iraq launched a successful offensive in the extreme south with a liberal use of chemical weapons, and recaptured the Fao peninsula. This marked a dramatic break in the Iraqi defensive posture of the past several years. Almost simultaneously, Iran found itself in confrontation in the Gulf with the US Navy which disabled or destroyed two of its four frigates.

On 27 April, Saudi Arabia severed its diplomatic links with Iran. The immediate reason was Tehran's refusal to accept Riyadh's curtailment of Iranian pilgrims for the hajj from 155,000 to 45,000 – based on the newly adopted formula of 1,000 pilgrims per million Muslims in a country, which had earlier been approved by the Islamic Conference Organization at its meeting in March. Riyadh accused Tehran of 'an enemy-like stand toward Saudi Arabia and intentional harm to its basic interests'. While disputing Riyadh's right to limit the numbers of pilgrims and impose conditions on the hajj, Iran stated that a major factor in the Saudi decision was its coordination with the US policies in the region to help Iraq.[3] Aware of his religious duty to maintain relations with all Muslim countries – if only to facilitate the performance of the hajj by their Muslim nations – King Fahd let it be known he had secured the consent of the Council of the Ulama for his action against the Islamic Republic of Iran.

Politically, this was a sensitive time for the Iranians, who were in the midst of their parliamentary elections. The second round finished on 13 May, with radical and reformist deputies emerging as the dominant force.

On 25 May the Iraqis overpowered the Iranians in

ferocious artillery and rocket barrages, mixing conventional shells with those filled with cyanide gas or deadly nerve gases, and expelled them from the Shalamche bridgehead east of Basra. A month later the Iraqis used similar tactics to regain their Majnoon Islands in the marshy border area in the south.

Tehran called for volunteers to rush to the battlefields. But the response was poor, mainly because of the prominence given in the Iranian media to Iraq's extensive use of poison gas weapons.

Tension between the Iranian and American navies in the Gulf continued unabated. On 3 July a minor skirmish occurred between the two sides in the Hormuz Straits. In this charged atmosphere an Iranian Airbus, with 290 passengers aboard, commenced its scheduled flight from Bandar Abbas to Dubai. It was mistaken by an American warship in the area as a warplane and shot down.

Iran accused America of deliberately striking the aircraft. But instead of initiating retaliatory action against the US in the region and outside, it complained to the UN Security Council. At home, top Iranian leaders held secret talks contemplating the acceptance of the UN Security Council ceasefire Resolution 598. They were able to obtain Khomeini's verbal consent on 15 July. The next day the Assembly of Experts discussed the war and formally recommended a ceasefire to Khomeini who alone, as the supreme leader and the commander-in-chief, had the constitutional power to decide matters of war and peace.

Once Khomeini had given his consent to a truce, reportedly in writing, President Khamanei acted to implement his decision. His letter to the UN secretary-general, Javier Perez de Cuellar, accepting the ceasefire, was made public on 18 July.

By all accounts, the news of Tehran's acceptance of the ceasefire resolution was received by Iranians with astonishment and disbelief. Nothing had prepared them for the dramatic decision taken by their government. They awaited a word from Khomeini.

This came on 20 July, the first anniversary (by the

Islamic calendar) of the massacre of the Iranian pilgrims
in Mecca, in the form of a 90-minute-long statement read
on Tehran Radio. 'Because of the events and factors which
I will not discuss for the time being and considering the
advice of all ranking political and military experts of the
country . . . I agreed to accept the ceasefire resolution,' said
Khomeini. 'I consider it to be in the interest of the
revolution and the system at this juncture. God knows that,
were it not that all our honour and prestige should be
sacrificed for Islam, I would never have consented [to the
ceasefire].' In other words, as he put it elsewhere: 'The new
decision was made only on the basis of expediency. I
renounced whatever I had said [in the past] only in the
hope of God's blessing and satisfaction.' Khomeini was
well aware of the confusion and discontent his decision was
likely to create among those who had admired and followed
his uncompromising stance throughout the war. 'Some
people, led by emotions, might talk about the whys and
wherefores of the decision, which is a beautiful thing in
itself, but now is not the time to deal with it,' he stated. 'I
repeat that accepting this [resolution] was more deadly for
me than taking poison. I submit[ted] myself to God's will
and drank this drink for His satisfaction.'[4]

Among the subjects Khomeini apparently did not wish
to discuss was the mounting difficulty Iran experienced in
its military procurements abroad. It found itself unable to
replace the losses it had suffered in the course of the 1987
Basra offensive in such crucial items as engines and guns
for its tanks and artillery shells. Washington's attempts to
stem the flow of arms and spares to Iran in the wake of the
Irangate scandal (of late 1986) had proved increasingly
effective in depriving it of sophisticated weaponry and
ammunition. Matters were made worse by the financial
stringency imposed on Tehran due to a continuing depression in petroleum prices, which had fallen steeply in
1985–86 due to the flooding of the international market by
Saudi Arabia. Iran's oil revenue in 1988 was running at
about three-fifths of Iraq's. Finally, according to Hashimi-
Rafsanjani, the parliamentary speaker and acting commander-in-chief, the US and Iraq had made it crystal clear

that they would resort to any means to prevent an Iranian victory, and that Iraq had taken to large-scale use of chemical weapons in its offensives.[5]

Iran found itself unable to counter the shift in the military balance by bolstering its military manpower and morale. Indeed, volunteers for active duty in the early summer of 1988 were about a third down on the previous year. Part of the reason was that those who did their three-month stint at the front found no major activity there. This discouraged their friends in civilian life from volunteering for front-line duties. The political indecisiveness, in turn, stemmed from the formidable firepower that Iraq had built up since the spring of 1987; the reluctance of the international community to penalize Baghdad for its continued and extensive deployment of poison gases; the heavy diplomatic price that Tehran would have to pay at the UN for launching a major offensive; and the Iranian leaders' unwillingess to impose further austerity on the people. In short, Iran was no longer able to overcome its inferiority in arms, financial strength and diplomatic backing with manpower and high motivation.

Khomeini's decision was generally well received. Many among the upper and middle classes had wished to see the war end earlier. The working and lower middle classes were too loyal to Khomeini to question his judgement. The prospect of some revolutionary guards officers defying the government receded when the Islamic Revolutionary Guards Corps commander, Muhsin Rezai, in the course of his meeting with Khomeini on 22 July, handed him a letter accepting the ceasefire decision and reaffirming his loyalty to him.[6]

The war had proved bloody and expensive. Conservative Western estimates put the number of total war dead at 367,000 – with Iran accounting for 262,000 and Iraq 105,000. With over 700,000 injured, total casualties were put at over one million. The official figures given two months later by Iran's minister of Islamic guidance put the Iranian dead at 123,220 combatants, and another 60,171 missing in action. In addition, 11,000 civilians had lost

their lives.[7] According to the Stockholm International
Peace Research Institute, excluding weapons imports, at
current prices Iran had spent between $74 and $91 billion
to conduct the war, and Iraq between $94 and $112 billion.
The military import bill for Iraq was $42 billion, and for
Iran $11 billion.[8]

It was not until 20 August that a formal ceasefire came
into effect. Peace talks between the two sides, which began
on 25 August 1988 in Geneva under the chairmanship of
the UN secretary-general, reached a deadlock when Iraq
demanded an immediate clearance of the Shatt al Arab by
the UN. Iran rejected this, arguing that according to the
1975 treaty this task was a joint responsibility of the two
signatories. Iraq replied that this treaty no longer existed.
Iran disagreed, arguing that as a border treaty it applied
for ever, and that it could not be abrogated unilaterally.

Militarily, Baghdad sounded as bullish at the end of the
war as it did at the start. But the Iranian regime and
society were stronger and far more cohesive, militarily and
politically, than they were eight years earlier.

Baghdad's invasion came at a time when revolutionary
ardour was waning in Iran. It provided the clerical rulers
with a platform from which to rejuvenate the drive for
national unity and Islamic revolution. Defending the
Islamic base of Iran and expelling the aggressor became
highly effective rallying cries. The war inhibited fractious
debate and dispute. It engendered an environment conducive to a dramatic rise in the strength and importance of
the ideologically oriented Islamic Revolutionary Guards
Corps.

By early 1984 the war had turned into a prolonged
conflict between national wills, a contest – military, politico-ideological and economic – between rival social systems: secular, socialist Baathism on one side, and
revolutionary Islam on the other. It came to dominate
society and politics in both countries; and its progress
became bound up with the future of the two regimes.

Iran's leaders portrayed war and the restrictions imposed
by it as providing an incentive to accelerate the process of

self-dependence and self-realization. The conflict gave rise
to many new local industries in defence and non-defence
fields. Military industry in Iran registered an impressive
growth, both in the output of old products and the production of new and sophisticated hardware.

All along, the Tehran regime's primary concern was to
deepen and broaden the Islamic revolution. So long as the
war served that purpose, repeated offers of a ceasefire by
Iraq or the United Nations or the Islamic Conference
Organization were spurned. Only when Khomeini realized,
through his on-going communication with the widespread
religious network functioning under him, that ordinary
Iranians were getting war-weary did he accept a truce. He
realized that imposing further economic austerity on the
people, combined with a measure of coercion to prosecute
the war effectively, would erode the mass base that his
regime enjoyed; a stage had been reached when continuing
hostilities would damage the revolution rather than buttress
it. Another major factor was the poor health of 86-year-old
Khomeini. He seemed to have appreciated that, following
his death, his successor, Montazeri, would not be able to
tackle the twin problems of the war and the power vacuum
created by his departure. Khomeini therefore decided to
end the conflict and thus ensure the future of the revolution
while he was still alive.

In the final analysis, therefore, only the domestic factors
had an impact on Khomeini, who had ignored pressures on
his regime by such diverse forces as Saudi Arabia, Libya,
the Soviet Union, America, the Islamic Conference Organization and the UN Security Council. Significantly, in his
20 July 1988 statement he specifically said: 'Iranian officials
independently made the decision to accept the [UN] resolution; and no other person or country had a role in this.'[9]

Tehran was all along concerned with the power equation
in the Gulf. Given its large area and population, it visualized itself as the regional superpower. The adoption of
Islam as its political ideology was seen by Iran as a
powerful tool with which to gather the states on the western
side of the Gulf under an Islamic umbrella, since their

ruling elites too claimed to derive their legitimacy from this faith. But Tehran experienced strong opposition to the realization of this scenario. Firstly, there was a historic animosity and distrust between Arabs and Persians. Secondly, there was the Shia-Sunni schism, with all the Arab Gulf rulers being Sunni and having poor regard for Shias. Finally, and most importantly, all these states had strong military, economic and political ties with the US, an adversary of revolutionary Iran, which had encouraged Iraq to invade the Islamic Republic.

The Iraqi effort to destabilize and overthrow the Khomeini regime through its invasion misfired. Equally, the Iranian attempt to turn the warfare into a prime instrument for exporting the Islamic revolution failed.

However, the Iraqi regime emerged as a much-changed entity as a result of the war. It de-emphasized ideology in general and the Baathist elements of secularism, republicanism and socialism in particular. To withstand the barrage of Islamic propaganda emanating from Tehran, Baghdad tried to appear more religious than its foe. It exploited early Islamic history and routinely described the current conflict as 'Saddam's Qadasiya', referring to the battle in 637 when Muslim Arabs overpowered the (Zoroastrian) Sassanian army of Persia at Qadasiya in southern Iraq. It introduced a programme of mosque construction and renovation, with Saddam Hussein making widely publicized visits to holy shrines. More importantly, unlike any of its previous gatherings, the Ninth Congress of the Baath Party in June 1982 described Islam as 'a great revolution in the history of mankind' and stated that, 'The modern Arab must be inspired by the spirit of Islamic mission.'[10] To that extent Iran could claim moral victory in the Gulf War. On the other hand, with the Sadam Hussein regime firmly in power in Iraq at the end of the hostilities, it was obvious that Iran's revolutionary Islamic fundamentalism had been contained.

Now that the Khomeini government had been deprived of the chance to export its revolution through forces of arms, it had no option but to develop revolutionary doctrine socially and economically in one country to provide a model to other Muslim states. This meant concentrating on reconstruction at home.

But focussing his attention on regenerating Iran's economy did not prevent Khomeini from functioning as a spiritual leader of Muslims at large, ready to provide guidance if the situation demanded it.

The need for such an action arose with the publication of *The Satanic Verses*, a novel by Salman Rushdie, an Indian-born writer resident in London. In the second chapter of the book the author portrayed Prophet Muhammad – thinly disguised as a fictional character called Mahound (meaning false prophet) – as an unscrupulous, lecherous imposter who hoodwinked his followers. Later, Rushdie suggested that Mahound included in the Quran certain verses which turned out to be the work of devil: the satanic verses. In the fourth chapter of the book, Mahound was portrayed as 'spouting rules, rules, rules until the faithful could scarcely bear the prospect of any more revelations'. (This was seen by Muslims as a symbolic attack on the Sharia.) Later the writer offered a long fantasy about 'the Curtain', the most popular brothel in Jahilia (i.e., Mecca). Here, in order to attract clientele, the prostitutes acquired the names of the wives of the prophet.

Soon after the publication of the book in late September 1988, certain Muslim leaders in Britain requested the prime minister, Margaret Thatcher, to ban it and prosecute Rushdie for slandering Islam. Thatcher replied that there was no legal ground to do either. To gain backing in the Muslim world these leaders mailed photocopies of the objectionable passages in the book to the London embassies of the 45 member-states of the Islamic Conference Organization. Given that blasphemy against Christianity is a criminal offence, they approached the home secretary, Douglas Hurd, to take action. In response, Hurd said that prosecution for such cases was the legal duty of the country where Islam was the main religion, and not a minority faith as in Britain. The issue caught the public eye, at home and abroad, on 14 January 1989, when Muslims in Bradford burned a copy of the book at a rally.

On 12 February, on the eve of publication of the American edition of the novel, there was a violent demonstration in Islamabad, the capital of Pakistan, where the book had been banned. It led to the deaths of at least six people. This marked the internationalization of the issue. Following this, it seems that one or more acolytes of Ayatollah Khomeini approached him to give a fatwa (religious decree) on the matter.

He did so on 14 February. 'I would like to inform all the fearless Muslims in the world that the author of the book entitled *The Satanic Verses*, which has been compiled, printed and published in opposition to Islam, the Prophet and the Quran, as well as the publishers, who are aware of the contents, have been sentenced to death. I call on all zealous Muslims to execute them quickly, wherever they find them, so that no one will dare to insult Islamic sanctity. Whoever is killed on this path will be regarded as a martyr.'[11]

Rushdie, a British national, went into hiding in London, and was given police protection. British foreign secretary Sir Geoffrey Howe decried Khomeini's action as 'interference in the international affairs of another country'. As the Friday prayer leader of Tehran, President Khamanei welcomed Khomeini's edict in his sermon on 17 February. 'The author may repent and say 'I made a blunder', and apologize to Muslims and the Imam [i.e., Khomeini],' he added. 'Then it is possible that the [Muslim] people may pardon him.' The next day Rushdie stated: 'I profoundly regret the distress that the publication [of my book] has occasioned to sincere followers of Islam.' To this Khomeini's office replied: 'Even if Salman Rushdie repents and becomes the most pious man of all time, it is incumbent upon every Muslim to employ his life and belongings to send him to hell.'[12] Earlier, Hojatalislam Hassan Sanai, head of the 15 Khurdad (5 June) Foundation in Iran[13], had offered a reward of $2.6 million to an Iranian and $1 million to a non-Iranian for the assassination of Rushdie.

Protesting against Khomeini's edict, the foreign ministers

of the 12-member European Community decided on 20
February to recall their heads of missions in Tehran and
'restrain' their economic relations with Iran. Britain withdrew all its five diplomats from Iran. In retaliation, Tehran
recalled its ambassadors from West European capitals.
Responding to the assertion of Western governments that
they stood for freedom of expression, President Khamanei
said that they had made the mistake of confusing 'freedom
of expression with the freedom to insult one billion
Muslims'.[14]

In an hour-long message addressed to the teachers and
students of religious seminaries, read out on Tehran Radio
on 22 February, Khomeini restated his views on the role of
the clergy in society and the inseparable link between
religion and politics, and attacked revisionism. 'Those who
continue to believe that we must embark on revisions in
our politics, principles and diplomacy and that we have
blundered and must not repeat our mistakes; those who
still believe that extremist slogans [of ours] will cause the
West and the East to be pessimistic about us, and that
ultimately all this has led to the country's isolation; those
who believe that if we act in pragmatic ways, then they
[the West and the East] will mutually respect the nation,
Islam and Muslims – to them this is an example,' Khomeini
said. 'God wanted this blasphemous book, *The Satanic Verses*,
to be published now so that the world of conceit, arrogance
and barbarism would bare its face in its long-held emnity
to Islam; to bring us out of our naïvety and prevent us from
attributing everything just to blunder, bad management
and lack of experience.' Khomeini was firm and clear-
headed. 'As long as I am around, I shall not allow the
government to fall into the hands of the [pro-West] liberals,' he declared. 'So long as I am alive, I shall cut off the
hands of the agents of America and the Soviet Union in all
fields.'[15]

Apparently, through this move, Khomeini tried to neutralize the pressure on his government from the pragmatic
camp at home to strengthen ties with West European
countries in order to facilitate the implementation of major

reconstruction projects following the Gulf War ceasefire. It is noteworthy that ten years previously (in November 1979) the seizure of the American embassy in Tehran by militant students reversed a move towards rapprochement between the Iranian government (then led by the 'liberal' Mahdi Bazargan) and America.

Khomeini's dramatic stance on the Rushdie affair sent his prestige soaring among the Muslims living outside Iran. According to Yaqub Zaki, an Islamic specialist at Harvard University, by articulating the feelings of Muslims about the Rushdie book, Khomeini 'recouped at one stroke everything lost in the war with Iraq, and emerged as the undisputed moral leader of the world's Muslims'. Support for Khomeini came not only from Muslim leaders in Western Europe, but also from within the Islamic world. Muhammad Ismail Qureshi, president of the World Association of Muslim Jurists, stated that Rushdie's action was 'unpardonable under the Islamic law'. The head preacher at Jama Masjid in Delhi, a leading mosque of India (with a Muslim population of about 100 million), said: 'We are supportive of the death sentence passed by the Ayatollah on the blasphemous dog.' Later Colonel Qadhafi of Libya expressed his support for Khomeini, and President Hussein Muhammad Ershad of Bangladesh demanded the trial and punishment of Rushdie.[16]

When British officials contacted various friendly Muslim states with a view to securing statements by political or religious leaders contradicting Khomeini's call to violence, they drew a blank. Even Turkey, a secular state led by President Kenan Evran – a rabid opponent of Islamic fundamentalism, keen to see his country join the European Community – refused to endorse the European condemnation of Khomeini. Apparently, Khomeini was on strong theological ground. He had based his judgement firmly in the Sharia and the Islamic tradition. The most pertinent verse in the Quran reads: 'Those who molest God's Messenger/for them awaits a painful punishment' (9:61). What sort of punishment is to be meted out to those who slander Allah's Messenger or His Word (the Quran) was specified, and practised, by Prophet Muhammad himself. Shortly after he had captured Mecca in January 630, he had Kaab ibn al Ashraf, a poet, decapitated for mocking the Quran.[17] Since then, Prophet Muhammad's example has been followed by his disciples.

By his action, Khomeini upstaged King Fahd of Saudi Arabia who, as 'The Custodian of the Holy Shrines', had been engaged in discreet lobbying against the Rushdie book. Four days after the Ayatollah's religious ruling against Rushdie, the Jidda-based Islamic Conference Organization warned his publisher, Viking-Penguin, that its member-states would boycott all its books if it did not withdraw *The Satanic Verses*. On 26 February, a seminar organized by the Saudi-funded World Muslim league in Mecca rejected Rushdie's apology as insufficient and demanded that he should confess openly that what he had written about Islam, Prophet Muhammad and his wives was 'pure lies and fabrication'. It condemned him as 'a heretic and a renegade', and called for a trial of the author and his publishers by 'relevant courts.'

It was obvious that Khomeini had set the pace in the matter; and other Islamic luminaries and organizations could do no more than either follow his lead or keep silent. Since the issue concerned Prophet Muhammad, the founder of Islam, there was no question of Sunni-Shia schism. Khomeini was seen simply as the leading Islamic figure on the world stage upholding the sanctity of Prophet Muhammad and Islam.

This was the line the Iranian delegation stressed, with considerable success, at the ICO foreign ministers' conference in Riyadh in mid-March. 'This publication [i.e., *The Satanic Verses*] transgresses all norms of civility and decency and is a deliberate attempt to malign Islam and the revered Islamic personalities', stated an ICO resolution. It declared the author an apostate, demanded the withdrawal of the book and called on the member countries to boycott the publishers if this was not done.[18]

Iran's delegates argued that since penalty for apostasy, according to Islamic law, is death, the ICO resolution more or less endorsed Ayatollah Khomeini's verdict of capital punishment against Rushdie. The Saudi hosts of the ICO conference stated that the ICO only expressed a political view, leaving the actual punishment for apostasy to Islamic jurists.

The ICO resolution signified a draw between Iran and Saudi Arabia, locked in a contest for the global leadership of Muslims: a rivalry which was being played out *inter alia* in the councils of the Afghan resistance. Following the Gulf War ceasefire, Iran had become active on that front.

Afghanistan

The failure of his administration to persuade the rebels to join a government of national reconciliation, during the latter half of 1987, did not stop Dr Muhammad Najibullah from diluting the Marxist form and content of the political system. The new constitution adopted in December 1987 dropped the term 'Democratic' from the country's name, reducing it to, simply, the Republic of Afghanistan. More significantly, the constitution declared Islam to be the state religion, and allowing a multi-party system.

Indeed, the results of the parliamentary election in April 1988 showed that the People's Democratic party had secured only 27 per cent of the seats, with the National Front, an umbrella body, gaining 28 per cent, and the popular organizations, such as the Workers Revolutionary Party, the Peasants Justice Party and the Islamic Party, obtaining 38 per cent. Premier Sultan Ali Keshtmand was replaced by a non-party politician, Muhammad Hassan Sharq. Addressing the PDP conference on 27 April 1988, the tenth anniversary of the Saur (April) Revolution, Najibullah criticized the party for not listening to the voice of the people and indulging in 'glib rhetoric' and 'deceitful verbiage' – and often mechanically applying models of advanced revolutions while ignoring the historical charac-teristics of Afghan society. He urged the party delegates not to underestimate the role of Islam and the prestige of the clergy, and declared that the objectives of the Afghan revolution could not, and should not, be realized by military means.[19]

Following a joint communiqué by Najibullah and Gorbachev in early February 1988, to the effect that Soviet troops would start pulling out from Afghanistan in May and complete the exercise in ten months, four agreements were signed under UN auspices in Geneva on 14 April by Afghanistan, the Soviet Union, Pakistan and America. The first three concerned the principles of non-interference, the declaration of international guarantees, and the basis for a voluntary return of refugees. The fourth agreement required Moscow to withdraw its 115,000 troops from Afghanistan between 15 May 1988 and 15 February 1989.

However, following these signatures, the two superpowers exchanged secret letters which allowed them to continue military supplies to their allies; that is, the Soviet Union agreed to let the US give arms and ammunition to the guerrillas based in Pakistan. But since Pakistan had signed the instrument on non-interference, it was required to bar transportation of military supplies into Afghanistan as well as close down the military training camps for the Afghan rebels on its soil. In the event, to the chagrin of Kabul and Moscow, Islamabad openly breached this agreement.

Having achieved Moscow's commitment on withdrawal of its troops from Afghanistan, the Islamic Alliance of Afghan Mujahedin decided to intensify its political challenge to the Kabul regime. Encouraged by the Pakistani Inter-Services Intelligence (ISI) Directorate – a military and internal security agency employing 100,000 people[20] – it formed an 'interim government' under the premiership of Ahmad Shah, a Wahhabi member of Professor Sayyaf's Islamic Alliance of Afghanistan. This went down badly with the moderate parties, which had proposed holding immediate elections in the refugee camps to choose an interim government. They had been encouraged by the results of a random poll in mid-1987 of 2,287 refugees in 106 of the 249 camps in Pakistan: it had shown 72 per cent favouring King Zahir Shah leading a post-war administration.[21] When the moderates were overruled they just ignored the newly formed government and its secretariat funded exclusively by the Saudis. This, and the refusal of Pakistan and America to recognize the Ahmad Shah administration, led to its quiet demise some months later.

Then there were deep differences among the resistance leaders on the question of the right strategy to capture Kabul. Two moderate and two radical parties wanted to let morale in the capital fall, encourage desertions from the Afghan army, and increase links with the civilian population, before staging an assault on the city under a united leadership. They were opposed by Hikmatyar's Hizb-e Islami which, backed by America and Pakistan, advocated an immediate attack on Kabul. In the end nothing came of these deliberations, partly because of the death on 17 August 1988 of Hikmatyar's chief patron, General Muhammad Zia al Haq, president of Pakistan, in an explosion aboard his aircraft.

With the Soviet military presence reduced by half by mid-August, the Najibullah government decided to vacate many border posts and garrisons in order to consolidate its strategic position and encourage refugees to return. On the socio-political front, it slowed down its programmes of land reform and women's emancipation. In contrast, it increased its budget for the religious affairs ministry, now employing 20,000 clerics, to the extent that it amounted to three times the budget for the foreign ministry. In Kabul alone the programme of repairing and refurbishing the city's 1,000 mosques was expected to cost the public treasury £20 million.[22] Addressing the People's Democratic Party central committee in October, Najibullah said that the PDP was prepared to put national reconciliation above party interests.

The resistance leaders rejected Najibullah's overture on the grounds that his government was a puppet of Moscow, and that they would therefore only talk with the Soviets. This came about in early December 1988 in Taif, Saudi Arabia, where the Mujahedin leaders conferred with Yuli Vorontsov, the Soviet deputy foreign minister posted to Kabul as the USSR's ambassador. But following their subsequent meetings with Vorontsov in Islamabad, they turned down his proposal of a coalition with the PDP, which they regarded as nothing more than a creation of Moscow. It was little wonder that they ignored Najibullah's offer of a unilateral ceasefire from 1 January 1989. Their fighters attacked Afghan soldiers, thus putting an end to the brief truce.

As the date of final withdrawal of the Soviet military approached, Moscow accelerated its diplomatic efforts to see a coalition government installed in Kabul. Vorontsov conferred with the eight Shia Afghan groups based in the capital of Iran: a country which sheltered about two million Afghan refugees.[23] As a result of his efforts, formal contacts were established between the Shia groups in Tehran and the Sunni groups in Peshawar.

Immense pressure was put on the Mujahedin parties in Peshawar by the US and Pakistani ISI (headed by General Hamid Gul) to hold a shura (consultative council) and form an interim government before the final Soviet pull-out from Afghanistan. But so acute were the differences among the Mujahedin Alliance constituents that this proved an impossible task.

Indeed, many observers predicted the Mujahedin Alliance breaking up, since the cement that held it together – the Soviets in Afghanistan – dissolved. In the event it did not. The chief reason was that the US, under the new administration of President George Bush, promised to continue supplying weapons to the Alliance to the tune of £1,000 million a year (with Saudi Arabia matching the American aid to the same extent). A breakaway party would have lost its share of arms – and thus its followers in the field, whose loyalty rested largely on a steady supply of cash and arms.

Equally, on the other side, in the absence of a political settlement leading to a coalition government, the Soviets handed over their vast military stores to the Afghans and airlifted more arms and ammunition. The Soviet foreign minister, Eduard Shevardnadze, said that Moscow would honour its obligations to Afghanistan under the December

1978 treaty of Friendship and Cooperation, which specified mutual consultations about ensuring 'the security, independence and territorial integrity of the two countries'. This implied that, if asked, the Soviets would fly air sorties from their own bases in support of the Kabul regime and hit rebel positions: something they had done earlier to expel the guerrillas from the northern town of Kunduz.[24]

While the Afghan resistance could rightly claim that their jihad against Moscow had succeeded in ridding their country of foreign troops, it could not alter geography or existing international treaties.

After several postponements the Afghan shura finally met in Rawlpindi, Pakistan, on 10 February. Its strength of 526 consisted of 61 delegates each for the seven constituents of the Mujahedin Alliance, 80 representatives of the eight Tehran-based Shia groups, and 19 'good Muslims' from Kabul. Describing the shura as unelected and unrepresentative, Mujaddidi, the current president of the Mujahedin Alliance, resigned. His successor, Muhammad Nabi Muhammadi, suspended the session.

What lay behind Mujaddidi's resignation was his failure to win the approval of his colleagues on the seven-member Mujahedin Alliance's Supreme Council for the pact he had signed earlier with Muhammad Karim Khalili, the leader of the Tehran-based Afghan groups. Responding to Khalili's demand for 120 seats, Mujaddidi had compromised by raising the initial 60 delegates to 100 for the Tehran-based groups. The pro-Saudi Sayyaf and the pro-Pakistani Hikmatyar refused to go along with this, fearing that the enlarged delegation from Tehran would coalesce with the Peshawar-based moderates and frustrate their own designs.

It was only after the delegation led by Khalili had departed, in frustration, for Tehran on 19 February that the shura finally got down to business. Each of the 439 delegates present was given two votes and told to cast them for any of the seven leaders of the Mujahedin Alliance.

The results, announced on 23 February, were: Mujaddidi (president) 174; Sayyhaf (prime minister) 173; Muhammadi (finance minister) 139; Hikmatyar (foreign minister)

126; Khalis (defence minister) 102; Rabbani (interior minister) 99; and Gailani (reconstruction minister) 66. This meant an end to the practice of rotating the chairmanship of the Mujahedin Alliance's Supreme Council every three months.

Significantly, Gailani, who had been the most vociferous critic of the Pakistani interference in Afghan affairs – blatantly illustrated by the large presence of the Pakistani ISI personnel inside the venue of the shura – received the lowest number of votes. On the other hand, thanks to the Saudi funds spent lavishly on his behalf, Sayyaf, the Wahhabi leader of the smallest party in the Mujahedin Alliance, was nearly at the top of the poll.[25] This was a dramatic measure of the influence of Saudi money and the Pakistani military on Afghan politics.

Islamabad, Riyadh and Washington visualized the formation of the interim government in Peshawar as an essential, but transient, step. The next move for it was to establish itself inside Afghanistan. Jalalabad, a city of a quarter million people, was seen as the most suitable venue for its secretariat. Situated only 45 miles from the Pakistani border, along a road that connected it to Kabul 80 miles to its west, it had been vacated by the Soviet troops in May 1988. Since then, the rebels had steadily captured the road from Pakistan, reaching the vast state farm at Gaziabad to the east of Jalalabad in January 1989. But the city had a deep defensive perimeter of minefields and gun emplacements, as well as the natural barrier of the Kabul River. It was guarded by some 15,000 Afghan troops, backed by more PDP militia. The rebel strength was put at 15,000 with most of the guerrillas belonging to Gailani's National Islamic Front of Afghanistan and Khalis's Hizb-e Islami. Their field commanders repeatedly resisted Pakistani pressure to mount an immediate frontal assault on the city on the grounds that this would lead to high civilian casualties.

The Afghan regime was determined to keep open the Jalalabad-Kabul road. Indeed, this was part of the overall strategy that it had, in conjunction with Moscow, followed throughout the civil war. The 100,000-plus Soviet troops

deployed in Afghanistan were just enough to enable the
Kabul government to control the key urban centres and
airfields, and the roads connecting them. Soviet air power
was deployed, in conjunction with Afghanistan's, to raid
guerrilla bases, and penalize and intimidate the people
supporting the rebels. That explained why, in nine years of
warfare, Moscow lost only 15,000 soldiers and airmen.

In contrast, the civil war claimed the lives of 70,000
members of the Afghan security forces and the PDP. When
the estimated deaths of the guerrillas and civilians, at about
300,000, were added to the above figure, the total of the
Afghan dead amounted to about 10 per cent of the country's
adult population.[26] A substantial proportion of these
human, and material, losses could be laid at the door of the
guerrillas. The magnitude of their military activity could
be gauged by the fact that, according to the government,
during the nine months after the signing of the Geneva
accords, they had conducted 557 attacks, 403 bombing
incidents, and fired 201,000 rockets, heavy artillery shells
and mortar shells.[27]

On the eve of the departure of the last Soviet troops,
including 20,000 from Kabul and its airfield, while the
Western embassies quit the capital predicting the imminent
fall of the Najibullah administration, the president acted
swiftly and firmly.

In Kabul, the government handed out 30,000 Kalashni-
kov assault rifles to the young Defenders of the Revolution,
thus partially mobilizing the PDP membership, aged 14 to
58. It implemented its plan to raise the Special Guard, with
30,000 of its personnel to be posted in Kabul and another
15,000 in the provincial capitals. In addition, there were
the regular armed police, 20,000 to 25,000 strong; and the
secret armed police (Khad), 15,000 to 20,000 strong. This
force of 80–90,000 out of an overall total of 150,000 troops,
paramilitary personnel and tribal militias was considered
the hard core of the Kabul regime, expected to fight to the
bitter end the 70,000 full-time combatants in the opposite
camp.[28]

Both sides had political and military strengths and

weaknesses. While the Mujahedin Alliance had held together despite the blandishments of Kabul and Moscow, it was judged by many observers to be hopelessly heterogenous, with its leaders hardly on speaking terms with one another[29], unrepresentative, and under the influence of foreigners. Its interim government, composed of disparate elements and lacking a constitution, failed to win the recognition of either Pakistan or America. It remained divided on socio-political policies, including the degree of Islamisation, and military strategy.

Militarily, the guerrillas had achieved success in capturing the capitals of some provinces along the Pakistani border. But they dared not establish a high profile in any major town for fear of becoming a sitting target for the enemy air force. This was the lesson they had drawn from the events in Kunduz, a northern town, which they seized in August 1988. They had to flee when Soviet warplanes hit Kunduz not only from Kabul but also from USSR air bases across the border. Politically, their behaviour in Kunduz aroused fear and bitterness among the residents. They looted the settlement to the extent of removing electricity poles. In the border town of Torham they butchered 70 government soldiers after the latter had surrendered.[30] They carried out similar massacres in the eastern province of Kunar vacated by the central government. Their propensity for vengeance damaged the effectiveness of the general alliance strategy of encouraging defections from the opposing side with promises of amnesty. Fear of bloody reprisals by their opponents was an important factor in motivating government supporters to take up arms and offer stiff resistance to the guerrilla attacks.

Aware of the Mujahedin Alliance's plan to infiltrate Kabul with men and weapons before besieging it, Najibullah grabbed the first opportunity to strike at his adversaries and prepare his followers for combat. Following the discovery on 18 February of weapons and explosives in the capital, the President declared that national sovereignty, political independence, and territorial integrity were under threat due to the machinations of Pakistan and America.

He imposed a state of emergency, and suspended the constitutional rights pertaining to public assembly, labour strikes, house searches and phone tapping, and set up military courts to try those charged with breaking the law. He appointed a new 20-member Supreme Council for the Defence of the Homeland consisting of military and party officials. He dismissed eight non-party ministers, including Premier Sharq, and replaced them with PDP members. Tanks and armoured personnel carriers guarded crossroads in the capital, where certain districts were sealed off as the armed police undertook house searches, arresting many 'agents loyal to Hikmatyar and Rabbani'.[31]

As before, the PDP government focussed its hostility on Hikmatyar's Hizb-e Islami and Rabani's Jamaat-e Islami. This meant that it was open to negotiations with the other components of the Mujahedin Alliance, as well as the Tehran-based groups. As it was, the exclusion of the latter from the Peshawar-based interim government made them amenable to considering Kabul's repeated appeals for national reconciliation.

The Afghan government had some success in its campaign for national reconciliation. An official source in Kabul revealed that the government had been in contact with 575 groups representing 45,000 armed guerrillas inside the country, and that several local ceasefires were already in place.[32]

The departure of the Soviets enabled Najibullah to present himself as a nationalist. A majority of the Mujahedin leaders, in contrast, were widely seen as the clients of Pakistan, Saudi Arabia and America. The holding of the Afghan shura in Rawlpindi, the twin of Islamabad, a foreign capital, was illustrative, and deeply wounding to many Afghan nationalists.

Since the Mujahedin leaders continue to reject a political settlement and opt exclusively for a military solution, they must wait for snow to melt in spring and early summer to pursue that option. Undoubtedly, their followers have proved their worth as guerrillas with their successes in ambushes and mountain combat. But capturing and holding urban centres is another matter. Their decentralized structure was an asset so long as they were engaged in guerrilla activity, but it is not suitable when it comes to engaging a heavily armed conventional army: that sort of combat requires a unified command structure that is not yet in sight.

This became transparently clear when the Mujahedin forces, about 10,000 strong, tried to seize Jalalabad in early March 1989. They attacked the city on 5 March with a view to capturing it on 8 March and using it as a venue for a meeting of their interim government on Friday, 10 March to prepare the ground for its recognition at the ICO foreign ministers' conference opening in Riyadh on 13 March. Their plans failed. Instead of staging a combined offensive under a centralized command, the different guerrilla factions mounted small, individual attacks. The heavily armed Afghan troops, facing conventional assaults, stood firm and performed better than expected. A fortnight after their initial assault the rebel commanders conceded they had become bogged down in a stalemate and that 'It will not be easy to take Jalalabad'.[33] The only consolation the Mujahedin had was that Hikmatyar, the foreign minister of their interim administration, was allowed to occupy Afghanistan's seat at the ICO conference in Riyadh. However, the Mujahedin government failed to win the recognition either of Pakistan or America.

Most observers agree that there is only a slim chance that the PDP administration will collapse from within shortly and let the Mujahedin interim government instal itself in Kabul. Nor is there any chance that the armed rebellion against the present regime will stay away in the near future. By now, such opposition field commanders as Ahmad Shah Masoud and Ismail Khan (both attached to the Jamaat-e Islami) have established an administrative infrastructure in the areas they control. Ismail Khan's edicts hold sway in the north-west, around Herat. Masoud, based in the Panjshir valley north of Kabul, is the leader of the Supervisory Council of the North, which includes four of Afghanistan's 31 provinces.

In the circumstances, the most likely scenario is of a country divided into various zones under different commanders, with the PDP government forces entrenched in major urban centres connected by roads. But this is an inherently unstable situation. Given the degree of power, political and military, a regime based in Kabul is capable of exercising, the ultimate initiative lies with it. In this it will be further aided by the fact that Afghanistan contains about 70 ethnic groups – a situation tailor-made for an ongoing 'divide and rule' policy by the central authority.

Already, inter-factional feuds, which had been suspended due to the jihad against the infidel invader, have resurfaced in certain parts of the country. With its population now more heavily armed than anywhere else in the world, the prospect of Afghanistan turning into a bigger and bloodier Lebanon cannot be ruled out.

It is possible that as the country sinks further into violence the move to bring back the former king, Muhammad Zahir Shah, to lead an interim government, will gather momentum. His return would allow the People's Democratic Party leaders and most field commanders to save face, and would, in addition, satisfy a popular demand.

Taking a general view of the Afghanistan crisis, it is obvious that Islam was the prime mover in getting nationalist and religious Afghans to mount a jihad against the Soviet military. It was successful in bringing about the Soviet withdrawal in February 1989. To that extent the events in Afghanistan were complementary to what had happened in February 1979 in adjoining Iran. There, the Islamic revolutionaries had overthrown a regime tied to the other superpower, America. Taken together, therefore, the Islamist forces in Iran and Afghanistan have proved the validity of the slogan 'Neither East nor West'.

There was yet another parallel. The Islamic holy war in Afghanistan brought about a dramatic change in the leftist ruling party. From a position of militant secularism it moved to the point where it adopted Islam as the state religion and initiated a programme of mosque construction and renovation. Likewise, while conducting a war against the Islamic Republic of Iran, the secular regime of Saddam Hussein turned religious, with the ruling Baath Party pledging to create a state which was 'inspired by Islam as a mission and a revolution'[34], and the government setting up the Islamic Higher Institute to train preachers, prayer leaders and theological students, and instructing its officials to sponsor fast-breaking banquets during Ramadan.

These examples well illustrate the growing power of Islam as a living socio-political ideology.

Notes

1. *The Middle East*, February 1988, p. 17.
2. *Tehran Times*, 21 and 23 January 1989.
3. *Guardian*, 28 April 1988; and *Middle East Economic Digest*, 6 May 1988, p. 8.
4. BBC World Service, 20 July 1988; and *Independent*, 21 July 1988.
5. *Middle East Economic Digest*, 29 July 1988, pp. 13–14.
6. Tehran Radio, 22 July 1988.
7. *The Times*, 19 July 1988; and Tehran Radio, 19 September 1988.
8. Stockholm International Peace Research Institute, *SIPRI Yearbook 1988* (Oxford and New York: Oxford University Press, 1988), p. 178; and US Arms Control and Disarmament Agency, *Military Expenditure and Arms Transfers 1987*, Washington, DC, Table II, p. 105.
9. *Independent*, 21 July 1988.
10. Baghdad Radio, 27 June 1982.
11. Tehran Radio, 14 February 1989.
12. *Guardian*, 20 February 1989.
13. For the significance of 15 Khurdad, an Iranian month, see p. 160.
14. Cited in *Time*, 6 March 1989.
15. *Independent*, 24 February 1989; and *Guardian*, 6 March 1989.
16. Rioting by Muslims in Bombay, the birth-place of Rushdie, led to twelve deaths by police firing. The book had been banned in India in early October 1988. *Guardian*, 25 February and 8 March 1989; and *The Times*, 28 February and 7 March 1989.
17. The other pertinent Quranic verses are:

'The hypocrites are afraid, lest a sura should be
sent down against them, telling thee what is in
their hearts. Say 'Mock on; God will bring forth
what you fear'. (9:6); and

'Those who molest god and His Messenger –
them God has cursed in the present world and
the world to come, and has prepared for them
a humbling punishment.' (33:57)

Kaab ibn al Ashraf was one of the six people to be executed
in Mecca for mocking the Quran or Prophet Muhammad.
The fact that he was not a Muslim means that attacking the
sanctity of the Prophet or the Quran was as much a capital
offence for non-Muslims as it was for Muslims. This explains
why Khomeini included the publishers of *The Satanic Verses* in
his religious decree. See further *Judgement of Ulama, Traditionalists and Other Authorities concerning Punishment for the Slander of the
Prophet*, Muslim Students Association (Persian Speaking
Group), Berkeley, C., 1989.

18. *Independent*, 17 March 1989.
19. *Observer*, 15 May 1988.
20. *Sunday Times*, 26 February 1989.
21. *New Statesman and Society*, 20 May 1988. Individual Mujahedin
    leaders, discredited by persistent reports of black marketing
    in foreign arms aid and drug-trafficking, polled one per cent
    or less.
22. *Guardian*, 19 October 1988.
23. Of these, some 600,000 Afghans had been resident in Iran
    before the 1978 revolution in Afghanistan.
24. See p. 253; and *Guardian*, 7 February 1989.
25. So far Riyadh had invested $850 million in Sayyaf's Islamic
    Alliance of Afghanistan, and provided him with hundreds of
    Wahhabi volunteers to fight the Kabul regime. *Independent*, 2
    February 1989.
26. *Guardian*, 16 and 27 February 1989; and *Observer*, 19 February
    1989. The last estimate is based on assuming half of the 15
    million Afghans inside the country to be adults.
27. *Daily Telegraph*, 3 February 1989.
28. *The Times*, 15 February 1989; and *Guardian*, 16 February 1989.
29. The extent of ill-feeling that existed between the moderate
    and hard-line factions within the Mujahedin Alliance was
    well conveyed by the following remark made by the spokes-
    man of Gailani's National Islamic Front: 'The extremists are
    more savage than the Communists because they kill and loot
    under the cloak of Islam. If they take power the bloodbath

will continue for another ten years.' *Financial Times*, 3 February 1989.

30. *The Middle East*, October 1988, p. 11.
31. *Sunday Times*, 19 February; and *Guardian*, 20 and 21 February 1989.
32. *Guardian*, 25 and 27 February 1989.
33. *Independent*, 18 March 1989; and *Sunday Times*, 26 March 1989.
34. Baghdad Radio, 27 June 1982.

NOTES

I THE RISE OF ISLAM: SUNNISM AND SHIAISM

1. The 'Presence' said to Muhammad: 'Read.' Muhammad replied, 'What shall I read?' The 'Presence' shook him and crushed him until he felt drained of all strength. Twice this happened. Finally the words came to him. Later these appeared as the opening of Chapter 96:

   Recite: In the name of thy Lord who created,
   Created man of a blood clot.
   Recite: And thy Lord is the Most Generous,
   Who taught by the pen,
   Taught man that he knew not.

   Arberry, Arthur J. (trans.) *The Koran Interpreted* (Oxford and New York: Oxford University Press, 1964), 96:1–5.
2. *Ibid.*, 5:49.
3. *Ibid.*, 4:3.
4. *Ibid.*, 4:19.
5. Watt, W. Montgomery *Islamic Political Thought: the Basic Concepts* (Edinburgh: Edinburgh University Press, 1968), pp. 5 and 132.
6. Cited in Shipler, David K. *Arab and Jew: Wounded Spirits in a Promised Land* (New York: Times Books, 1986), p. 141. Since Jews and Christians are mentioned in the Quran, they are known in Islam as 'People of the Book'.
7. Of these obligations, prayers, charity and fasting during Ramadan are mentioned in the Quran, the rest in the Hadiths.
8. Arberry, *op. cit.*, 9:60. The 2.5 per cent rate applies to the believer's cash and ornaments of precious metals. The rates for cattle and agricultural and mineral output vary. Sarwar, Ghulam *Islam: Beliefs and Teachings* (London: Muslim Educational Trust, 1982), p. 75.
9. One of the several verses on resurrection in the Quran reads:

   Say: 'God gives you life, then makes you die,
   Then He shall gather you to the Day
   Of Resurrection, wherein is no doubt,
   But most men do not know.'

Arberry, *op. cit.*, 45:25.

10. Ruthven, Malise *Islam in the World* (Harmondsworth: Penguin Books, 1984), p. 97.
11. *Ibid.*, p. 98.
12. The first four Shia Imams are: Ali, Hassan, Hussein and Zain al Abidin.
13. The first six Shia Imams, according to Twelvers, are: Ali, Hassan, Hussein, Zain al Abidin, Muhammad al Baqir and Jaafar al Sadiq.
14. The rest of the twelve Imams are: Musa al Kazim, Ali al Rida (Reza, in Persian), Muhammad al Taqi Javad, Ali al Naqi, Hassan al Askari and Muhammad al Muntazar.

2   ORTHODOX ISLAM AND SUFISM

1. Asad, Muhammad *The Principles of State and Government in Islam* (Gibraltar: Dar al Andalus, 1980), pp. 48 and 106.
2. Ruthven, Malise *Islam in the World* (Harmondsworth: Penguin Books, 1984), p. 160.

3   ISLAM IN MODERN TIMES

1. Cited in Ziadeh, N. A. *Sanusiyah* (Leiden: E. J. Brill, 1958), pp. 41–4.
2. In contemporary Iran he is known as Jamal al Din Asadabadi.
3. Smith, Wilfred Cantwell *Islam in Modern History* (Princeton, NJ: Princeton University Press, 1957), p. 49.
4. Mortimer, Edward *Faith and Power: the Politics of Islam* (London: Faber & Faber, 1982), p. 115.
5. See Enayat, Hamid *Modern Islamic Political Thought* (London: Macmillan, 1982), pp. 70–83.
6. Mortimer, *op.cit.*, p. 250.

4   THE MUSLIM BROTHERHOOD IN EGYPT AND SYRIA

1. Mitchell, Richard P. *The Society of Muslim Brothers* (Oxford and New York: Oxford University Press, 1969), p. 4.
2. Bayyumi, Zakariyya Sulaiman *The Muslim Brothers* (in Arabic) (Cairo: Wahbah Library, 1979), p. 90.
3. Mitchell, *op. cit.*, p. 14.
4. Ali, Said Ismail *Al Azhar: A Participant in Egyptian Politics* (in Arabic) (Cairo: Dar al Thaqafa, 1974), p. 104.
5. Ali, *op. cit.*, p. 299.
6. Ghazali, Muhammad *Our Beginning in Wisdom* (Washington, DC: American Council of Learned Societies, 1953), pp. 30–31.
7. Cited in Ajami, Fouad 'In the Pharoah's Shadow: Religion and

Authority in Egypt' in James P. Piscatori (ed.) *Islam in the Political Process* (Cambridge and New York: Cambridge University Press, 1983), p. 25.

8. *Majallat al Azhar*, February 1968 and October 1968.
9. Shoukri, Ghali *Egypt: Portrait of a President, 1971–81* (London: Zed Press, 1981), p. 296.
10. *Ibid.*, pp. 292–3.
11. Hiro, Dilip *Inside the Middle East* (London: Routledge & Kegan Paul, and New York: McGraw Hill, 1982), p. 112.
12. Shoukri, *op. cit.*, p. 201.
13. *The Times*, 16 November 1978.
14. Dekmejian, R. Hrair *Islam in Revolution: Fundamentalism in the Arab World* (Syracuse, NY: Syracuse University Press, 1985), p. 105.
15. *Al Ahram*, 10 May 1979.
16. Cited in *8 Days*, 25 July 1981.
17. This was all the more striking in contrast to the death of Nasser which had led to unprecedented scenes of public grief.
18. Dekmejian, *op. cit.*, p. 104.
19. *Ibid.*, p. 106.
20. *International Herald Tribune*, 27–8 June 1987.
21. Cited in Batatu, Hanna 'Syria's Muslim Brethren', *MERIP Reports*, November–December 1982, p. 12.
22. Cited in Petran, Tabitha *Syria: a Modern History* (London: Ernest Benn, 1978), p. 197.
23. Cited in van Dam, Nikolaos *The Struggle for Power in Syria* (London: Croom Helm, 1981), p. 106.
24. Batatu, *op. cit.*, p. 20.
25. Cited in van Dam, *op. cit.*, p. 114.
26. *Guardian*, 12 March 1980.
27. *Foreign Broadcast Information Service*, 24 March 1980.
28. Drysdale, Alasdair 'The Assad Regime and Its Troubles', *MERIP Reports*, November–December 1982, p. 8.
29. *Le Monde*, 11 April 1981.
30. The Programme was incorporated into the Islamic Front's Charter issued in January 1981.
31. Qutb, Sayyid *Conflict between Islam and Capitalism* (in Arabic) (Beirut: Dar al Shuruq, 1975), p. 66.
32. Batatu, *op. cit.*, p. 20, and Dekmejian, *op. cit.*, p. 106.
33. Drysdale, *op. cit.*, p. 9.
34. Batatu, *op. cit.*, p. 20.
35. Drysdale, *op. cit.*, p. 10. Hama's governor claimed, 'We have built more mosques in Hama than have been built since its foundation.'
36. Cited in Ayoub, Mahmoud Mustafa *Islam and the Third Universal Theory: the Religious Thought of Muammar al Qadhdhafi* (London and New York: KPI Limited, 1987), p. 98.
37. Cited in *ibid.*, p. 49.

5 SAUDI ARABIA: THE OLDEST FUNDAMENTALIST STATE

1. Ibn Taimiya, Taqi al Din *Politics of Legitimacy* (in Arabic) (Beirut: Dar al Kutub al Arabiya, 1966), p. 106.
2. Cited in Mortimer, Edward *Faith and Power: the Politics of Islam* (London: Faber & Faber, 1982) p. 166.
3. Helms, Christine Moss *The Cohesion of Saudi Arabia: Evolution of Political Identity* (London: Croom Helm, 1981), p. 137.
4. The appropriate verse reads: 'So pardon them, and pray forgiveness for them, and take counsel with them in the affair; and when thou art resolved, put thy trust in God.' Arberry, Arthur J. (trans.) *The Koran Interpreted* (Oxford and New York: Oxford University Press), 3:153.
5. *Arab World File*, No. 100, 16 October 1974.
6. Cited in Piscatori, James P. 'The Roles of Islam in Saudi Arabia's Political Development', in John L. Esposito (ed.) *Islam and Development: Religion and Socio-political Change* (Syracuse, NY: Syracuse University Press, 1980), p. 134.
7. *The Times*, 15 September 1975. The trend continued. In March 1979 American universities alone had 15,000 Saudi students on their rolls. *The Middle East*, May 1979, p. 31.
8. Hiro, Dilip *Inside the Middle East* (London: Routledge & Kegan Paul, and New York: McGraw Hill, 1982), p. 342.
9. *Time*, 29 May 1978, p. 20.
10. Maududi, Sayyid Abul Ala *A Short History of the Revivalist Movements in Islam* (Lahore: Islamic Publications, 1963), p. 33.
11. Houtsma, M. Th., A. J. Wensinck, E. Levi-Provencal, H. A. R. Gibb and W. Heffering (eds) *The Encyclopaedia of Islam, Vol. III* (Leiden: E. J. Brill, 1936), p. 115.
12. Dekmejian, R. Hrair *Islam in Revolution: Fundamentalism in the Arab World* (Syracuse, NY: Syracuse University Press, 1985) p. 142.
13. Cited in Holden, David, and Richard Johns *The House of Saud* (London: Sidgwick & Jackson, 1981), p. 522.
14. *Le Monde*, 4 May 1981.
15. *Daily Telegraph*, 20 December 1980.
16. *8 Days*, 8 March 1980, p. 16.
17. Cited in Dekmejian, *op. cit.*, p. 147.
18. Hiro, Dilip *Iran Under the Ayatollahs* (London and New York: Routledge & Kegan Paul, 1985), p. 335. In 1983 Saudi Arabian nationals were estimated at 5.5 million, of whom 440,000 were Shia. Bill, James A. 'Resurgent Islam in the Persian Gulf', *Foreign Affairs*, Washington DC, Fall 1984, p. 120.
19. Hiro, *Inside the Middle East*, p. 87.
20. Cited in Mortimer, *op. cit.*, p. 174.
21. Cited in Haddad, Yvonne Y. 'The Arab-Israeli Wars, Nasserism and Islamic Identity', in John L. Esposito (ed.), *op. cit.*, p. 239, note 23.

22. *Guardian*, 26 January 1981.
23. Qutb, Sayyid *Conflict between Islam and Capitalism* (in Arabic) (Beirut: Dar al Shuruq, 1975), p. 25.

6 IRAN: REVOLUTIONARY FUNDAMENTALISM IN POWER

1. Arberry, Arthur J. (trans.) *The Koran Interpreted* (Oxford and New York: Oxford University Press, 1964), 2:117.
2. *Ibid.*, 7:125.
3. *Ibid.*, 21:105.
4. *Ibid.*, 28:4.
5. Keddie, Nikki R. *Roots of Revolution: an Interpretive History of Modern Iran* (New Haven, CT, and London: Yale University Press, 1981), pp. 21–2.
6. This is the popular term used for the Hidden Imam.
7. Cited in Akhavi, Shahrough *Religion and Politics in Contemporary Iran: Clergy-State Relations in the Pahlavi Period* (Albany, NY: State University of New York Press, 1980), pp. 29–30.
8. Arberry, *op. cit.*, 24:31.
9. Keddie, *op. cit.*, p. 111.
10. *Bakhtar-e Emruz*, 6 March 1952.
11. Khomeini articulated his views on the subject in a pamphlet entitled *Local Government Administration in the Islamic Manner*.
12. *Ittilaat*, 7, 8 and 9 March 1963.
13. Anon. *Biography of the Leader, Vol II* (in Persian) (Tehran: 15 Khurdad Publications, 1979), p. 42.
14. *Payam-e Emruz*, 10 June 1963.
15. Algar, Hamid 'The Oppositional Role of the Ulema in the Twentieth Century in Iran' in Nikki R. Keddie (ed.) *Scholars, Saints and Sufis: Muslim Religious Institutions Since 1500* (Los Angeles and Berkeley, CA: University of California Press, 1972), p. 253. Since there was no dynastic rule in Iran from 641 to 1501, the Shah's claim of 2,500 years of continuous monarchy was false.
16. Cited in Khumayni, Ruh Allah *Islam and Revolution* (trans. by Hamid Algar) (Berkeley, CA: Mizan Press, 1981), p. 202.
17. Khomeini, Ruhollah *Islamic Government: Rule of the Religious Jurist* (in Persian) (Najaf, 1971), p. 48.
18. *Ibid.*, p. 75.
19. 'The Ideological Conditions for Khomeini's Doctrine of Government' in *Economy and Society*, May 1982, London and Boston, MA, p. 149.
20. *Iran Almanac, 1975* (Tehran: Echo of Iran), p. 395. Part of the increase was no doubt due to the rising prosperity of Iranians during that period.
21. *The Dawn of the Islamic Revolution* (Tehran: Ministry of Islamic Guidance, no date), pp. 254–5.

22. *Ibid.*, p. 257; and Nobari, Ali-Reza (ed.) *Iran Erupts* (Stanford, CA: Iran-America Documentation Group, 1978), p. 196.
23. Cited in *Sunday Times*, 13 April 1980.
24. *Ibid.*
25. Among those who witnessed this phenomenon at first hand was a Tehran businessman, who acted as presiding officer at a polling station in a southern part of the city. Interview in Tehran in December 1979.
26. Fischer, Michael M. J. *Iran: From Religious Dispute to Revolution* (Cambridge, MA, and London: Harvard University Press, 1980), pp. 221–2.
27. *Inqilab-e Islami*, 1 September 1979.
28. *Ibid.*, 10 October 1979.
29. *International Herald Tribune*, 24 October 1979.
30. The wording of the constitution is either from *Constitution of the Islamic Republic of Iran* (trans. Hamid Algar) (Berkeley, CA: Mizan Press, 1980) or *Constitution of the Islamic Republic of Iran*, published in *Middle East Journal*, Washington DC, Spring 1980, pp. 184–202.
31. This was later changed to Islamic Consultative Assembly. But the popular term, Majlis, remains unchanged.
32. *8 Days*, 6 December 1980, p. 17; and *The Middle East*, February 1981, p. 20.
33. *Inqilab-e Islami*, 4 February 1981.
34. *The Times*, 1 June 1981.
35. *Selected Messages of Imam Khomeini Concerning Iraq and the War Iraq Imposed upon Iran* (Tehran: Ministry of Islamic Guidance, 1981), p. 68.
36. Taleqani, Mahmud *Society and Economics in Islam* (Berkeley, CA: Mizan Press, 1982), p. 28. This books contains an English translation of the significant chapters of Taleqani's *Islam wa Malikiyat* (in Persian) first published in Tehran in the early 1960s.
37. *Ibid.*, p. 52.
38. *Ibid.*, p. 58.
39. Sadr, Muhammad Baqir *Iqtisad-e Ma, Vol. II* (in Persian) (Tehran: Borhan Press, 1978), p. 63. The original, *Iqtisaduna* (in Arabic), was published in Beirut in 1961.
40. *Ibid.*, p. 341.
41. *Constitution of the Islamic Republic of Iran* (trans. Hamid Algar), pp. 43–5.
42. Bakhash, Shaul *The Reign of the Ayatollahs: Iran and the Islamic Revolution* (London: I.B. Tauris, 1985), p. 176; and Hiro, Dilip *Iran Under the Ayatollahs* (London and New York: Routledge & Kegan Paul, 1985), p. 361.
43. Of the thirty-seven banks in pre-revolution Iran, the govern-

ment owned nine wholly, and six partly. *The Middle East*, September 1979, p. 42.

44. *The Iranian*, 17 October 1979, p. 5.

45. *New York Times*, 30 September 1981.

46. *Sunday Times*, 26 September 1981.

47. *Arabia: the Islamic World Review*, August 1982, p. 19.

48. *Guardian*, 11 and 12 April 1982; and National Voice of Iran Radio, 28 March 1983.

49. *BBC Summary of World Broadcasts*, 30 December 1982.

50. Tehran Radio, 5 January 1983.

51. *Sunday Times*, 11 April 1982.

52. Zabih, Sepehr *Iran Since the Revolution* (London: Croom Helm, 1982), p. 99.

53. The lower figure was given by *Newsweek*, 3 March 1980, p. 12, and the higher by Hashimi-Rafsanjani in an interview with *Arabia: the Islamic World Review*, August 1982, p. 89.

54. A village was defined as a place with less than 5,000 people. Of the 65,000 villages, only 18,000 had more than 250 inhabitants. *Iran Almanac, 1975* (Tehran: Echo of Iran), p. 415.

55. *Kayhan International*, 4 March 1984.

56. *The Middle East*, February 1982, p. 30.

57. *Daily Telegraph*, 11 June 1980.

58. *Ibid.*, 19 July 1980.

59. *MERIP Reports*, February 1982, p. 23.

60. *Daily Telegraph*, 5 July 1980.

61. To Shias the First Martyr is Imam Ali and the Second is Imam Hassan, his eldest son.

62. Interviews in Tehran, April–May 1983.

63. Abrahamian, Ervand *Iran Between Two Revolutions* (Princeton, NJ, and Guildford: Princeton University Press, 1982), p. 433; and *Sunday Times*, 4 April 1982.

64. Graham, Robert *Iran: the Illusion of Power* (London: Croom Helm, 1978), p. 206.

65. *Jumhouri-ye Islami*, 1 December 1985.

66. *Iranvoice*, 30 July 1979.

67. Islamic Republic News Agency, 2 November 1983.

68. See above, p. 131.

69. *Sunday Times*, 30 December 1979.

70. *Foreign Broadcast Information Service*, 28 January 1982.

71. *The Middle East*, February 1982, p. 14.

72. *Guardian*, 31 May 1982.

73. *BBC Summary of World Broadcasts*, 24 June 1983.

74. Riyadh Radio, 24 July 1983.

75. *Guardian*, 5 December 1983.

76. *BBC Summary of World Broadcasts*, 11 August 1984.

77. *Kayhan International*, 10 December 1985.

78. *Iran Press Digest*, 11 November 1985.
79. Islamic Republic News Agency, 1 April 1986.
80. This account is based on an eye-witness report by Mushahid Hussain, a Pakistani editor, published in the *Washington Post* and reprinted in the *International Herald Tribune* of 24 August 1987.
81. *Guardian*, 29 January and 10 April 1980.
82. *New York Times*, 2 March 1981.
83. *Sunday Times*, 15 January 1984.

7 AFGHANISTAN: CHANGING FORTUNES OF FUNDAMENTALISM

1. Established in 1867, Deoband is the second oldest Islamic university in the Muslim world, the first being Al Azhar.
2. Dupree, Louis *Afghanistan* (Princeton, NJ, and Guildford: Princeton University Press, 1980), pp. 126–7.
3. See above, p. 152, for Iranian ulama's reaction to European dress.
4. *Al Falah*, Seventh Year, No. 7, pp. 62–3.
5. Of the 113,000 tourists in Afghanistan in 1971, more than half were western. Dupree, *op. cit.*, p. 656.
6. Maududi, Sayyid Abdul Ala *Purdah and the Status of Women in Islam* (Lahore: Islamic Publications, 1979), p. 23.
7. *Ibid.*, pp. 197–8.
8. Roy, Olivier *Islam and Resistance in Afghanistan* (Cambridge and New York: Cambridge University Press, 1986), p. 83.
9. *The Area Handbook of Afghanistan* (Kabul, 1973), p. 36.
10. For the Iranian Guardians Council's view on the state's acquisition of excess land, see above, p. 203.
11. Hyman, Anthony *Afghanistan under Soviet Domination, 1964–83* (London: Macmillan, 1984), p. 90.
12. *Kabul Times*, 9 December 1978.
13. *Ibid.*, 11 October 1979.
14. *Kabul New Times*, 1 January 1980. After the Soviet intervention the *Kabul Times* became the *Kabul New Times*.
15. Amin, Tahir *Afghanistan Crisis: Implications and Options for Muslim World, Iran and Pakistan* (Lahore: Institute of Policy Studies, 1982), pp. 96–7.
16. *Aims of Hizb-e Islami* (Peshawar, no date), p. 14.
17. *Kabul New Times*, 21 April 1980.
18. Hyman, *op. cit.*, pp. 203 and 204.
19. *Ibid.*, p. 204.
20. Arnold, Anthony *Afghanistan: the Soviet Invasion in Perspective* (Stanford, CA: Hoover Institution Press, 1985), p. 100. Soviet deaths probably amounted to 6,000 to 8,000.
21. *Sunday Times*, 8 February 1987.

22. *Guardian*, 26 February 1987.
23. *New York Times*, 28 April 1987.
24. *Observer*, 10 May 1987; and *Independent*, 26 May 1987.
25. *Washington Times*, 23 April 1987.

CONCLUSION

1. See above, p. 63.
2. The Shah died within eighteen months of the revolution, on 27 July 1980.
3. Arberry, Arthur J. (trans.) *The Koran Interpreted* (Oxford and New York: Oxford University Press, 1964), 3:164.
4. The actual figures for war expenditure in 1985 were: Iran, 14 billion dollars, and Iraq, 12.87 billion dollars. The corresponding figures for their gross national products were 163 billion dollars and 22.5 billion dollars. *The Military Balance 1986–87* (London: International Institute of Strategic Studies, 1987), pp. 96 and 97.

SELECT BIBLIOGRAPHY

Abd-Allah, Umar F. *The Islamic Struggle in Syria* (Berkeley, CA: Mizan Press, 1983)

Akhavi, Shahrough *Religion and Politics in Contemporary Iran: Clergy-State Relations in the Pahlavi Period* (Albany, NY: State University of New York Press, 1980)

Amin, Tahir *Afghanistan Crisis: Implications and Options for Muslim World, Iran and Pakistan* (Lahore: Institute of Policy Studies, 1982)

Arberry, Arthur J. (trans.) *The Koran Interpreted* (Oxford and New York: Oxford University Press, 1964)

Arnold, Anthony *Afghanistan: the Soviet Invasion in Perspective* (Stanford, CA: Hoover Institution Press, 1985)

Asad, Muhammad *The Principles of State and Government in Islam* (Gibraltar: Dar al Andalus, 1980)

Ayoub, Mahmoud Mustafa *Islam and the Third Universal Theory: the Religious Thought of Muammar al Qadhdhafi* (London and New York: KPI Limited, 1987)

Bakhash, Shaul *The Reign of the Ayatollahs: Iran and the Islamic Revolution* (London: I. B. Tauris, 1985)

Beling, Willard (ed.) *King Faisal and Modernisation of Saudi Arabia* (Boulder, CO: Westview Press, 1980)

Constitution of the Islamic Republic of Iran (trans. Hamid Algar) (Berkeley, CA: Mizan Press, 1980)

Dekmejian, R. Hrair *Islam in Revolution: Fundamentalism in the Arab World* (Syracuse, NY: Syracuse University Press, 1985)

Dupree, Louis *Afghanistan* (Princeton, NJ, and Guildford: Princeton University Press, 1980)

Enayat, Hamid *Modern Islamic Political Thought* (London: Macmillan, 1982)

Esposito, John L. *Islam and Politics* (Syracuse, NY: Syracuse University Press, 1984)

Esposito, John L. (ed.) *Islam and Development: Religion and Socio-political Change* (Syracuse, NY: Syracuse University Press, 1980)

Esposito, John L. (ed.) *Voices of Resurgent Islam* (Syracuse, NY: Syracuse University Press, 1983)

Fischer, Michael M. J. *Iran: From Religious Dispute to Revolution*
(Cambridge, MA, and London: Harvard University Press,
1980)

Ghazali, Muhammad *Our Beginning in Wisdom* (trans. Ismail el
Faruqi) (Washington DC: American Council of Learned
Societies, 1953)

Heikal, Mohamed *Autumn of Fury: the Assassination of Sadat*
(London: André Deutsch, 1983)

Helms, Christine Moss *The Cohesion of Saudi Arabia: Evolution of
Political Identity* (London: Croom Helm, 1981)

Hiro, Dilip *Inside the Middle East* (London: Routledge & Kegan
Paul, and New York: McGraw Hill, 1982)

Hiro, Dilip *Iran Under the Ayatollahs* (London and New York:
Routledge & Kegan Paul, 1985)

Holden, David, and Richard Johns *The House of Saud* (London:
Sidgwick & Jackson, 1981)

Hudson, Michael C. *Arab Politics: the Search for Legitimacy* (New
Haven, CT, and London: Yale University Press, 1977)

Hyman, Anthony *Afghanistan Under Soviet Domination, 1964–83*
(London: Macmillan, 1984)

Ismail, Tareq Y. *Iraq and Iran: Roots of Conflict* (Syracuse, NY:
Syracuse University Press, 1982)

Keddie, Nikki R. *Sayyid Jamal al Din 'al Afghani': a Political
Biography* (Los Angeles and Berkeley, CA: University of
California Press, 1972)

Keddie, Nikki R. *Roots of Revolution: an Interpretive History of
Modern Iran* (New Haven, CT, and London: Yale University
Press, 1981)

Keddie, Nikki R. (ed.) *Scholars, Saints and Sufis: Muslim Religious
Institutions since 1500* (Los Angeles and Berkeley, CA: University
of California Press, 1972)

Kerr, Malcolm H. *Islamic Reform: the Political and Legal Theories of
Muhammad Abduh and Rashid Rida* (Los Angeles and Berkeley,
CA: University of California Press, 1966)

Khomeini, Ruhollah *Selected Messages of Imam Khomeini Concerning
Iraq and the War Iraq Imposed upon Iran* (Tehran: Ministry of
Islamic Guidance, 1981)

Khumayni, Ruh Allah *Islam and Revolution* (trans. Hamid Algar)
(Berkeley, CA: Mizan Press, 1981)

Lewis, Bernard *Arabs in History* (5th ed.) (London: Hutchinson,
1970)

Maududi, Sayyid Abul Ala *Towards Understanding Islam* (Lahore:
Islamic Publications, 1960)

Maududi, Sayyid Abul Ala *A Short History of the Revivalist
Movements in Islam* (Lahore: Islamic Publications, 1963)

Maududi, Sayyid Abul Ala *Purdah and the Status of Women in Islam*
(Lahore: Islamic Publications, 1979)

Mitchell, Richard P. *The Society of Muslim Brothers* (Oxford and New York: Oxford University Press, 1969)

Mortimer, Edward *Faith and Power: the Politics of Islam* (London : Faber & Faber, 1982)

Piscatori, James P. (ed.) *Islam in the Political Process* (Cambridge and New York: Cambridge University Press, 1983)

Qutb, Sayyid *Islam: the Religion of the Future* (Kuwait: New Era Publishers, 1977)

Qutb, Sayyid *Milestones* (Kuwait: New Era Publishers, 1978)

Qutb, Sayyid *This Religion of Islam* (Kuwait: New Era Publishers, 1977)

Rahman, Fazlur *Islam* (2nd ed.) (Chicago and London: University of Chicago Press, 1979)

Roy, Olivier *Islam and Resistance in Afghanistan* (Cambridge and New York: Cambridge University Press, 1986)

Ruthven, Malise *Islam in the World* (Harmondsworth: Penguin Books, 1984)

Sadr, Muhammad Baqir *Our Economics, Vol. I* (Tehran: World Organization for Islamic Studies, 1982)

Sadr, Muhammad Baqir *Our Economics, Vol. II* (Tehran: World Organization for Islamic Studies, 1984)

Smith, Wilfred Cantwell *Islam in Modern History* (Princeton, NJ: Princeton University Press, 1957)

Taleqani, Mahmud *Society and Economics in Islam* (Berkeley, CA: Mizan Press, 1982)

Trimingham, J. Spencer *The Sufi Orders in Islam* (Oxford and New York: Oxford University Press, 1971)

van Dam, Nikolaos *The Struggle for Power in Syria* (London: Croom Helm, 1981)

Watt, W. Montgomery *Islamic Political Thought: the Basic Concepts* (Edinburgh: Edinburgh University Press, 1968)

Wendell, Charles (ed.) *Five Tracts of Hassan al Banna (1906–49)* (Los Angeles and Berkeley, CA: University of California Press, 1978)

Zabih, Sepehr *Iran Since the Revolution* (London: Croom Helm, 1982)

Index

Born in Larkana, Pakistan, Dilip Hiro received his higher education in India, Britain and America, where he obtained his Master's degree. He has been living in London since 1964, and is a full-time writer and journalist. His articles on the Middle East and allied subjects have appeared in many leading British and American publications, including the *Sunday Times, Guardian, Washington Post, Wall Street Journal* and *Atlantic Community Quarterly*. He has published several books including *Inside India Today* (1976), *Inside the Middle East* (1982) and *Iran Under the Ayatollahs* (1985). He is a member of the Middle East Studies Association of North America. He is a frequent commentator on Islamic affairs on British and American radio and television.